# JERO TAPAKAN: BALINESE HEALER
*An ethnographic film monograph*

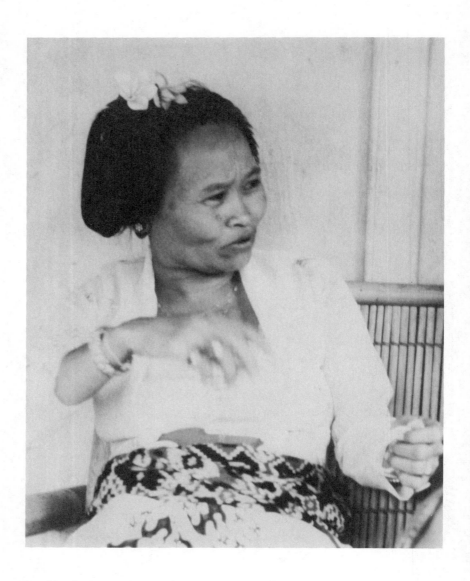

Jero Tapakan.

# Jero Tapakan:
# Balinese healer

An ethnographic film monograph

LINDA CONNOR,
PATSY ASCH,
*and*
TIMOTHY ASCH

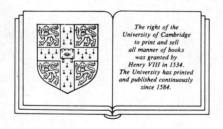

The right of the
University of Cambridge
to print and sell
all manner of books
was granted by
Henry VIII in 1534.
The University has printed
and published continuously
since 1584.

CAMBRIDGE UNIVERSITY PRESS
*Cambridge*
*London New York New Rochelle*
*Melbourne Sydney*

Published by the Press Syndicate of the University of Cambridge
The Pitt Building, Trumpington Street, Cambridge CB2 1RP
32 East 57th Street, New York, NY 10022, USA
10 Stamford Road, Oakleigh, Melbourne 3166, Australia

First published 1986

Printed in the United States of America

*Library of Congress Cataloging-in-Publication Data*
Connor, Linda, 1950–
Jero Tapakan, Balinese healer.
Bibliography: p.
Includes index.
1. Jero Tapakan.   2. Healers – Indonesia – Bali
(Province)   3. Folk medicine – Indonesia – Bali
(Province)   4. Moving-pictures in ethnology.
I. Asch, Patsy.   II. Asch, Timothy.   III. Title.
GN635.I65C66   1986   615.8'82'095986   85–19046

*British Library Cataloguing-in-Publication Data*
Connor, Linda
Jero Tapakan, Balinese healer : an ethnographic
film monograph.
1. Balinese (Indonesian people)   2. Spiritual
healing – Indonesia
I. Title   II. Asch, Patsy   III. Asch, Timothy
306'.46   DS632.B25


ISBN 0 521 32295 2 hard covers
ISBN 0 521 31144 6 paperback

*To Jero Tapakan's grandchildren*

# Contents

# Illustrations

# Preface

THIS book was written to provide detailed information on Balinese healing and to complement four films on a particular healer, Jero Tapakan:

*A Balinese Trance Séance,*

*Jero on Jero: "A Balinese Trance Séance" Observed,*

*The Medium Is the Masseuse: A Balinese Massage,* and

*Jero Tapakan: Stories from the Life of a Balinese Healer.*

We hope to demonstrate the value of having an anthropologist, who is familiar with the participants, their society, and their language, examine a filmed event. Films that try to present an overview of a society tend to be superficial and usually incorporate lengthier narration than the images can bear. We feel that it is more useful, for both research and teaching, to film specific events or interactions in detail and to complement the film with thorough written documentation than to try to present a general ethnography within the film itself. Because the final products provide a new type of teaching resource, we welcome critical comment.

Our book and films represent collaborative ethnographic documentation that involved both filming and writing. Jero Tapakan is the most important person in this collaboration: Her life and work are the focus of this project, and her skills as a healer and her enthusiastic support were necessary. Linda Connor, Jero's friend and a researcher of Balinese healing, provided the written ethnographic content and a translation of recorded dialogue and action. She also recorded most of the sound. I, Timothy Asch, stubbornly committed to integrating film and written materials in anthropology and ethnographic film, initiated the project, found the necessary funding, and shot all the footage. Patsy Asch, besides editing and producing the films and monograph, provided much of the energy necessary to complete them. We could each be assigned a title – subject, anthropologist, filmmaker, editor – but that was not the way it worked. Ideas, suggestions, and questions flowed from one of us to another, and it is no longer clear (or important to us) who is responsible for what.

The Anthropology Department of the Research School of Pacific Studies, The Australian National University, has been our most generous benefactor, providing salaries, equipment, and a studio, as well as funding for research. Documentary Educational Resources and its donors provided funds for production and a film distribution network. The Anthropology Department of the University of Sydney supported Linda Connor's fieldwork and, with the Anthropology Department of the University of Southern California, contributed to our production costs and allowed us the use of their film-editing facilities. The Wenner–Gren Foundation for Anthropological Research also contributed, particularly to our return to Bali in 1980, and the East–West Center, Hawaii, has supported Linda's final work on this monograph. Judith Wilson struggled with our clumsy prose; Ria van de Zandt, Ann Buller, and Ita Pead helped prepare the manuscript and the many versions of the subtitles. The staff at Cambridge University Press – Susan Allen-Mills, Michael Gnat, and Barbara Palmer – provided invaluable assistance in the final editing of the manuscript.

There are many others who deserve our thanks: among them, Dr. Douglas Miles, Linda's supervisor at the University of Sydney; Mr. Komang Suweta, who transcribed many of our tapes; Dr. Anak Agung Gede Muninjaya, a Balinese doctor and friend who looked at early versions of the films and helped Linda subtitle some of the more obscure dialogue; Dr. E. Douglas Lewis, who put up with our interruptions of another filming project when we dashed off to Bali to film *Jero on Jero*; and our many friends who suffered through version after version of both the films and this manuscript – particularly Nick Higginbotham, who provided constant encouragement.

We thank Jero's daughter-in-law, Men Toko, who frequently cooked for us and gracefully put up with our erratic comings and goings. We thank, too, the many Balinese in the films, particularly Ida Bagus and Dayu Putu. We especially record our gratitude to Jero's son, Wayan Data, whose generosity, intelligence, and kindness we shall cherish all our lives.

*Los Angeles*                                                    Timothy Asch

# PART I

*Introduction*

# ONE

## *The monograph and films*
PATSY ASCH

### A. Organization

WE envisage this monograph and the four films on Jero Tapakan as a resource for students of anthropology and related disciplines. Rather than a book that should be read in chronological order or a single, long film that must be viewed in its entirety, from the outset we intended to create an integrated set of materials that different people could use in a variety of ways, depending upon their particular interests. Some will want only to view a single film once; others may want to see all four films, perhaps studying a particular passage by repeatedly viewing and examining shots in detail. There will be those who want only to read the film synopses, others who want to read Linda Connor's chapters on healing without reference to the films, and still others who wish to study a film in relation to our written documentation and analysis. We suggest that our materials – films and monograph – may be used to optimal advantage in teaching by projecting one or more films as an integral part of a lecture, with appropriate reading assigned, and by making this book and videocassettes of the films available in libraries for independent study.

This monograph has been organized into four parts: an introduction and three parts related specifically (and respectively) to the films on séances, massage and traditional Balinese medicines, and aspects of Jero Tapakan's life.

Part I includes, in Chapter 2, a very brief introduction to Indonesia and Bali intended for people who know little about the region. Others may wish to turn directly to Chapter 3, an introduction to Balinese healing, which provides background on social organization and religion for all four films and helps to place Jero Tapakan's life within her social world. In Chapter 4, Timothy Asch discusses how and why we made these films, giving an account of the history of this particular endeavor and how it fitted into his goals and experiences as an ethnographic filmmaker and anthropologist. Some technical information is included. It is in this chapter that the rationale for the project lies and our goals are most clearly articulated. The project

3

has been a collaborative effort and would not have been possible without the particular combination of our individual experiences and training.

Part II, on the films *A Balinese Trance Séance* and *Jero on Jero: "A Balinese Trance Séance" Observed*, is the most detailed in the monograph because it grew out of part of Linda's Ph.D. thesis and deals with complex ideas. Synopses of the two films are followed by Linda's ethnographic notes (Chapter 5), which provide background on such topics as offerings, sorcery, death rituals, and linguistic usage. Viewers of *The Medium Is the Masseuse* and/ or *Jero Tapakan: Stories from the Life of a Balinese Healer* may want to read about several of these topics, since the information is not repeated later when these two films are discussed. In Chapter 6 there is a brief discussion of the circumstances that led to the filming of *Jero on Jero* and of the way it was edited. This is followed by a detailed shot list of *A Balinese Trance Séance*, in which the subtitles and narration of that film are juxtaposed with the comments Jero and Linda made as Jero watched the séance film for the first time; it was from this dialogue that we edited *Jero on Jero*. Also included are comments about the content and significance of each shot as well as notations about our editorial decisions. The chapter concludes with excerpts from the discussion Jero and Linda had after viewing the séance film. In Chapter 7 Linda provides an annotated translation of the *complete* recording of the séance (not just the segments included in the film).

Part III pertains to the film *The Medium Is the Masseuse: A Balinese Massage*. Again a synopsis is followed by ethnographic background (Chapter 8) that focuses on Balinese concepts related to the human body and the symptoms, causes, and treatment of illness. We have placed emphasis on information collected from observations Linda made of Jero's practice as a masseuse and dispenser of medicines as well as discussions she had with Jero and her patients; many quotations from the film are included. Chapter 9 is a brief discussion of the editorial decisions made and includes specific notes about each scene from the film.

Part IV provides background on *Jero Tapakan: Stories from the Life of a Balinese Healer*. A synopsis of the film is followed, in Chapter 10, by a discussion of Jero's life, with information to help the viewer interpret Jero's words. There are long excerpts from the translations of recordings of Jero's account, many of which were not included in the film. In Chapter 11 each scene in the film is discussed briefly, and the reasons behind our editorial decisions are given.

We have compiled a bibliography of writings on Bali that includes a few films. This list is not intended to be exhaustive but is meant to provide a starting point for further reading about Balinese society and culture as well as more detailed information on subjects raised in the monograph. With one noticeable exception (Weck's *Heilkunde und Volkstrum auf Bali* [1976]), we have not included the many important works on Bali written in languages other than English.

## B. Relation to anthropology

We have not tried to write (or film) an ethnography of Bali or even a definitive account of Balinese healing. We began by filming particular interactions that were of interest to Linda in her research on possession, magic, and healing, and we have tried to make these interactions comprehensible to others. We focus on one particular Balinese woman (whom we have called by her title, Jero Tapakan) because Linda knew her well and Jero was an able and eager teacher. Of all the healers Linda studied (58 were observed and interviewed, and intensive work was undertaken with 12), Jero was the one with whom Linda developed the warmest friendship. Her practice, incorporating as it did skills as both spirit medium and masseuse, was one of the most interesting. She was also one of the most popular *balians* (healers) in her district. We found Jero's practice fascinating and became involved in a friendship that grew more and more important to us.

In our most confident moments we conceive of the monograph and films as a model of one way to balance what film can do best – present visual, sound-synchronous, ethnographic data of particular events involving specific people – with the powerful, analytical, generalizing capabilities of print, which permit one to bridge temporal and spatial constraints in order to juxtapose and interpret with flexibility.

In editing these four films we have frequently sacrificed image quality for continuity in dialogue, but we have not included everything said. We have cut scenes when we felt the conversation was represented fairly without including all the dialogue. We began by editing the sound track and worrying only marginally about the images. Where we felt that to cut the sound, even though we did not have synchronized picture, would violate the meaning of the dialogue, we used cutaways (in our case, pictures of the same event but taken either before or after the sound that is heard). We did have to be realistic about the limits of editing based on conversation. For instance, we decided to cut out the long dream sequences in *Jero Tapakan: Stories from the Life of a Balinese Healer* (see section 10D) because we did not have sufficient film of this segment. In our writings we have also paid primary attention to what people say rather than to their other behaviors.

Frequently there is a cleavage among anthropologists between those interested in looking at what people actually do and those interested in the symbolic content of what people say and in their stated beliefs. Film is generally thought to be best suited to the former. We have attempted a synthesis because we feel it is a false dichotomy: Speech is action, and evidence of people's beliefs can be found in many other kinds of action. In *A Balinese Trance Séance* the viewer sees the event from a distance, as though through a window. There are times when it seems appropriate to sit quietly and observe without participating; this séance was such an occasion, and so the presence of the filmmakers is not made explicit in the film. *Jero* on Jero: "A Balinese Trance Séance" Observed was filmed while Jero was watching the séance film for the first time, in order to convey her reflections about her own behavior as well as her explanations of whatever she felt was problematic. Certainly Linda asks Jero questions, and the long history of their relationship and Linda's research interests strongly influence Jero's comments, but it is clear, particularly when Jero ignores many of Linda's gestural and facial clues, that Jero herself is determined to make certain things explicit. In commenting on what she is seeing, Jero chooses to explain not the particular séance but rather her own experiences as a medium for deities and spirits: What seems to be at issue, for her, is her right to be a medium at all.

In the film The Medium Is the Masseuse: A Balinese Massage the viewer watches a massage while listening to Jero, her patient, and Linda discussing the history and treatment of the patient's illness. At the end of the film we include an interview with the patient and his wife, another attempt to elicit discussion of concerns the subjects in the film wish to present to Linda and, by extension, to the viewer. Their account is a retrospective construction of a personal history that provides interpretive meaning. However, in these last two films we cannot assume that what people say is necessarily what they would present to other Balinese. Their statements are almost certainly influenced by what they think is important to present to a foreign audience, and their consciousness of this audience is apparent in the numerous interpolations of statements such as: "This is the Balinese way."

In Jero Tapakan: Stories from the Life of a Balinese Healer, we may get closer to Jero's actual beliefs – at least to those sanctioned by her community. Jero is telling stories that she has recounted many times in the past. Among other things, these stories are a charter of her right to practice as a balian, and for Jero and her audience they have taken on a mythic quality. The fluid and dramatic style in which her tales are recounted, their detail and continuity, their similarity to traditional folk tales and dramatic performances, and Jero's impatience whenever Linda interrupts the flow of the account are all indications of stories that have become a reality for the teller, existing in prescribed form. I say "a reality," for no doubt segments of her experiences are used and thought about in different ways on other occasions, and there are people of Jero's acquaintance who would view her history differently because their perspectives are not hers. However, these stories do seem to provide information about Jero's view of the world and view of herself that is less concerned with Linda and a foreign audience than are her statements in Jero on Jero or The Medium Is the Masseuse. The interpretation that Jero uses in the stories (particularly the labeling of certain behavior as "blessed madness") is one that is culturally available; this retrospective rationale has become crystallized into a standardized version of the event.

By focusing on one person, the films also raise the question of the relationship of the individual perspectives to collective actions and representations. Fieldwork is considered by many anthropologists as their own rite of passage, distinguishing their discipline from other social sciences. Through participant observation the ethnographer is expected to come to understand the way a particular group of "others" views the world and organizes its social relationships. Observations collected in the field refer to specific incidents involving particular people. Even a generalization, such as "A Balinese should marry his/her father's brother's daughter/son," is either a quote from one, six, or twenty particular Balinese or a reference to a statistical analysis based on particular cases, usually a small sample of the group to which the generalization is applied.

Much of what Linda has written can be directly related to her observations of and discussions with Jero. Linda also has drawn conclusions from her study of many healers and her experiences living in Bali for more than three years. In the monograph Linda has tried to link general statements about Balinese to data about the life of a *specific woman*, Jero Tapakan, and to her practice as a healer; but Balinese healers do not necessarily hold views identical with those of Jero, nor do they behave in exactly like ways. Because Westerners, or non-Balinese, cannot apprehend or distinguish immediately what is typically Balinese from what is idiosyncratically Jero, people who have looked at these films, especially *A Balinese Trance Séance*, have expressed uncertainty about the relationship between individual behavior and collective beliefs and, perhaps, practices.

Film deals with specific events involving a limited number of people at a moment or moments in time. Debate has arisen about the accuracy of ethnographic film, not only because all film is highly selective (in focal length, framing, and choice of subject as well as temporal and spatial manipulation), but also because film isolates and specifies. On the other hand, one tends to assume that the filmmakers have chosen a particular event because they feel it is typical and reveals important ideas and feelings about another group of people. The power, and the danger, in using film is that to see is often to believe, and to believe is frequently to generalize. Furthermore, beneath the question of what is typically Balinese (or general) and what is unique to Jero lies the issue of what is universally human. Unconsciously we tend to interpret certain behaviors and events observed on film as conveying universal meaning: For example, when the father in *A Balinese Trance Séance* cries, we assume he is feeling sad about the death of his son, and when Jero laughs upon seeing herself on film for the first time, we assume she is both pleased and embarrassed. Corroboration or refutation may be sought through further examination of the films and written documentation, just as anthropologists in the field must continually test their spontaneous interpretations by observation and discussion.

We stress these problems because this project is a blatant example of the dichotomy in ethnography between the individual and the general. Most ethnographers gather data through particular experiences with specific others, but such participant observation does not guarantee that what is "typical" or "collective" will be revealed. When anthropologists examine their field notes carefully, many find that the majority of entries, particularly those to which they later refer, relate to the activities and statements of a very small number of people, often people from the same social category (e.g., that of elder, male, ritual leader, aristocrat, or female healer); yet in their publications this dependence is rarely made explicit, and questions about the distribution of both knowledge and beliefs, or about how their analysis derives from their data, are rarely addressed. In this monograph, focusing as it does on one aspect of one person's life (Jero's profession), there is no way we can avoid this problem. Nor do we wish to. At points in the films it is clear that Jero's perspective is not that of her clients or patients and that they do not fully understand one another, yet there is evidence that they do agree about many things that we might not.

In the ethnographic sections Linda often generalizes about Balinese belief and practice. There is a definite contrast between the films, which record and elaborate upon the particular, and the more analytical sections of this monograph, which attempt to discern patterns and meaning within the welter of particularities of Linda's own experiences and discussions.

For purposes of pedagogy, the viewer may wish to consider the films as empirical data. Bear in mind that these films were made by us, with our particular biases, and that, like all films, they are *not* mirrors of reality (neither the Balinese reality nor that of the filmmakers). By asking questions about what can be seen and heard in the films and then using the monograph as a reference book to try to answer some of these questions, the reader/viewer may explore how much can be learned about the lives of the people observed in the films from a very limited set of interactions, as well as pinpoint some of the potential dangers in attempting this.

In ethnographic fieldwork and documentation there are tensions between the particular and the general, between empiricism and abstraction, and between the subject and the analyst. We hope readers, by examining the films in relation to the material in this monograph, will have an opportunity to experience some of the ways these tensions affect their thinking. There is no substitute for fieldwork, but the acquisition of some of the observational and analytical skills necessary can be fostered through a careful and informed study of certain films.

Films provide vicarious experiences, such as what it feels like to raft across a raging river or participate in a Balinese séance. The film images are usually all the audience will ever know of the events depicted. This contrasts with the multiplicity of embedded meanings – historical and sociological – that we each bring to direct experiences. We have tried to foster the illusion that the viewer is an observer at these events by presenting Jero's professed views without constant qualification. For example, in the narration for *A Balinese*

*Trance Séance*, statements such as "Jero is possessed three times," are based on Jero's interpretation; we wanted to present the logic of her arguments.

But do the films present Jero's perspective? Every frame and every word spoken were selected by us, either consciously or unconsciously, so the films represent *our interpretation* of Jero's perspective. We assume that if we maintain temporal continuity (particularly in our translations of recorded dialogue) and use long shots, and if we include Jero's comments as she watches the film, the resulting materials will present her perspective more accurately than if we were to make films composed of short shots with no attempt to maintain spatial or temporal continuity or to present Jero's comments about the film. But the differences remain relative; films and books are only interpretations.

Our attempts to understand Jero and the nature of her social world have challenged many of our basic assumptions and have been exciting experiences both intellectually and emotionally. Our goal is to allow our audience to have similar experiences as they work through the material, rather than to preempt their discoveries by didactic interpretations. However, unless the reader/viewer should meet her, Jero will remain a character in film, known only through a few structured scenes. The challenge is to see how much can be deduced from the films and accompanying written documentation.

# TWO

# *Indonesia and Bali: a brief background*

## LINDA CONNOR

INDONESIA lies at the eastern end of the Indian Ocean between Australia and mainland Southeast Asia. It straddles the equator in an arc of over 3,000 islands stretching east to northwest for almost 3,500 miles (see Map 1). The archipelago, with more than 100 active volcanoes, has the greatest concentration of volcanic activity of any place on earth. Bali, an island eight degrees south of the equator, is in the middle of the archipelago, approximately two kilometers east of Java (see Maps 2 and 3).

Indonesia, with a population in 1980 of almost 148 million, is the world's fifth most populous country, where more than 300 distinct languages are spoken in as many different regional cultures. As much as 60 percent of the population lives on only 7 percent of the total land area, the island of Java, which has some of the densest population concentrations in the world (about 1,000 per square kilometer in certain rural areas). The tiny island of Bali, 93 miles from east to west and 50 miles from north to south, is also densely populated, with approximately two and a half million inhabitants in 1980.[1]

More than 85 percent of the population of Indonesia consists of farmers whose staple crops are rice, sweet potato, corn, and sago. Indonesia also contains huge urban centers: Jakarta (population 6.5 million in 1980), Surabaya (population 2 million in 1980), Bandung (population 1.5 million in 1980), and Medan (population 1.4 million in 1980). The populations of the cities and towns are continually swelled by rural–urban migration (both seasonal and permanent) of impoverished farmers and landless laborers seeking employment. Government promotion of capital-intensive, high-yield, new rice agriculture has not prevented these population movements from occurring. In fact, it has been argued that the new rice agriculture, which depends on modern technology (machinery, patented hybrid seeds, fertilizers, and pesticides) as well as on a monetized system of credit, has accelerated the decline of many poor farmers and rural laborers.[2]

[1] The population figures cited here and elsewhere are from publications of the Biro Pusat Statistik [Indonesian Central Bureau of Statistics] (Jakarta, 1981).
[2] For further information, see W. L. Collier, "Food Problems, Unemployment, and the Green Revolution," *Prisma: Indonesian Journal of Social and Economic Affairs*, no. 9 (1978), pp. 38–52, and Poffenberger and Zurbuchen 1980.

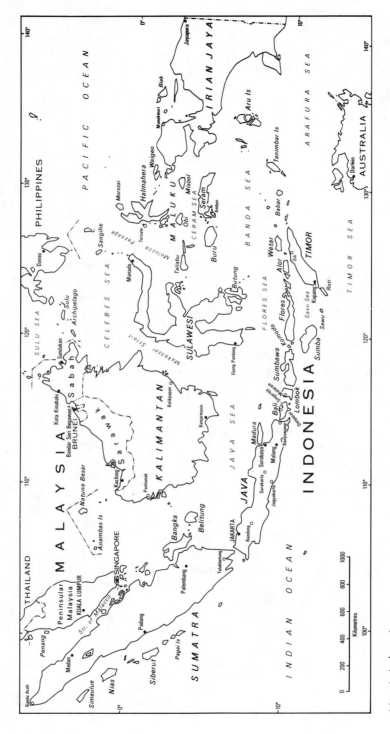

Map 1. Indonesia.

The past two decades have seen a considerable development of light and medium industries, but the rate of industrialization has not been great enough to absorb the unemployed or underemployed rural work force. The development of heavy extraction industries (mining, petroleum, lumber) by the Indonesian government in association with foreign corporations has generally been capital- rather than labor-intensive and has characteristically been located away from the main centers of population. Thus these developments have had little effect on employment conditions in most rural and urban areas.

The majority of Bali's population lives in the central lowlands and southern coastal plain, where the most fertile irrigated land, the center of the pre-colonial court culture, and most of the island's populous towns including the provincial capital, Denpasar, are situated. The main centers of tourism, which provide employment for a small percentage of the work force and a haven for hundreds of thousands of visitors each year, are also located on the island's southern coast.[3] The other main area of population concentration is the old colonial capital of Singaraja and its hinterland, situated on the narrow coastal plain of northern Bali (see Map 2). The town was developed by the Dutch in the latter half of the 19th century and the first half of the 20th century.

The majority of Balinese are still tied in some way to agricultural production as either owner/cultivators, sharecroppers, or landless laborers. Increasingly, however, Balinese live in rural households whose members obtain only a small part of their livelihood from agricultural production. As there is very little industrialization on the island, members of peasant families have diversified into a variety of occupations such as wage labor (road repair, construction work, public transport), peddling of foodstuffs and other cheap commodities (at marketplaces and roadside stalls), and service employment (in tourism or as servants in urban households).[4]

The population of Indonesia is 90 percent Muslim or nominally Muslim. The remainder adhere to Christian, Buddhist, Hindu, or indigenous religions. Bali's early history is marked by Hindu and Buddhist influences. These came from India via the Sumatran maritime empire Srivijaya, which flourished between the fifth and ninth centuries A.D., and from its neighbor Java, where eighth- and ninth-century dynasties created the magnificent Buddhist monument of Borobodur. Most Balinese identify the inland Javanese Hindu kingdom of Majapahit (13th to 16th centuries A.D.) as the single most important external influence on their culture, and textual and artistic sources document Java's long-standing cultural and political influence. This influ-

---

[3]   Bendesa and Surkarsa (1980) discuss the economic significance of tourism in Bali. See also Noronha 1979.
[4]   Poffenberger and Zurbuchen (1980) describe in some detail the patterns of economic diversification of Balinese rural families.

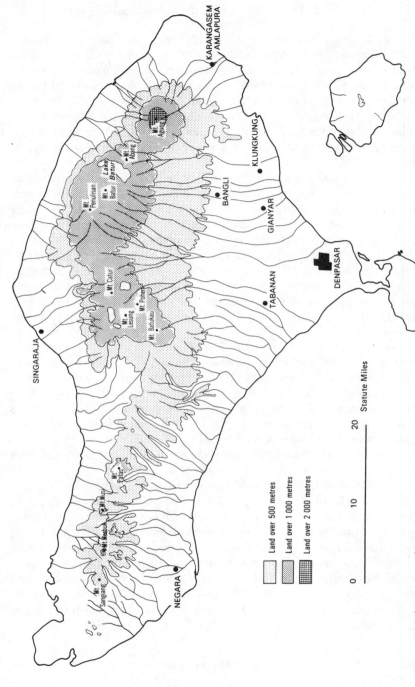

Map 2. Bali: topography.

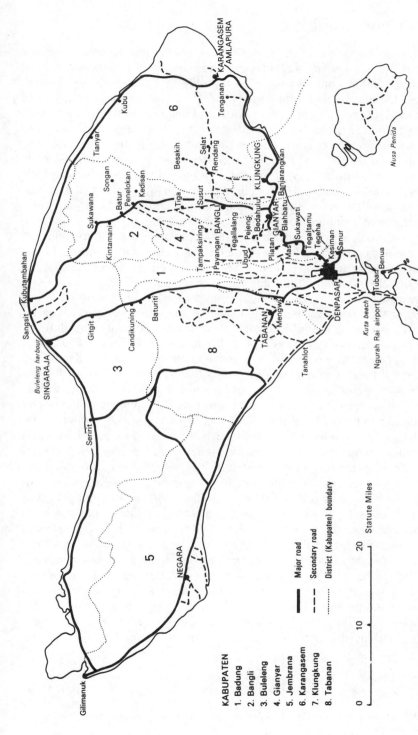

KABUPATEN

1. Badung
2. Bangli
3. Buleleng
4. Gianyar
5. Jembrana
6. Karangasem
7. Klungkung
8. Tabanan

———— Major road

– – – Secondary road

.......... District (Kabupaten) boundary

Statute Miles

0        10        20

Map 3. Bali: districts.

ence was strengthened in the late 10th century by the dynastic marriage between the Balinese prince Udayana and the Javanese princess Mahendradatta, a union commemorated to this day in Balinese artistic performances. During the mid 14th century the great East Javanese kingdom of Majapahit brought Bali under its control, and thenceforth the ruling houses of Bali claimed ancestry from Majapahit nobility. In the late 15th and early 16th century, in the declining days of Majapahit, Brahmana priests fled the last Hindu courts of Java, as political power there passed to the Islamic, mercantile states on the Javanese coast. Virtually all Balinese are now adherents of a unique form of Hindu religion in which Brahmanic and Buddhist elements have been combined with the animism and ancestor worship that are characteristic of much of the Malay culture area.

Balinese religion is complex, with different social groups holding different and sometimes conflicting ideals. A small courtly elite of Brahmana scholar-priests and other traditional literati have reinforced the scholarly, ascetic trends in Balinese religion. It is this aspect of religious life that has received most emphasis in Western scholarly accounts of the island's culture, because communication between the indigenous elite and foreigners is much easier than between peasants and foreigners. The peasant population of Bali, for the most part, had no direct access to the traditional *lontar* texts.[5] Peasant religion, though by no means a separate form, is under the day-to-day guidance of local temple caretaker priests (*pamangku*) and other religious officiants, many of whom are neither literate nor of gentry status. Village religion emphasizes the more ecstatic and magical elements of belief and practice. Since the 1920s this picture has been complicated further by the growth of religious reform movements, usually initiated by an urban-based bourgeoisie, which has promoted rationalizing and modernizing trends. These reformists are committed to establishing their religion as monotheistic, with a uniform written doctrine and, in many cases, a less elaborate ritualism. This group was particularly vocal in the 1950s in attempting to promote Balinese religion as one of the "great world religions" in the eyes of the government of newly independent Indonesia. The reformists were finally successful in this aim in the early 1960s, thereby opening up the provincial religious bureaucracy to new sources of funds and freeing Balinese Hinduism from the stigma of central government classification as "indigenous animism."[6] Religious reformists (who are often restorationists of various persuasions) continue in their efforts to modify the character of Balinese religion.

Despite these pressures, Bali still appears to be an island where gods, temples, and lavish ceremonies abound. Tens of thousands of temples and

---

[5]  There are numerous descriptions and discussions of the *lontar*, mostly in Dutch. Some English-language works include Robson 1972; Worsley 1972; Pigeaud 1975; Vickers 1982*a*, 1982*b*.

[6]  Such funds were not so readily available for the promotion of "indigenous animism."

small shrines dot the countryside and the villages and towns: in houseyards, marketplaces, fields, graveyards, and caves, on beaches, or by lakes. Temples, whether of modest proportions in houseyards or on a grand scale, are basically open-walled courtyards containing clusters of roofed shrines of stone, brick, or wood, oriented inland to the sacred mountains. Every Balinese belongs to several temple congregations, each of which celebrates an anniversary festival occupying several days in each Balinese *wuku*-calendar (210 days).[7] In addition, Balinese spend considerable time and resources on the many elaborate rites of passage that guide them safely into this world, through it, and into the next. The culmination of the cycle is the magnificent cremation ceremony and other death rituals for which Balinese culture is renowned.[8]

The elaborate forms of Hindu-Balinese culture developed for centuries in relative isolation from the rest of the archipelago, whose islands were increasingly subject to the inroads first of Islamic and then of Western mercantile powers. The Dutch East India Company was already reaping great profits in Java in the 17th century. The indigenous economy was rapidly transformed into a plantation system, which supplied raw materials to the industrial markets of the Dutch metropolis. Dutch control gradually spread to other islands of the archipelago and was consolidated in 1816 when the Netherlands government formally declared the East Indies a colony. Bali was economically peripheral compared with islands to the east and west. It was too small for large-scale plantation agriculture and lacked the precious spice groves of the eastern islands. Not until the mid 19th century, when an increasingly threatening British presence in the archipelago region prompted a consolidation of colonial control in hitherto peripheral areas, did the Dutch turn their attention to Bali. Intense colonial intervention in the Bali–Lombok area culminated in a series of military expeditions (1846–89) against the raja of Buleleng (now Singaraja) where the Dutch managed to gain a firm foothold. The colonial administration gradually extended its authority in the second half of the 19th century and by the first decade of the 20th century the wealthy and populous southern kingdoms were also under Dutch control.[9]

Bali, with Lombok, formed a separate colonial residency, administered from the northern Balinese town of Buleleng. Because the Dutch consolidated their control at a time when the Ethical Policy (proclaiming native advancement and social welfare) was officially endorsed in the Netherlands,

[7]   Discussions of the Balinese calendars and concepts of time can be found in Goris 1960*a*; C. Geertz 1973*b*; Covarrubias 1973. Belo (1953), Goris (1960*b*, 1969*a*, and 1969*b*), and Lansing (1983*b*) discuss the Balinese temple system.

[8]   Covarrubias devotes a chapter to death and cremation (1973, pp. 359–88). Mershon (1971, pp. 177–258) includes seven chapters on death rituals.

[9]   For more detailed accounts of Balinese history, see Hanna 1976; Boon 1977; Kraan 1983; Lansing 1983*a*, 1983*b*.

colonialism did not effect as radical a transformation of the indigenous economy as it had in other parts of Indonesia. The island was largely untouched by plantations, which transformed social and economic relationships in other areas of the colony. Nor did the Dutch missionaries enjoy any great success in converting the populace to Christianity. The Netherlands government accorded Bali the status of a huge native reservation and intended it to be seen as a testimonial to the benevolence of imperial rule, especially by those at home who were becoming increasingly concerned about colonial ethics.

The Dutch presence in Bali signaled a decline in traditional bases of courtly wealth and power. Many former functionaries of the precolonial courts were deprived of their positions. Others, as in Java, became members of the indigenous civil service, mediating between Dutch authorities (whose numerical presence in Bali was never very great) and the peasantry. There has been very little systematic examination of the far-reaching structural changes in the relations between peasantry and elites that must have been effected by the Dutch colonial presence.[10] The new rulers transformed the structure of the indigenous administration system, made increasingly onerous tax collections, and were responsible for the increasing monetization of the economy that accompanied Dutch mercantilism.

As early as the 1920s, Bali had joined with other parts of the Dutch East Indies in agitating for national independence. The liberation movement continued to be supported by guerrilla struggle through the 1930s and into the war years. It was not until 17 August 1945, after three years of Japanese occupation of the former colony, that the leaders of the new republic declared independence. However, Bali remained part of the Dutch-controlled Republic of East Indonesia until 1949. After five years of prolonged fighting and diplomatic wrangling, the unitary Republic of Indonesia came into being in 1950, with Sukarno as its first president.

Far-reaching changes were wrought in Balinese society following its incorporation as a province of the independent republic. National development policies and government institutions (including schools and clinics at the subdistrict and village level) have been established. Balinese are being drawn beyond the shores of their island by educational and employment opportunities in larger urban centers. The first language of the majority of the population is Balinese, but Indonesian is being spoken in the towns with increasing frequency. It is the medium of communication in nearly all schools,[11] in government offices, and in provincial and national media. Nevertheless, as in many parts of Indonesia, a substantial proportion of

[10]   Vickers (1980) has examined the implications of Dutch colonial control for the relationship between artists and court patrons.
[11]   In rural primary schools it is still common for Balinese to be the language of instruction.

Bali's rural population, especially women and the elderly, does not speak the national language.

Despite the many changes in Balinese society over the last few decades, more than four-fifths of the island's population still live in small rural hamlets where residents cooperate in the many tasks of daily living as well as in managing life crises and their associated ceremonies. Most peasants are members of many different customary organizations (often with conflicting interests and different membership), such as irrigation societies for the management of wet-rice agricultural resources and temple associations for the maintenance of local temples and the performance of rituals.[12] However, it is important to note the inevitable transformation of these customary social relations as more of the rural populace becomes irreversibly drawn into the cash economy and the demands of modern forms of employment.

[12] The variety of local organizations in Balinese villages is discussed in C. Geertz 1959 and H. Geertz 1959.

# THREE

# *Balinese healing*
## LINDA CONNOR

OUR four films focus on the life story, beliefs, and practices of a Balinese healer, a woman who is known by the title Jero Tapakan. Each film deals with a different aspect of this woman's life: the events that preceded her becoming a healer, her practices as a masseuse and as a spirit medium, and her response to seeing herself on film working as a spirit medium. In the following chapters we shall present information intended to enlarge the reader's understanding of each film. We also hope to deepen the reader's appreciation of practitioners like Jero. Balinese healers are worthy of intensive study not only because of the intrinsic interest of their healing techniques but because of the opportunity they provide to learn about the way people in different cultures think about the place of human beings within their cosmos. Balinese, like many people, are likely to show an urgent and active concern with philosophical, spiritual, or cosmological matters when they are involved in a crisis situation. By far the most common crises that overtake people in the course of their lives are those concerned with their own or their close relatives' morbidity and mortality. Healers confront these crises on an everyday basis and thus can be expected to have a more systematic cosmology and to be more articulate in communicating it to others. Observing healers and their patients deepens our understanding of cultural ideologies about the nature of self and other, the workings of mystical power in the cosmos, and the essentials of bodily and spiritual well-being.

## A. Balians in Balinese culture

The Balinese word *balian* has generally been translated as "traditional healer" in ethnographic literature, but the significance of balians' activities extends beyond this sphere: They are consecrated practitioners who perform many priestly functions, and they are often highly esteemed people (as the honorific title "Jero" indicates) with some influence in the affairs of Balinese rural communities. There are probably several thousand balians working in Bali today.

Balians operate in a diverse range of healing capacities, none of which are mutually exclusive; any one practitioner may perform a variety of functions. Among the Balinese gentry (*triwangsa*), and to a lesser extent outside these strata, there are balians who specialize in reading, transcribing, and interpreting archaic Javanese–Balinese manuscripts about medicine, magic, and mysticism. Their texts consist of inscribed palm leaves (*lontar*), which have been dried, treated, and bound. These experts dispense advice, medicines, charms, and instructions for offerings. Divining (*matenung*) may be incorporated into their skills.

Most balians are not members of the gentry but "outsiders," commoners (*jaba, sudra*) who are usually illiterate in classical texts, although an increasing number have spent at least a few years in the national educational system. They include midwives, spirit mediums, masseurs, and bonesetters. There are also numerous practitioners who traffic in charms and rituals to render the body invulnerable to both physical and magical attack, who peddle love potions, and who sell protective amulets with accompanying ceremonial prescriptions for almost any purpose.

Unlike, for example, Ayurvedic practitioners in India, balians do not form an instituted body. They are folk healers who are individually recruited to their vocation through scholarship in a teacher–pupil relationship (usually with a senior male relative), through inheritance of a practice, or through divine inspiration. Collaboration and formal exchange of knowledge are uncommon between healers, except for literate practitioners. Survival and popularity as a balian depend on the ability to attract a clientele that will pass on word-of-mouth recommendations.

### Historical evidence for the position of balians

Evidence for the existence of specialists referred to as balians goes back to the 19th century. From the classical texts (chronicles, poetry, and genealogies) of the 19th-century courts we learn of the balians whom rajas employed as functionaries of the courts, and who were rewarded with land for their services. These specialists were usually literate males, members of Brahmanic priestly families patronized by the small courts scattered throughout the fertile wet-rice-producing areas of southern Bali. But not all balians were tied to the courts, a fact often obscured by evidence for the 19th century (which emphasizes elite representations of history). Most balians, then as now, were probably illiterate peasants, deriving most of their livelihood from private donations in cash, kind, or labor. Much of the evidence for the existence of these practitioners of the 19th century and earlier can only be inferred from representations that recur in the arts – theater, painting, and folktales – as well as in mythology and in a few chronicles.[1]

Images of female balians in art and myth often portray a witchlike image, ultimately derived from Durga, the underworld goddess adopted from the Hindu pantheon. Such images define women as peripheral to orthodox

---

[1] This evidence is discussed in Connor 1982a, pp. 78–86.

(scholarly) bases of knowledge (which are transmitted patrilineally) and thus as susceptible to illicit alternatives. Images of male balians, on the other hand, may be either benevolent or malevolent, and they show greater variability, from coarse and bumpkin-like (*kasar*) to refined and polite (*alus*).

In the arts, myths, and indigenous chronicles, people with curative and magical powers frequently intervene in affairs of state and are sought out by royal authority, but all the evidence suggests that those with this sort of influence were the high priests of the courts (*purohita, bagawanta*) or other Brahmanic priests (*pedanda*) renowned for their spiritual powers. Balinese chronicles (*babad*) also contain evidence for the consultation of high priests by rajas intent on using magical as well as military warfare to extend their sphere of influence and vanquish their rivals. Although at lesser moments of history (for which there are no records), humble social status may not have debarred a balian of repute from consultation by a raja, it does seem that the more elevated Brahmanic scholar-priests have a privileged situation in this respect. The few references to commoner balians in the Balinese historical record associate them with threats against the realm rather than with the defense of the court.

Bali came under Dutch control relatively late in the history of Dutch presence in the archipelago – the mid 19th century for northern Bali and the early 20th century for southern Bali. There was a decline in courtly wealth and power associated with colonial control, and the central place of the courts as a source of cultural creativity was eliminated. Those balians and other specialists who had relied primarily on court patronage were forced to turn for support to private individuals and the institutions of village communities.[2] It is likely, however, that most balians were not supported by royal patronage; thus the incorporation of Bali into the colonial state probably had little effect on their livelihood or on their relations with clients. It is only when we examine the contemporary evidence for the social situation of balians that we can build up a more detailed picture of their recruitment and practice.

## Balian recruitment and client networks

Balians are recruited to their vocations in different ways and engage in a variety of therapeutic techniques. Both of these factors influence the social relations they enter into with their clients and with each other. The sphere of social relations constituted by service and recruitment can be divided into four main dimensions:

1.  practice as a literate medical specialist, requiring neither secrecy nor unfamiliarity with clients;
2.  broadly therapeutic skills not requiring literacy and founded on divine inspi-

---

[2] An example of the decline of the courts in relation to Balinese art is discussed in Vickers 1980.

ration to the calling, or inheritance of a practice, without pressures for either secrecy or unfamiliarity;

3.    spirit mediumship, with preferential unfamiliarity but not secrecy; and

4.    the peddling of spells, charms, and rituals that enhance spiritual strength (kemasukan kekuatan), with preferential secrecy and unfamiliarity.

In the films A Balinese Trance Séance and The Medium Is the Masseuse, we see Jero Tapakan working as a spirit medium and as a masseuse. It is evident from the films that Jero's relationship with her clients in each of the two situations is quite different. In the former case, the interaction is premised upon her unfamiliarity with the predicament of the clients who ask for the séance, and their dependence on her as therapist is a transient one. In the latter case, it is apparent that Jero has an ongoing, long-term relationship with the client and his wife, as she does with many of the people who come to her for massage and associated treatments. Practitioners in each of the four categories described above have different relationships with their clients, depending on the type of service offered:

### 1. LITERATE MEDICAL SPECIALISTS (BALIAN USADA)

All balian usada are males. Their practices are founded on possession of classical texts about healing (usada).[3] Balian usada acquire their skills by a formalized learning process. Usada and other texts enshrine the mythological charter for balian usada, that is, the teachings of the first balian, Buda Kecapi. Not all balian usada are in fact literate. For some the main qualification is the possession of medical texts rather than the ability to read them. Such is the spiritual potency of any material manifestation of the written word that holy water blessed by contact with lontar manuscripts (wangsuan) is itself believed to be curative.

Balian usada who do attain literacy receive their training from a senior male relative, usually a father or patrilateral uncle. Many of the most renowned balians in Bangli district, where I worked, are from gentry families, who predominated in precolonial occupations requiring classical literacy, but some peasant balians also base their practices on lontar texts. At present in the Bangli district a balian usada can be found, on average, in every second or third hamlet (banjar). The less renowned practitioners draw on a stable clientele from the surrounding settlements whereas those of high repute also attract new clients from greater distances. Clients consulting balian usada may receive only holy water blessed by contact with lontars and holy oil (tutuh) for the nose, eyes, mouth, or ears. Some literate practitioners will elicit symptoms and then consult texts for diagnosis and ther-

---

[3]  A review of the Balinese medical literature can be found in Goris 1937. For a more exhaustive treatment, see Weck 1976.

apy, which usually consists of both medicines and propitiatory offerings. The procedure may vary depending on the nature of the client's case.

Even when rigorous textual learning precedes consecration and practice as a balian, the ultimate legitimation, as the practitioner often tells it, is through divine omens, if not direct communication with deities. Such experiences testify to the individual's spiritual endowment (*kasaktian, kasakten*) and are considered a necessary complement to formal training if his treatments are to have any efficacy.

## 2. BALIANS WITH BROADLY THERAPEUTIC SKILLS

This category of therapists includes bonesetters (*balian tulang*), masseurs (*balian apun, balian uat*), midwives (*balian manak*), peddlers of curative substances (*balian paica*), and the many diviners (*balian tenung*) who are not literate and do not possess *lontar* manuscripts. Visionary experiences alone, when publicly recognized and endorsed by a consecration ceremony, are enough to establish their claim to be balians. Inheritance of a practice, although not necessary, further strengthens this qualification and the likelihood of public endorsement. However, many successful balians, like Jero Tapakan, have no inherited claim to the vocation, nor is there any formal apprenticeship. The experience of being a patient or of frequently observing the treatments of a near relative is usually not in itself considered adequate preparation for a healing vocation.

After establishing an identity as a practitioner, these balians must develop a clientele, unlike *balian usada*, who more often than not inherit one. Most balians build up a reputation slowly and attract the bulk of their clients from within their own district. A few balians experience dramatic and public divine revelations or gain a reputation for miraculous cures, and they may attract clients from all over the island. It is rare, however, that such a clientele can be sustained over a long period of time. Generally, none of these practitioners requires anonymity or secrecy.

## 3. SPIRIT MEDIUMS

Spirit mediums (referred to most commonly as *balian taksu* or *balian tapakan*), like the balians with broadly therapeutic skills, come to their calling by a process of divine inspiration; but they differ from other balians in that their clients often prefer to remain strangers vis-à-vis the practitioner. This means that clients will usually travel some distance to reach the house of a spirit medium whom they do not know personally. Spirit mediums are at the center of client networks based on ties of kinship, friendship, and economic relations. Although interactions with any particular client group are rarely repeated, clients do not have to be unfamiliar with each other, so the medium often builds up a reputation in certain locales. This is the case in the film *A Balinese Trance Séance*, where the clients filmed chose Jero on the basis of recommendations from other residents of their village.

By virtue of their geographically extended networks, many spirit mediums have access to general information about matters of local *adat* (customary law and practice) in many areas of Bali. This in turn facilitates their ability to handle many of the problems raised in séances. This breadth of knowledge is apparent in Jero Tapakan's discussion with her clients in *A Balinese Trance Séance*, examined in Part II.

## 4. BALIAN KEBAL

In the case of *balian kebal* the constraints of both secrecy and anonymity operate. Some of these balians engage exclusively in *kemasukan kekuatan* procedures ("the introduction of strength"), whereas others practice them covertly in combination with other forms of healing. Most come to the calling by divine inspiration, but a few use manuscripts about magic in their practices.

*Balian kebal* are widely considered to be endowed with spiritual power, which they use in a morally ambiguous, even dangerous, way. Secrecy under these circumstances is mutually desirable on the part of the balian and the client. The balian seeks secrecy because of the threat of police surveillance, the moral disapprobation of the local community, and the possibility of a challenge to his powers by other balians. Clients prefer some measure of secrecy because of the widespread disapproval of such practices and because the "strength" so gained by the balians' ceremonies is meant to be a covert form of protection against enemies. For the same reasons, clients seek to maintain their anonymity vis-à-vis other clients and the balian. However, the pressures for anonymity and secrecy are limited by the necessity to disseminate information about the practice so that the balian may acquire clients.

*Balian kebal*, typically, are middle-aged men who have had some experience of life outside of rural areas. They may have served in the armed forces or worked as itinerant traders, casual laborers, or boat hands on interisland shipping. These experiences render them more sophisticated than many of their fellow villagers and usually give them fluency in the national language, Indonesian.

Their clients are, typically, males in modern occupations (e.g., police, soldiers, civil servants) whose work requires a degree of mobility. Many come from outside Bali. In catering to this clientele, *balian kebal* base their practices not only on Balinese magic but on variants of pan-Indonesian mysticism (Ind.: *kebatinan*) and martial arts (Ind.: *silat* ).

*Balian kebal* are at the center of widely dispersed social networks, not only because of the need for unfamiliarity and secrecy but because of the mobility of their clientele, which provides these practitioners with access to much information about different aspects of their society.

## B. Religious foundations of healing

The generic appellation *balian* indicates that Balinese perceive a common function among a diverse array of practitioners: mediation between the realms of "darkness" (*peteng*) and "light" (*lemah*). "Darkness," the domain of mystical activity, need not have sinister connotations; rather, the term indicates that this realm is largely opaque to human understanding. "Light" is the domain of everyday life. Mystical forces constantly impinge upon the realm of human activity; darkness and light are separated only in the abstract, never in practice.

For Balinese, mystical power has two aspects. It is a quality imminent in the natural world, especially in the form of *sakti*, as an essential quality of certain objects, people, places, and substances. It is also "supernatural" in the transcendent sense, as a force at the command of deities, ancestors, and demons who are usually removed from the world of everyday social relations. Balinese conceive human fate as intertwined with the wills of the beings who compose the supernatural realm.

For a practitioner to refer to himself or herself by the title balian is to lay claim to public recognition as a person who is *sakti*, "spiritually powerful." *Sakti* equips balians with the personal power to intervene on behalf of clients with a variety of mystical forces.[4] More humble practitioners are cautious in acknowledging that they have such power. They may deny that they are balians, although they work as healers. Many people are reluctant to use the term *balian* in describing others because *sakti* can be used for good or evil ends; it is a morally neutral force. Thus it is not necessarily a compliment to describe someone as *sakti*.

On behalf of individuals and communities, balians struggle with misfortune, disease, and death by deploying their spiritual powers in mediation between the domain of mystical activity (to which they have privileged access) and their clients' immediate concerns. The specialty of balians lies in their healing expertise: Any person who tries to alleviate others' suffering is likely to be referred to as a balian, no matter what other social identity he or she possesses. In a broader sense, balians interpret events in the world to their clients in terms of religious ideologies that are essentially similar to those of other types of consecrated village specialists such as caretaker priests (*pamangku*), customary officials (*kelian adat*), and puppeteer priests (*dalang*).

Mystical power in the cosmos

The most fundamental ordering of the Balinese universe is the distinction between the *buana alit* (lit.: "small world") and the *buana agung* (lit.: "great world"). The *buana alit* is the universe of the human body as an anatomical

---

[4]  McCauley (1984b) discusses the concept of *sakti* in relation to healers' practices.

structure and as a vessel for the diverse manifestations of supernatural forces; for example, the human soul (*atma*) can be viewed as the manifestation of God in each individual. The *buana agung* is the whole of existence. Each element of the body has many correspondences in the natural universe. The two structures are defined by the energy flow between them: They are isomorphic, interacting and modifying each other, with the direction of causation not predetermined. Both the *buana alit* and the *buana agung* are suffused with mystical power. Balians, in their healing ceremonies, attempt to influence the condition of their patients by deploying spiritually powerful elements of the *buana agung*, such as medicines, offerings, and mantra syllables. People with great spiritual power may also effect changes in the natural universe by the correct manipulation of mystical forces within their own bodies. Balinese myths and chronicles contain many stories about deities and seers whose meditations changed the course of nature.

The principle of correspondence between the microcosm (or small world) and the macrocosm (or great world) influences popular belief only in the broadest terms. Control over the relations between the two domains is left in the hands of those skilled in textual analysis and ritual practice. For these people, knowledge of the correct way to manipulate natural objects allows control over their corresponding cosmic elements and thus creates and defines the person of power (*wong sakti*). For example, members of a temple congregation who plan an important ceremony may employ a priest who prays and meditates to bring about fine weather. For ordinary folk, uninitiated into the mysteries of cosmic correspondences, offerings (*banten*) are the material means by which they can influence the supernatural determination of their fate.[5] Offerings are potent symbols in which contents of the natural world are arranged in an attempt to communicate with supernatural sources of ultimate authority (see Section 5F).

### The *kanda mpat*, the four spiritual siblings

In popular understanding the most potent fusion of the great world and the small world lies in beliefs and practices regarding the four spiritual siblings associated from conception and birth with each human being. A person's welfare is as dependent on nurturing his or her spiritual siblings through ritual as it is on food and shelter. These siblings link the individual with the macrocosm and the realm of supernatural beings. Each sibling has concomitants in the microcosm and the macrocosm: For example, apart from their physical manifestations at birth – the placenta, blood, amniotic sac, and amniotic fluid – each sibling is represented by a part of the body, a symbol of the alphabet, a mantra syllable, texts, temples, dances, and topographical

---

[5]   Stuart-Fox (1974) discusses the variety and use of offerings in Balinese ceremonies. Offerings also receive detailed discussion in Belo 1953; Mershon 1971; and Hooykaas 1977.

and natural features. Authoritative tracts abound on the siblings, referred to in the texts as *kanda mpat* (from *kanda*, "elder sibling," and *mpat*, "four"). In everyday usage the spiritual siblings are frequently referred to as *nyaman tiange* ("my siblings"), a phrase that does not differentiate between one's spiritual and one's natural brothers and sisters. A multitude of illiterate practitioners, who base the legitimacy of their procedures on divine inspiration, ritually address these four spiritual siblings.

The *kanda mpat* preside over the welfare of their human host throughout his or her life and must be given offerings at every important rite of passage. Like the human brother or sister, the four spiritual siblings are gradually socialized to be fit to live in Balinese society. This process in the life of a child is marked by an elaborate series of childhood rites of passage. Jero Tapakan, commenting on the significance of the many childhood life-cycle ceremonies in Bali, says:

They are to purify the *nyama* [siblings] which are born with the child. With each ceremony, they are purified a little more and take a different form. When the child is born, they are *pemali agung* [a great curse]. After the *lepas aon* ceremony [to celebrate the drying up and dropping off of the umbilical cord] they are known as *kala yoni* [the demons of the womb], and after the 42-day ceremony [*tutukambuhan*] they are called *nyama kakeregin*. After the three-month ceremony [*nelung bulanin*] they have new names and status. After the six-month ceremony [*otonin*] they are fully purified and called the usual names [Angapati, Marajapati, Banaspati, and Banaspati Raja].

When a balian is consecrated, his or her *kanda mpat* are consecrated also. In the film *Jero on Jero*, Jero Tapakan discusses the importance of her "siblings within" in the performance of a séance (see section 6B, shot 16). Worldly foibles and talents are often attributed in the palm-leaf tracts to the relative strengths and weaknesses of an individual's four siblings. In illness, all four siblings, or one or more of them, are considered to have been weakened through ritual neglect, and they must be refortified by healers. In magical manipulations they are withdrawn by the sorcerer and must be retrieved by powerful countermagic. Relevant texts contain prescriptions for offerings and invocations for their retrieval, propitiation, and strengthening.[6]

In both popular understanding and traditional religious doctrines Balinese conceive of the person not as an isolated, indivisible unit but as a nexus of interacting forces, macrocosmic and microcosmic, natural and spiritual, always in a delicate balance. For most people, such a view forms a taken-for-granted, unarticulated background for their interactions with others and their intrapersonal psychic processes. Balians interpret the significance of clients' experiences in terms of the connections between the individual "self" and cosmic forces. They are able to communicate their insights to

---

[6]  Discussions of the *kanda mpat* from different perspectives can be found in Mershon 1970; Hooykaas 1974; and Connor 1982c.

their clients through healing ministrations and rituals and, thus, contribute to forming their clients' consciousness of their predicament. Nonspecialists' interest in such matters is circumscribed, limited to the contexts of crises such as rites of passage, illness, and misfortune. Clients seek out the specialist who is judged the best manipulator of mystical power. Participants in this process, as the films reveal, are not just individual clients but households, hamlets, descent groups, or temple congregations.

Case studies of illness and healers' practices, around which this monograph and the four films about Jero Tapakan revolve, raise the important question of how Balinese conceive of agency in human affairs. It is evident from our material that the conceptual importance of an active and individual "secular" human ego, familiar in the West, is attenuated in Bali. Agency in Balinese practice is multidimensional and, although purely secular motivations are recognized, spiritual forces are intrinsic to the human personality through the system of cosmic correspondence.

The relationship that Balinese conceptualize among macrocosm, microcosm, and mystical power contributes to the view that every event is potentially charged with meaning that may not be immediately manifest. Thus mere contingency is not drawn upon as an explanation for phenomenal appearances. This is pronounced, for example, in the way Jero Tapakan interprets the events of her own life (see section 10D), but it is also evident in interpretations by nonspecialists of the misfortunes and problems they encounter (see, for example, Ida Bagus's and Dayu Putu's interpretation of their situation in section 8D or the discussion of the séance in Chapters 5 and 6). People do not invoke "luck," especially "bad luck," as an explanation for their circumstances. Things do not just happen; they are caused. The ultimate agents of causation (supernatural beings) are not under direct human control but may be approached through ritual specialists and offerings.

## C. Balians and everyday economics

In contemporary Bali, many balians rely on their practice as the primary or an important subsidiary source of income. Jero Tapakan and her family have several small pieces of poor agricultural land whose produce is only enough to support them for a few months of the year. The most substantial part of their livelihood is provided by income Jero earns as a balian. Clients' contributions in cash, kind, and labor over the past twenty-five years have enabled Jero gradually to lift the family out of its former debt and poverty and to become moderately prosperous by village standards.

There is little evidence concerning the economic situation of balians during the precolonial and colonial years, but the vocation probably contributed to the livelihood of many practitioners. Up until the 1940s and the end of Dutch rule in Bali, land was still plentiful in relation to the population. It is doubtful whether there was the same degree of occupational diversification that is evident in the last few decades; the accelerated monetization of the economy has only taken place since the 1940s. Compared to the indirect and attenuated forms of economic power exerted today, courts in the colonial period exercised more control over processes of production and exchange at all levels of society. However, most balians were not tied to court patrons, and so it is doubtful whether the decline of the courts during the colonial period would have affected adversely the livelihood of these practitioners in any direct way.

Although we know little about the economic position of balians in the precolonial and colonial period, it must have been different from their present situation. Whereas in the 1970s and 1980s balians receive a large part of their remuneration from clients in cash, this was probably not the case prior to the 1940s. We can surmise that most balians relied on donations, as they do today, but that most payments were in kind or in the Chinese coins (*kepeng*) used in rituals. It is not clear whether the severe shortages of land today have intensified the economic pressures that lead people to select healing as a form of occupational diversification or whether this vocation has long been a desirable option.

Since the end of the colonial period, a doubling of the population and the intensified participation of the Indonesian economy in international capitalism have given rise to a situation where the majority of agricultural producers have too little land to support even their own subsistence. In Bali, as in Java, the most dramatic transformation of production relations in the last few decades has been through the introduction of new rice technology. Although the capitalization of wet-rice cultivation may improve gross yields,[7] it also contributes to the impoverishment of a so-far undefined proportion of the peasantry and promotes gross differences in access to strategic resources within the peasantry. Producers become increasingly dependent on imported technology (e.g., mechanized rice hullers instead of hand hulling) and on supplies of hybrid seed, petrochemical fertilizers, chemical insecticides, pesticides, and fungicides, none of which are produced within local communities. Small landowners may compete on disadvantageous terms for the necessary credit and may be forced out of production. Moreover, a variety of income-earning activities associated with traditional rice production are eliminated altogether.

Similar changes have occurred where the introduction of industrially produced manufactured goods has eliminated traditional productive activities. Some home industries, for which there are no commodity import substitutes, have survived, and in Bali especially a few have been regenerated by the tourist market. But although there have been high hopes for tourism as a

---

[7] Yield improvement is debatable. See Collier, "Food Problems"; Poffenberger and Zurbuchen 1980; and J. C. Scott, *The Moral Economy of the Peasant: Rebellion and Subsistence in Southeast Asia* (New Haven: Yale University Press 1976).

source of employment, these aspirations have not been fulfilled: Tourist numbers, contrary to predictions, have not grown significantly during the past few years.[8] As there is very little industrial development on the island, the primary impact of the penetration of commercial capital has been to stimulate economic diversification unaccompanied by industrialization, which would provide employment for otherwise redundant labor.

What then, in these circumstances, are the options open to members of peasant households in order to maintain their livelihood? Economic survival depends on supplementing or replacing customary subsistence activities with a number of alternative occupations, many of which draw household members into relations of petty commodity production and exchange. These jobs typically are labor-intensive, require little investment of scarce cash resources, provide few opportunities for capital accumulation, and return very small profits. The only other opportunity open to peasants for earning nonagricultural income is wage labor, usually poorly paid. Petty commodity production and wage labor are key elements in a process of occupational diversification in which people are prepared to invest large amounts of the most abundant resource, labor, for minuscule returns.[9]

A balian requires no formal education in the modern school system and no capital to establish a practice. This is typical of many peasant income-earning activities. Balians depend on a preexisting demand for their services. Jero Tapakan's occupation as a hawker – an itinerant vendor of goods acquired with capital not her own – helped her develop a social network that later facilitated her practice as a balian. It also gave her confidence in dealing with strangers. Some aspects of her earlier occupation are related in the film *Jero Tapakan: Stories from the Life of a Balinese Healer*. Jero and other balians are not unlike craftsmen and women (*tukang*) who constitute a pool of skilled labor and peddle the products of their own specialized skills in the marketplace (from a relatively advantageous position). However, Jero and many other balians do stand in a special economic relationship to their clients. Although peasant occupations are increasingly subject to the rationale of the marketplace, many balians are ideologically committed to a donation form of payment for their services. The reliance of many balians on customary social networks for clients (as described above) places constraints on the sort of economic relations they establish and hinders any rationalization of payment procedures. All but the most renowned balians have a standard of living with a range similar to that of other members of the peasantry. Because of this, practice as a balian may be one of a number of income-earning activities in which members of a household engage: For some the income earned as balians is negligible, but for others it provides the bulk of subsistence needs.

---

8   See Noronha 1979; Bendesa and Sukarsa 1980.
9   See Poffenberger and Zurbuchen 1980.

## Women as balians

Women form a minority of practitioners, with estimates from different areas of Bali placing them at between 10 percent and 33 percent of total balian numbers.[10] There are several reasons why women are underrepresented as balians. The lack of female access to medical literacy means there are no women among the *balian usada*, who make up about 50 percent of balians in Bali. But other factors also affect the general situation of women as healers.

In Bali a moderately successful practice as a healer may be more rewarding financially than the small-scale peddling on which many peasant women rely for their main source of income. The advantage of peddling, however, is that it can be accommodated to the demands of childrearing and house-work, for which women conventionally hold primary responsibility. Most women in rural hamlets live in extended-family households where young children can be cared for by close relatives for the hours the mother is away from the home. Some mothers take very young babies to market with them. Families of women with permanent food stalls not far from the houseyard virtually move into the stall, eating there and often sleeping there as well. Peddling, which involves very little investment of cash resources, can be put aside for the demands of household crises, preparations for major rituals, or the opportunity to earn income more lucratively, for instance in the harvest season.

Healing places demands on practitioners that prevent many women from considering it as an option. Midwives may be called out to attend clients at any time of day or night. Spirit mediums on auspicious days may hold seven or eight séances, each lasting half an hour to one and a half hours. Massaging is physically exhausting, and some masseurs of high reputation work from dawn to dusk in response to client demand. Clients come to the house of a balian with no forewarning but cannot be turned away without good reason such as illness or ritual pollution (e.g., from menstruation, childbirth, or social proximity of a death).

In the case of women, the earning of income has to be accommodated to the reproduction of labor within the family. Because of these constraints, it is doubtful whether work as a healer would satisfy the requirements of many women for an economically viable occupation, especially wives with children. The same circumstances do not constrain men's participation as healers.

In the majority of cases I recorded (69 percent), women with successful practices as healers were unmarried, childless, or older widows with ado-lescent or adult children. Older women have daughters, daughters-in-law, nieces, and grandchildren to take over housework tasks. For single women,

[10] See Connor 1982*a*, p. 97. Issues concerned with women as balians are discussed in more detail in Connor 1983.

continuation in the calling may mean they remain unmarried. When the woman chooses not to marry, her enhanced status and income compensates in some measure for failure to conform to high normative values placed on female reproduction.

## D. Balian therapies and modern medicine

During the interview at the end of *The Medium Is the Masseuse* we learn that the patient and his wife have made a complex series of choices about their consultations with balians and with modern medical personnel. During the massage of this patient, Jero herself compares some of the qualities of Balinese treatments with those of the doctors. In *A Balinese Trance Séance* we find her providing different clients with an alternative explanation of their relative's death to that provided by the hospital doctors. Balians' therapies are different from, and often at odds with, those of modern medicine. The differences are important for balians when we consider the implications for balians of future developments in the health bureaucracy.

Several decades ago, under colonial administration, the emphasis in health care was on individual curative services, mostly concentrated in urban areas. In the rural areas of the Indies the functions of the traditional healers continued unimpeded. In the 1950s and 1960s there was a heightened development of public health programs and maternal and pediatric health care facilities. In those years the first impetus came for the involvement of traditional healers in the modern health sector, but the programs were limited in scope.

In 1968 the National Health Conference framed initial policy on the Community Health Centers (Puskesmas [Pusat Kesehatan Masyarakat]) to be implemented in the first five-year development plan of President Suharto's New Order (1969–73). The aims were an increase in the number of trained medical personnel serving rural areas and promotion of rural community involvement in health care. The funding during the first five-year plan, and since, has been enormous, with increasingly large sums contributed to Indonesia by international agencies (e.g., WHO, UNICEF), U.S. aid programs (e.g., U.S. Agency for International Development [AID]), and the Inter-Governmental Group for Indonesia (IGGI).

These trends continue into the 1980s and the fourth five-year development plan. During the 1974–8 plan, the target of one Puskesmas (clinic) per subdistrict was exceeded. From 1975 onward the emphasis has been on "primary health care" as formulated at WHO/UNICEF conferences. The official Indonesian Primary Health Care Project aims to maximize community involvement in health care as part of a more comprehensive program of community development. It involves the recruitment of community leaders as mediators between the bureaucracy and the village. Primary health care policies ideally promote the universal provision of low-cost basic health care by training locally selected community members in elementary medical procedures as well as educating community members to be responsible for their own public health services. Such policies ostensibly aim to equalize and decentralize the allocation and control of limited health care resources.

These policies have the potential to exercise a profound influence on the position of balians in rural Balinese society. Attitudes toward balians on the part of health care practitioners and administrators vary and change over time, both at an informal level and as embodied in official policy decisions.[11] Up until the early 1970s, when community health programs began to be implemented, balians (and traditional healers throughout Indonesia) were largely ignored by the health administration. Many doctors inherited the prevalent Dutch attitude that literate medical practitioners who used classical medical texts were to be admired whereas the illiterate midwives, spirit mediums, and other healers were to be despised for their primitive practices.

Indonesian doctors work with a very high patient:doctor ratio in rural areas and are aware that they can handle only a minority of cases.[12] For many poor peasant families in the more inaccessible areas of Bali the only viable option is treatment by balians or no treatment at all. Some doctors have studied the techniques of balians and worked with them on cases, arguing that the functions of balians and doctors are complementary, not competitive. A majority, however, deny that traditional healers have any important role to play except perhaps as "faith healers" who offer a last resort in hopeless cases. Many doctors, in support of the argument that such treatment should be eliminated or at least strictly monitored, are quick to cite cases where patients have been irreparably harmed by balians. They propose a licensing system, which they recognize would be extremely difficult to implement because balians are scattered and professionally unorganized.

Whatever the orientation of modern practitioners, most are forced to recognize and reckon with the local influence of balians, especially in rural areas. For many Balinese the hospitals and clinics are a last resort for reasons of cost, inaccessibility, or fear of unfamiliar procedures. This is counter-balanced, however, by patients' pragmatic orientation to health care: Many people are willing to attend clinics, particularly for conditions known to respond to clinic treatments and where cost and distance are not prohibitive. Nevertheless, many problems are thought to require the ministrations of balians, either because clinic treatments have proved unsuccessful or as an alternative to them.[13] Government midwives often are not available when

---

[11] Pounds (1982) provides a thorough anthropological perspective on national primary health-care policies as they have affected rural Balinese communities.
[12] For example, see Thong 1976.
[13] McCauley discusses health-care decision making by Balinese villagers (1984a, chap. 4). See also Connor 1982b.

needed. Strains and sprains, muscle and joint pains, and broken bones are often taken to masseurs and bonesetters in preference to clinics. Some complaints are construed as "Balinese," or they may develop into "Balinese" complaints if they prove refractory to clinic treatment. Balinese complaints need to be treated by balians, it is believed, because they are likely to be caused by sorcery or ancestral or divine curse. In such cases offerings and prayers, under the balian's guidance, are thought to be essential to recovery even if medical treatment is sought at the same time. Thus, in the film *A Balinese Trance Séance*, the clients consult Jero because they are dissatisfied with the doctors' explanations of their son's death and wish to find out the "real" reason at the séance. Illnesses with sudden onset and dramatic symptoms, or sudden or premature death, are particularly likely to be construed as having a "Balinese" cause.

Cases of madness or stress are rarely taken to clinics or mental hospitals until several balians have been consulted. Generally balians resolve such cases to the family's satisfaction. My survey of patients at the provincial mental hospital in Bangli revealed that almost 80 percent of patients and their relatives had visited one or more balians before admission.[14] Culturally, the psychotherapeutic models currently utilized by medical practitioners are inappropriate and incomprehensible to the majority of clients. Doctors usually explain the patient's complaint to relatives as some variant of "weak nerves" (*syaraf lemah*), and the drugs given are explained as a remedy for this complaint; they also give some brief counseling when disrupted psychocultural patterns are obvious. Among most of the rural Balinese families I interviewed, "weak nerves" were seen as the consequence of a deeper problem of spiritual origin. Consequently, most of the mental hospital's clientele consisted of chronically unmanageable patients and those who manifested extreme aggression, for which there is a low tolerance in the culture.[15]

### Incorporation of balians into the health bureaucracy

Throughout Indonesia formal attempts to incorporate traditional healers into the health bureaucracy have had their greatest success with midwives. The specific health-related tasks of midwives are easily recognizable. Government-trained midwives can work closely with traditional midwives in the villages, through upgrading courses at local health clinics and through follow-up consultations. In some cases the village midwives receive a small financial incentive to participate and are equipped with a kit to promote elementary hygiene. The success of the program depends on the ties government midwives have with the local populations and on the receptivity of individual midwives. Some "upgraded" midwives in the district where I

[14]  Connor 1982*b*.
[15]  See Higginbotham 1984, chap. 7, pp. 228–53.

lived always used their kits and were familiar with the functions of each object; others had never even opened the package except to remove the implements that were useful for ordinary household purposes.

Enlisting the services of other types of balians in modern-style health care is more difficult. Spirit mediums, for example, have functions that resist definition in modern health care terms. These practitioners have so far escaped medical attention, although there have been tentative suggestions that their activities be brought under closer scrutiny by the Department of Religion. The significant factor affecting attempts to incorporate balians into the health bureaucracy is that, for modern medical practitioners and planners, the manipulation of mystical powers is at the periphery of healing processes; for balians and their clients it is the very foundation of therapy.

# FOUR

## How and why the films were made
TIMOTHY ASCH

### A. Introduction: ethnographic film and anthropology

FEW anthropologists have taken film seriously, a fact both regrettable and surprising given film's potential value as a tool for research and teaching. Without examples to illustrate this potential, anthropologists will continue to ignore film. This project attempts to provide one such example to serve as a model for other anthropologists. We hope this book and the four related films will stimulate interest among ethnographic filmmakers, researchers, and teachers of anthropology (as well as related disciplines) and generate a dialogue that will promote broader and more scholarly use of film in anthropology.

No one disputes the value of detailed visual records of interesting social events. Although such events have been studied by anthropologists, visual records with any great ethnographic value for anthropologists are tragically few. This is largely because most so-called ethnographic films have been made not by trained anthropologists but by filmmakers intent on creative expression. Such films tell us more about the filmmakers and their cultural biases than about the people filmed. Seldom have anthropologists regarded these films as an asset because few ethnographic films have been linked to research or to written publications.

Excellent films of other societies do, of course, exist. In the great tradition of the feature film, some extraordinary films convey to members of one society an understanding of the social relationships within another: films such as Pagnol's trilogy, *Marius, Fanny,* and *César* (Marseilles in the 1930s), Ray's *Pather Panchali* (rural India in the 1940s), and Guney's *Yol* (Turkey in the 1980s). Yasajiro Ozu's *Tokyo Story* portrays relationships within a postwar Japanese family, emphasizing the gap between the older and younger generations. A sensitive script, fine actors, and a great director produced a film designed to reveal certain social relationships with simplicity and clarity, free of the mundane distractions – the "noise" – one experiences when observing the daily relationships of people living their own lives. These feature films, made by members of diverse cultures, depict the beliefs and world views of their creators, as does all art, but the best of them speak across cultural boundaries; they permit others to feel they understand important aspects of social relationships in foreign societies. They may also provide insights into the viewer's own life.[1] These films can and should be used to teach anthropology, but because they are scripted, acted, and directed, I hesitate to call them ethnographic films. It is precisely the absence of scripting, acting, and direction (as developed in the theatrical film tradition) that characterizes many documentary films and all ethnographic films.

Feature films depend on dialogue to provide insights into the lives of their characters. Feature films, however, have always incorporated dialogue (even in the silent era, dialogue frames were interspersed between shots), whereas the documentary film tradition has been more concerned with images and with using images to tell a story. For three decades after the introduction of "talkies" only the feature film industry, using cumbersome and expensive equipment, could afford to make films with lip-synchronous sound. Today anybody with training can shoot footage – whether on 16mm, super 8mm, or videotape – whose subjects speak about the central concerns of their lives and participate in spontaneous conversations.

Although the portable, sound-synchronous camera rig was invented in 1960, it was 1970 before many ethnographic filmmakers realized that they should include sound-synchronous dialogue in their films. Some of us had already used subtitles in our earlier films, but probably David and Judith MacDougall's films of the Jie of northeastern Uganda were the most compelling examples of the value of sound-synchronous filming and subtitling of dialogue.[2] I gained as much insight into Jie life from the subtitled conversation in their films as I did from the visual images of daily activities.

The addition of dialogue permits us to make potentially more valuable films. It is no longer sufficient to edit miscellaneous images into a general montage when it is possible for the subjects to speak for themselves (although their words are filtered through the transcription, translation, and condensation required by subtitles). It is the dialogue rather than the beauty of the images that should dictate the filming and editing of a scene.

In filming conversation we may obtain extensive oral texts, because conversations can be tape-recorded without interruption even when the visual record is not as complete. But all conversation is socially and physically situated. Filmed conversations combine a sound-recorded text with a visual record of the behavior of the speakers and listeners, their nonverbal communication, and much of the social context. Understanding the dialogue

---

[1]   See G. Bateson, "An Analysis of the Nazi Film *Hitlerjunge Quex*," in Margaret Mead and Rhoda Metraux, eds., *The Study of Culture at a Distance*, pp. 302–14 (Chicago: University of Chicago Press, 1953).

[2]   *To Live with Herds, Under the Men's Tree*, and *Nawi* (distributed by Extension Media Center, University of California at Berkeley).

recorded during a Balinese séance, for example, depends on knowing whether the healer is considered – both by herself and by her clients – to be possessed; in other words, on knowing whom the clients think they are addressing and who is answering. The visual record indicates exactly when the spirit enters or departs (see section 6B, shot 39).

The first and most valuable activity an ethnographer undertakes is to learn the language of the people with whom he or she is living. For ethnographers, fluency in a language means acquiring the social skills to use the language appropriately in varied social contexts with a variety of native speakers. Using these skills, ethnographers collect data about a group of people at certain points in its history. Such data should be accessible for reanalysis or comparison by future generations of anthropologists.[3] But very few original data are available, and what there is tends to be idiosyncratically coded and hence incomprehensible to others.[4] The same can be said of most ethnographic film; rarely has anyone analyzed someone else's ethnographic footage. Edmund Leach has advocated the inclusion of case-history material "in sufficient quantity for the reader to exercise his scepticism where and how he will" rather than merely a brief analysis, "a 'take it or leave it' solution."[5] So, too, ethnographic filmmakers should provide sufficient detail to permit viewers to interpret behaviors for themselves.

When we try to define ethnographic film, we must recognize the difference between ethnographic footage and the products made from it. Many films are composed of snippets of footage, recorded at different times and in different locations, strung together and linked by a narrative that provides a story. The original footage may be of naturally occurring social interaction among a group or groups of people (my definition of ethnographic footage), but edited film may so distort, misinterpret, or remove from context the snippets shown that it is impossible for viewers to go beyond the interpretation provided in the narration and to analyze for themselves behavior observed on film. Such documentaries should be labeled ethnographic films only insofar as they can be used in a study of the subculture of the filmmakers.

Given the time, money, and effort involved in producing a film, ethnographic film could support ethnography best by providing, as a minimum, a permanent record (perhaps in the form of a videotape) of all the footage shot, in the order in which it was shot, with accompanying annotations, either written or on tape, of as much of the context of the filmed behavior as the fieldworkers can provide. If possible, translations of the dialogue

[3] As Edmund Leach, e.g., has made such an analysis of Malinowski's material: see Leach, "Concerning Trobriand Clans and the Kinship Category *Tabu*," in Jack Goody, ed, *The Developmental Cycle in Domestic Groups*, pp. 120–45 (Cambridge: Cambridge University Press, 1958).

[4] See, e.g., Franz Boas's notes at the American Museum of Natural History.

[5] Edmund Leach, *Pul Eliya, A Village in Ceylon: A Study of Land Tenure and Kinship* (Cambridge: Cambridge University Press, 1961), p. 12.

should also be included. As most shooting ratios are high (sometimes an hour of film is edited from as many as 30 hours of footage), the vast percentage of footage remains unseen. If properly annotated, it would be a valuable resource for future generations.

In order to make ethnographic film that is both tied to research and technically adequate to produce instructional films for others, collaboration between an ethnographically trained filmmaker and an anthropologist is probably the best strategy. I prefer not to film with the intention of editing a documentary that paints a broad canvas to show a culture in one hour, as many have done: An hour-long film is unlikely to reveal the complexities of a group's social relationships. The audience needs to see enough of an event to identify the participants and learn something of their relationship to one another and the grounds of their apparent involvement. For example, Jero does not know the nature of her clients' problem in *A Balinese Trance Séance*, but they have come to contact the spirit of their dead son and the audience can see how their purpose slowly emerges and how, in the process, they are drawn into new concerns. In *Jero on Jero* it becomes clear that Linda has specific topics she wants to cover but that Jero is interested in quite different issues. The audience, like the participants, needs to work through the event to make sense of it. In a general film about a culture the audience need not work through anything; images are presented to them with a packaged presentation.

Myriad in range, unique in pattern, cultures are evidence of the ways human beings have organized their social relationships and of their interactions within diverse environments. As each culture changes, quickly or slowly but inevitably, what remains? What do anthropologists' records leave for future generations? The best example we have is John Marshall's many films of the !Kung bushmen, recorded over more than 30 years (1951–84), with accompanying study guides and linked to a vast and growing literature.[6]

## B. Background in ethnographic film

Before I arrived in Bali in 1978 I had been trying to develop effective ways to record and analyze social interactions utilizing different aspects of the audiovisual media – in Canada, then Africa, Trinidad, Venezuela, Afghan-

[6] Study guides are available for about 20 of Marshall's films, including among the most famous, *The Hunter, N!ai: Story of a !Kung Woman, N/um Tchai: The Ceremonial Dance of the !Kung Bushmen, An Argument about a Marriage,* and *Bitter Melons* (Watertown, Mass.: Documentary Educational Resources). Among the many books and articles on the !Kung, the following are probably the most useful, read in conjunction with the films: Lorna Marshall, *The !Kung of Nyae Nyae* (Cambridge: Harvard University Press, 1976); Marjorie Shostak, *Nisa: The Life and Words of a !Kung Woman* (Cambridge: Harvard University Press, 1981 [paperback ed., New York: Random House, 1982]); Richard B. Lee, *The !KungSan: Men, Women, Work in a Foraging Society* (New York: Cambridge University Press, 1979); Richard Lee and Irven De Vore, eds., *Kalahari Hunter-Gatherers: Studies of !Kung San and Their Neighbors* (Cambridge: Harvard University Press, 1976).

istan, and Indonesia. The Bali project was a direct and conscious outgrowth of my own history as an ethnographic filmmaker. When I first became interested in ethnographic film I was studying anthropology at Columbia University. I had been a still photographer, a student of Minor White's and Edward Weston's, and a photojournalist. In the early 1960s I went to Harvard to work with Robert Gardner and John Marshall. As I watched Marshall struggle to find a new form for some of his ethnographic footage – superb sequences of social interaction like those in *A Joking Relationship, A Rite of Passage*, and *Meat Fight* [7] – I began to think of new and more effective ways to integrate film into anthropological instruction. Lengthy narrated films told the viewer what to see and how to interpret it. Frequently these films were shown when the instructor was absent; they were not used to illustrate specific anthropological concepts, to provide a common data base for a group of students, or to stimulate classroom discussion. Most ethnographic filmmakers are intent on making one general film, and they expose their footage according to a script. Marshall's work shows the value of filming sequences that can be edited as discrete events or combined in more complex films. Short sequences can easily be integrated with lectures, much as anthropologists use case studies.

With this background, I joined Napoleon Chagnon to film among the Yanomamo Indians in southern Venezuela. The many short films we made,[8] as well as some of the longer films,[9] were attempts to provide rich visual material on one group of people. They were films with little or no narration that forced the viewer to play a more active role in making sense of the footage. I hoped the films could be used by instructors in a wide variety of courses.

By the time I began to film with Linda Connor in Bali I had four main reservations about the Yanomamo films.

1. Unnarrated films of people who look exotic can be, and frequently are, used to reinforce Western prejudices about "primitive" people (e.g., the Yanomamo shamans in *Magical Death* are often seen as inhuman and disgusting).
2. I had intended that the films be integrated with written materials that would provide the needed context to help counter such prejudice and to make the films more valuable for instruction. Films can only convey a certain amount of information. If too much is said the viewer ceases to try to comprehend what is occurring and, instead, expects to be told how to interpret behavior. Ethnographic film ought to be not an illustrated lecture but something quite different, something closer to the experience of a field observer, albeit an experience in which the images are framed by someone else's camera. Generating inter-

---

[7]  Distributed by Documentary Educational Resources, Watertown, Mass.

[8]  E.g., *Bridewealth, A Father Washes His Children, A Man and His Wife Weave a Hammock*, and *Dedeheiwa Weeds His Garden* (Watertown, Mass.: Documentary Educational Resources).

[9]  More complex films include *The Feast, The Ax Fight*, and the two films of the myth of Naro (Watertown, Mass.: Documentary Educational Resources).

esting questions without providing access to information that might help students to find some of the answers is not fair. Such information is best provided by written materials (although there are times when an additional film, such as *Jero on Jero*, is valuable). Given his other commitments, Chagnon was not able to do this, however, and seemed to believe his other publications would be sufficient.

3.    I regretted not filming more Yanomamo conversations, which would have allowed individual Yanomamo to reveal their thoughts and opinions more directly. It is disappointing that so few individual characters emerge in ethnographic films.

4.    I was sorry that we dared not take our film back to show to participants. Were Yanomamo to see images of dead relatives they would probably try to kill us, assuming that because we had stolen the dead people's souls (by taking their images) we were responsible for their deaths.

My involvement with the Bali project has been deeply influenced by these concerns: Balinese do not seem as exotic as Yanomamo, so there is less danger of the film's making caricatures of them. By filming events of interest to a graduate student (who would spend time on transcriptions, translations, and annotations because the films were part of her research), I had stumbled on a method for obtaining the written materials necessary to allow ethnographic films to be used effectively by anthropologists. Jero's character emerges clearly because viewers see her in a variety of social settings engaged in different activities. And Linda was as eager as I to return to Bali to show people footage of themselves and their neighbors.

The method works for me. However, an anthropologist who collaborates with a filmmaker, even one trained in anthropology, should not expect ethnographic filmmaking to be easy: Filming is often arduous (during the last few days of a cremation ceremony Linda and I had almost no sleep and carried our heavy equipment everywhere); the anthropologist must guide the filmmaker in local custom, not always an easy task, and act as translator; and the job of transcribing and translating recordings is often tedious and always demanding. Furthermore, a struggling anthropologist, who must publish or face unemployment, can ill afford to work on ethnographic films until such films and their accompanying written documentation are accepted as scholarly publications.

## C. History of this project

I first went to Indonesia in 1977 to film with James J. Fox on the island of Roti in eastern Indonesia. In July of 1978 I went to Bali to prepare for a second trip to Roti. While waiting for Fox to join me from Holland, I decided to make a short film in order to test my recently repaired camera and some old film stock. The previous year I had met Linda, a graduate student who was studying possession, magic, and healing in Bali. She was an ideal person with whom to collaborate because she was finishing two years' fieldwork and was almost ready to return home. She seemed heartened by the idea that I would want to make a film with her that focused on something she had been studying, something that would be valuable for her research. Crucial from my point of view was Linda's fluency in Balinese and Indonesian and her thorough knowledge of her subject.

Linda discussed filming with Jero Tapakan, a Balinese healer with whom she had worked closely. Jero was eager to assist Linda. Before we began, Jero performed a special ritual in her shrine house to ensure that our filming would be successful, and it was she who spoke to other Balinese about being in each film. Two days out of every three Jero practices as a spirit medium; on the third day she gives patients massages and related treatment. I watched these two aspects of Jero's practice carefully so that I could anticipate the sequence of actions and begin to predict the course of social interaction that transpired during Jero's séances and massage treatments. We decided to film Jero treating two patients with massage, in order to test my old film stock, and to film a séance with new stock to be sure the camera was working properly. From the Sydney laboratory report we learned that two of our three rolls on massage were too old and the third was marginal, but the séance footage, from which we edited *A Balinese Trance Séance*, was fine.

At this point I learned that Fox would probably not reach Indonesia for another six weeks. As Linda and I were enthusiastic about working together, we decided to use those weeks to make several more films: one about Jero's practice as a masseuse; a biographical film in which Jero explains how she came to be a spirit medium; and a longer film showing how half of Jero's hamlet organized a group cremation. As we did not have enough film to cover the cremation, during the first five weeks of preparation I took still photographs — often bursts of 10 to 15 pictures of a given activity — while Linda recorded sound and interviewed participants. I wanted to demonstrate that anthropologists could use still photographs with tape recordings to document an event without having to rely on cumbersome and expensive movie equipment. However, in the last few days of preparation and during the final cremation ceremony we filmed.

Linda and I sometimes lived at Jero's compound, sometimes in a neighboring town, 25 minutes away. We usually traveled on one motorcycle, although it is not easy for two people to carry a sound-synchronous camera rig on a motorcycle over treacherous muddy roads in driving rain, sometimes with a live chicken from the market for Jero's pot.

The séance film took four months to edit, but before it was finished we made a videocassette with subtitles to show to various audiences, primarily students. The feedback we received affected the final structure of the film and the narration. This process of testing is essential. It is important to know who the audience will be. No matter how well one thinks one has been able to communicate, feedback in a trial stage is an excellent way to evaluate what has and has not been communicated; it also gives the anthropologist an opportunity to test reactions to his or her interpretation.

Long before 1980 anthropologists like Alan Lomax and Jay Ruby had been arguing that ethnographic film should be more reflexive, that the presence of the filmmakers should be a conscious part of ethnographic film. But séances are formal events, and we did not feel it appropriate to participate. When I showed the film to Vincent Megaw's visual anthropology class at Flinders University, South Australia, three of his students were incensed at the seemingly ''imperialistic'' and ''voyeuristic'' quality of the film. They saw us as symbols of colonialism, using our implicit power to force the subjects of the film to participate. It did not help to explain that the massage and biography films would be different, because these had not yet been edited.

We had planned to return to Bali in 1980 to show our footage to the participants, as we had promised. It was in Megaw's class that I suddenly realized that a film of Jero's reactions to seeing herself in the séance film would reveal her attitude toward the project. Furthermore, Jero's reactions might be the best way to answer some of the many difficult questions raised among Western audiences when they watched the séance film, particularly the question of whether Jero is a charlatan. Such a film also would demonstrate the value of showing participants a film of themselves as a way of eliciting additional information and interpretations of past events. For these and other reasons we made *Jero on Jero*.

Before the filming, Jero asked the clients if they would mind being filmed. Because Jero obviously trusted Linda, they said: ''If it is all right with you, it's fine with us.'' They did not seem distracted by the camera, except once during the séance when the chief petitioner suddenly looked straight into the camera and once near the end when I drew attention to myself by asking the man on the floor to turn on his tape recorder again so the film's future audience could identify the source of the strange voices in the background.

*A Balinese Trance Séance* and *Jero Tapakan: Stories from the Life of a Balinese Healer* were case studies that Linda analyzed in her thesis; the work of annotation thus served two purposes. Because, in the end, Linda did not include detailed discussion of massage in her thesis, she spent less time studying the massage footage. Nonetheless, treatment by massage was an important aspect of her fieldwork because these informal occasions provided an opportunity both to observe healing sessions and to inquire about patients' and healers' concepts of the causes of illness, the nature of the human body, and techniques to restore health. Two of the filmed massage sessions illustrate Jero's views particularly well: The first concerned a woman with dysentery, who Jero said was suffering from a divine curse because as an adolescent she had been a temple dancer and had not asked the deity's permission to marry; the second was Ida Bagus, the patient in *The Medium Is the Masseuse.*

Patsy had edited a film from our 1978 massage footage, but we were dissatisfied with it for two reasons: The woman filmed was seeking treatment for simple aches and pains, so her case did not reveal those Balinese explanations for the causes of illness that contrast with Western explanations; and the footage showed little of the patient's perspective. The three of us returned to Bali in 1980 with a videotape of the original massage footage and the intention of shooting a second massage film. In *The Medium Is the Masseuse,* filmed after Jero had seen herself on videotape, there is evidence – her use of the Indonesian generic term for "healer" instead of the Balinese one, for example – that Jero is adjusting her performance to a new awareness of her audience and of how she appears on film. Patsy and I again returned to Bali in 1982 and showed *The Medium Is the Masseuse* to Ida Bagus and Dayu Putu and to Jero. Linda could not be there, but in her subsequent visits to Bali (1983 and 1984) she did have lengthy discussions with Jero about the massage footage. She was also able to follow up the case of Ida Bagus's illness and the couple's childlessness.

Perhaps the most exciting aspect of this project has been showing footage to participants and recording their reactions. The people we filmed in Bali are by far the most appreciative audience I have ever had. It is rare for anthropologists to be able to explain effectively what it is they are doing in the field, let alone share their work. Showing videotapes is one way of doing this, and it is a way to help repay our vast debt to the people with whom we work.

For Jero and Linda, videotape of the séance was a mnemonic, a way to trigger personal and joint reflection on a past event in which they both had participated. For anthropologists, the value of using film is the capacity of images and sounds to recall forgotten feelings and ideas. Repeated viewing and discussion of a sequence with participants may tease out embedded layers of meaning they each associated with the experiences depicted on film. Film also helps to objectify events. Linda and Jero, watching the séance film together, were able to appreciate the differences in their knowledge and their perspectives. Jero spontaneously remarked on things that startled her, such as her appearance, but she also tried to explain things she suddenly realized Linda might not understand. Film can help the participants go beyond some of their taken-for-granted assumptions to appreciate the problems outsiders may have in understanding the social dynamics of an interaction.

Our footage recording feedback (both that of Jero watching the séance film and that of people in Jero's hamlet watching footage of a collective cremation they had performed) provided non-Balinese with further insights into the views of the participants and their interpretations of what is occurring. *Jero on Jero* is the first film of its kind that I know of, and it is particularly apt for contemporary Western audiences who are concerned with notions of person and systems of explanation.

## D. Royalties

This project raised for us the moral question of royalty payments to the film subjects. For too long anthropologists and ethnographic filmmakers have made their reputations and sometimes their income from information about the lives of other people, usually without sharing royalties with these people. As far as film is concerned, our minimal debt to people filmed is twofold: We should maintain control over footage to prevent distribution of a distorted image of the lives of those we film, and we should share profits. It is rare for an ethnographic film to make a profit or, in fact, to cover costs and pay the filmmakers a salary. However, distribution companies do pay royalties, and a portion should go to the film subjects. But what portion?

The dilemma resides not in what we, as filmmakers, can afford but in the effect that money can have on people who live in small, subsistence-based communities. If, as with the Jero films, the subject is a single person, the social relationships between that person and her neighbors can be altered radically if she is given a large sum of money. Is this desirable? If a film focuses on a group of people, to whom in the group should the money be given? In other words, how is it administered and for whose gain? Are we justified in specifying that royalties be used for some purpose that we designate, such as education, health, or irrigation, rather than giving it to a local leader to spend at his discretion or to the regional government? Payment of royalties is a thorny moral question, but it is one that ethnographic filmmakers must consider.

The anthropologist who has worked with the people filmed is in the best position to evaluate the situation and recommend how much to pay and in what manner. On the basis of Linda's assessment of Jero's circumstances, we decided that Jero should receive a fixed percentage of the gross income from sales and rentals of all four films (even before expenses were recouped). This money is given to her privately whenever someone we know and trust is going to Bali and can take her the cash. When emergencies have arisen (such as a costly illness in her family) we have increased the amount to cover her debts. We anticipated that the percentage given would not have negative effects on her life, but we also wanted to ensure that she had additional resources when necessary.

Certainly this is a paternalistic decision but, given the financial difficulties of sending money to Indonesia, Jero's lack of understanding about things like royalties and percentages, and the tendency of the Balinese ritual cycle to absorb all known income, we felt this the most equitable way to handle her royalties. These films are about Jero's life, and she has a right to benefit, as should the subjects of most ethnographic films.

## E. Technology

Technical decisions reflect goals. I wanted to be unobtrusive but not to mystify or hide my activities while filming. I wanted to be able to move freely around a scene in order to sustain filming of social interactions. People soon find a camera and the person behind it more boring than an ethnographer with a notebook, perhaps because the photographer's eyes are hidden. I have found that if I am relaxed and feel comfortable about being present most people that I film begin to ignore me. I believe it is important for people to know when you are filming; I respond to any requests to stop, but I don't remind people that they are being filmed.

Thanks to the Australian National University, I was able to use a 16mm Arriflex SR camera. This is a dependable field camera. Film comes in rolls of three lengths – approximately 3 minutes, 11 minutes, and 30 minutes. For microanalysis of social behavior, these 30-minute rolls are essential, but one must use a tripod when filming with a 30-minute magazine because of the weight. Although there are times when I would like to be able to sustain a shot for 30 minutes, I use 11-minute rolls because I want to be able to carry my camera as I film and move about freely for long periods of time. The séance and massage films were shot entirely with a hand-held camera; the early interviews in *Jero Tapakan: Stories from the Life of a Balinese Healer* and the scenic pan of the rice fields were filmed from a tripod. Jean Rouch remonstrated with me for using a tripod, and after I attended some of his students' gymnastics classes, I abandoned tripods even for the interviews in *Jero on Jero* and the massage film. The trick is to brace your elbows so that you can hold the camera steady. I had five camera magazines so I could change film rolls in about 15 seconds, thereby minimizing gaps in my coverage of events. (Unfortunately, it takes longer to change sound rolls, but they last 30 minutes.) If I had all five magazines loaded with 11-minute film, I could film for 55 minutes. This was sufficient.

I had a 10–150mm Angenieux zoom lens, which I used in two ways: to focus and to show details. Because it is easiest to focus on a telephoto setting, I would zoom in to a close-up to focus and then either zoom out quickly, if I intended the close-up to be cut, or zoom out slowly if I wanted it to be usable. Usually I filmed at a wide angle to get the broadest coverage possible. The Angenieux lens has a major design flaw, probably a compromise to minimize the size: At extreme wide-angle settings, if one focuses on something close to the camera, the corners of the image appear black.

Black corners are visible in several shots in the massage film, where I was restricted by Jero's narrow porch.

There are those who advocate filming social interaction from a distance so that all participants are visible. For microanalysis of behavior, this may be essential, but a distant view is only one of the infinite views possible. I filmed as I might observe: At times I showed all the participants, but I also focused on particular interactions and on details of behavior that I thought would be valuable for Linda's research. By moving, by altering my focal length, I got a variety of perspectives. Subtle gestures often are visible only in a close-up or from a particular angle. The danger is that the more one moves around the more one introduces one's own biases, but bias is inevitable because film is the product of a particular person. My results depend on my understanding of what it is I am filming and of how film might be used as part of a particular research project. This, in turn, depends on my rapport with the anthropologist with whom I am collaborating.

This rapport is fostered by engaging the anthropologist in filmmaking. Linda was the logical person to record sound. Tape recorders pose more social problems than cameras do, particularly if one uses a long directional microphone (MKH 416 TU) as we did. It is hard not to appear aggressive as one thrusts this phallic object toward people. Linda was less threatening than a stranger, her fluency in Balinese was invaluable in selecting what to film and in predicting people's actions, and the fewer our numbers the less disruptive our film crew was likely to be. We decided that Linda should continue to join in conversation whenever she felt it appropriate and that I would film her when she participated. This felt natural to us, demonstrated our participation, and provided evidence of Linda's style of fieldwork.

Linda used a Nagra 4.2 tape recorder with a built-in 50-cycle pilotone sync signal. She recorded on quarter-inch tape, both 1mm, 30-minute tapes and 1.5mm, 15-minute tapes. The thicker the tape the less likely sound recorded at one point on the tape will later print through to another section, ruining the sounds originally recorded there. One-millimeter tape is the thinnest that should be used. Sometimes we had to identify each shot visually; at the head or tail of the shot I would film Linda as she struck the end of the microphone shield (an example is included in *Jero Tapakan* when Linda resumed tape-recording after Jero cried). At other times we used a radio signal from the camera to the tape recorder that put a beep on our sound track whenever the camera was turned on and at the same time flashed a light on the film, producing a clear frame that later could be synchronized with the beep.

The technical aspects of filming *A Balinese Trance Séance* were straightforward. The shrine house where Jero held her séances was very dark. With her permission, I removed the front door and opened the shutter, but it was still too dark. To light the back of the room, the shelves of medicines and holy water, and Jero's face, I used a 100-watt, 12-volt lamp in a standard sun-gun housing powered by a 12-volt car battery (there was no electricity in Jero's village). Sound-recording was a problem because the tiny shrine house was cramped; only one person besides Jero could maneuver within. Linda had to stand outside, to the left of the door; I could not see her to get any clues about when and when not to film or to learn whether she had to change tape rolls.

The group of relatives we filmed came for three different séances and stayed almost three hours, but I had only 35 minutes of film. I filmed the first séance fairly thoroughly, using two rolls of film (22 minutes during a 42-minute period). About 20 minutes (mostly of the second and third times Jero was possessed by a deity) were not filmed. I never filmed Jero coming out of a state of possession, probably because I could not predict when it would occur.

The most difficult postproduction problem we had was with subtitles. For *A Balinese Trance Séance* cards with the lettering for each title were made and photographed. Then I used an animation camera to film each negative the exact number of frames we wanted to use. I filmed them in the order in which they were to appear on the film so that I produced a film roll of titles the exact length of the film that could be superimposed on the film images when the laboratory made the internegative. A similar process was used for *Jero on Jero* and *The Medium Is the Masseuse*, except that by that time optical companies had computer typesetters and they could film directly from the long roll of titles produced by their computers. *Jero Tapakan: Stories from the Life of a Balinese Healer* posed a special problem because Jero was wearing a white shirt that would have made traditional titles illegible, and it did not seem possible to shift the location of the titles, as Patsy had done for the massage film. We are having the titles etched into each print, rather than putting them into the internegative, which means we can make a print without English subtitles if we want a version in another language. This method could become expensive, however, if more than 20 prints are sold. (For further technical information, particularly about the editing, see Chapters 6, 9, and 11.)

The technical quality of the film on Jero does embarrass and disappoint me; the footage is very grainy, the contrast is high, at times the exposure is incorrect, some of the footage is jiggly or out of focus, and I have not always had the camera pointed at the right place. Some of these weaknesses stem from my own history: I have no formal training as a cinematographer, and I have little filming experience between field trips, sometimes for periods as long as four years. In the field I have filmed extensively without being able to see any of the footage until the trip was over. Much of what I have learned is forgotten before I return to the field to film again.

The nature of ethnographic filming itself is a second source of problems. I try to sustain filming of social interaction up to some naturally occurring conclusion, which is often hard to predict and does not fit the length of film rolls. Since I try not to let my filming interfere with naturally occurring events, I often have to film in poor light, from an awkward angle, and without adequate warning – nothing is rehearsed, nothing is repeated, and no two events are ever exactly alike.

Circumstances surrounding this particular project were a third source of technical difficulties. When I began filming in Indonesia, reversal film rather than color negative film was still recommended by the Australian laboratories. Although it is certainly cheaper to produce subtitled films in reversal, the quality of the image is not as rich. During our filming the laboratories converted to equipment to develop negative film, and it became increasingly difficult to get satisfactory development and printing of reversal stock. (Because it is difficult to mix reversal and negative in a film, we had to continue using reversal film stock.) All four films were taken on location with minimal lighting but in circumstances where I felt it best to use fast film rather than flood the area with artificial lights. The fastest reversal film, 7250 with an ASA of 400, is a high-contrast, video-news film with very little latitude in exposure. With limited footage I could not film whole events, which I would have liked to do; I did not speak Balinese, and often I could not see Linda and hence could not follow her direction. I had a fever and stomach cramps and found it difficult to concentrate during filming of the massage film.[10] Jero's narrow porch, with its pillars, was an awkward place in which to film. And so on.

I list these problems to emphasize that ethnographic filming, especially of sustained interactions, always presents problems; the filmmaker has almost no control over who will interact or when, where, and for how long. Obviously, the better the filmmaker knows the people and the type of event, the better he or she can film it. In making ethnographic films, the longer the period spent with the subjects before filming, the better the film should be.

If the aim is to take useful ethnographic footage, the filmmaker should probably concentrate on a few people, on an event of manageable length and complexity – an event similar to others observed many times – and should avoid excessive camera movement, such as zooms and pans, that constantly detract from the film's content. With minimal training all anthropologists should be able to use portable video equipment to produce footage useful for their own research and for seminars. Video equipment has two advantages: The filmmaker can immediately see and evaluate what has been filmed, reusing the tape if it is not satisfactory; and the images can be shared with the participants, to give them pleasure and to generate new data. Super 8mm film is also a fairly easy medium in which to work effectively; 16mm, partly because of the ever increasing expense involved,

---

[10]  Jero did treat me with massage and an elixir afterward, but my recovery was too late to influence my filming.

as well as the weight and complexity of the equipment, requires formal training.[11]

Certainly I would not want my ethnographic film students to go to the field with as little training as I had. On the other hand, there is a danger in training ethnographic filmmakers in traditional film schools. The primary consideration is the integrity of the event and the people filmed; the urge to construct a creative work of art is in many respects an obstacle. It would be naive to imagine that I was not influenced by the craft – by every film I have seen, by the technical strengths and limitations of my equipment, by the conventions of my day – but my goal is to make films in which my own artistic drives are eclipsed by the subjects in the film. The challenge for us was to enable Jero, in talking about the central concerns of her work and life, to speak for herself.

[11] Some anthropologists who have used 16mm film or super 8mm without formal training have done valuable work; e.g., Napoleon Chagnon, William Geddes, and Karl Heider.

Part II

# A Balinese Trance Séance *and* Jero on Jero: "A Balinese Trance Séance" Observed

# FILM SYNOPSES

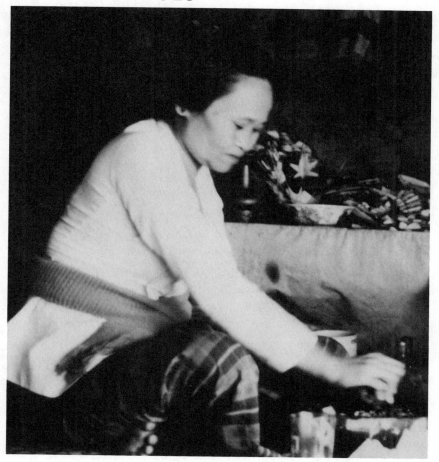

Jero, seated in her shrine house, preparing for a séance.

## A Balinese Trance Séance

JERO Tapakan, a spirit medium in Central Bali, is engaged in a consultation with a group of clients at the shrine house in her home. Before the main séance begins a narrated introduction provides a visual impression of the séance and background information on the medium and her profession. The clients wish to contact the spirit of their dead son to discover the cause of his death and his wishes for his cremation ceremony. Jero is possessed several times in the course of the séance: first by a protective houseyard deity, who demands propitiatory offerings that had previously been over-looked; then by the spirit of the petitioner's deceased father, who requests further offerings to ease his path in the other world; and finally by the spirit of the petitioner's son. In an emotional scene the son's spirit reveals the cause of his premature death (sorcery) and instructions for his forthcoming cremation. Between each possession the medium converses with her clients, clarifying vague points in the often ambiguous speech of the deities and spirits. The closing shots of the film show the final prayers and the clients' departure. The film attempts to present the participants' view of what is occurring, and all dialogue is subtitled.

A 30-minute, 16mm, color film by Timothy Asch, Linda Connor, and Patsy Asch
Available on videocassette from Cambridge University Press
Available on 16mm film from Documentary Educational Resources
5 Bridge Street, Watertown, Mass. 02172, USA

## Jero on Jero: "A Balinese Trance Séance" Observed

In 1980 we returned to Bali with videocassettes of our 1978 Balinese footage. Jero Tapakan, a healer whom we had filmed, looked at all the cassettes several times. This film presents some of her comments to Linda Connor and her reactions as she watched and listened to *A Balinese Trance Séance* for the first time.

By watching herself, Jero had a unique opportunity to reflect upon the experience of possession. Her comments provide insights into how she feels while possessed, her understanding of sorcery, and her humility in the presence of the supernatural world. She also voices more mundane thoughts, for example, the importance of the appearance of her home. Jero's approach to the videotapes and her spontaneous comments contrast with Linda's more controlled statements that reflect academic and filmmaking goals.

Audiences should see and discuss *A Balinese Trance Séance* before screening *Jero on Jero*, since they are likely to find Jero's comments more valuable after they have examined and discussed their own reactions to the séance film.

A 16-minute, 16mm, color film by Timothy Asch, Linda Connor, and Patsy Asch
Available on videocassette from Cambridge University Press
Available on 16mm film from Documentary Educational Resources
5 Bridge Street, Watertown, Mass. 02172, USA

# FIVE

## *Ethnographic notes on*
## A Balinese Trance Séance *and*
## Jero on Jero

### LINDA CONNOR

### A. Consultations with spirit mediums

CONSULTATIONS with spirit mediums are ritual events in which the practitioner brings clients into direct contact with supernatural powers believed by the participants to be responsible ultimately for the course of their lives. For a brief duration, spirits and deities express their wills, to be interpreted directly by their petitioners. From a Balinese perspective, this renders the situation a particularly authoritative one.

Séances construct a relationship between human beings and cosmological forces in terms of hierarchy. Supernatural beings dominate; humans are powerless and deferential. Within the structure of the séance, accommodation to the will of the deities and spirits is assumed but can be achieved only at the expense of considerable effort by the petitioners. Although there are many contexts in Balinese social life where egalitarian relations of cooperation and collective effort receive ideological emphasis, such relations are not salient during the séance. Humans are not merely the pawns of deities, however: The existence of spirit mediums such as Jero Tapakan bespeaks the possibility of compromise and of bargaining with supernatural wills. To some extent deities and spirits can be placated by means of the séance, which also gives recognition to the bonds of sentiment linking the spirits of the deceased to their living relatives. This linkage permits the petitioners some leverage in the supernatural realm, thus diminishing their perceptions of their own powerlessness.

In terms of the participants' ideology, mediums are conceived as the passive conduits of supernatural wills. However, practitioners such as Jero Tapakan, who actively interpret the deities' and spirits' utterances to their clients, are usually regarded as the most highly skilled. This reason is never given by Balinese, who attribute the specialist's success to the strength of his or her inner spiritual forces, which facilitate communication between the human and the supernatural realms. The medium (male or female) is nonetheless respected as a person of some influence and status (e.g., see Jero's comments in *Jero on Jero* on clients' perception of her status).

When discussing their own attributes, mediums usually portray themselves

59

as the humble vehicles of possessing agents and readily admit to their great ignorance in all spheres of human activity. In *A Balinese Trance Séance*, for example, Jero early remarks that "Others are literate, and can do anything," and several times during *Jero on Jero* she reiterates that "I'm just an ignorant commoner." Clients defer to the practitioner's knowledge as superior to their own, but all parties defer to the knowledge of deities and spirits, and between each episode of possession they attempt to make sense of the somewhat cryptic utterances.

Even the simplest séance is a delicate process of negotiation and exchange of information, in which mediums perform crucial functions. Because skepticism is rare, about both the existence of deities and spirits and the capacity of these beings to make their will known through mediums, the main concern of would-be clients is to select a skilled medium who will not make a clumsy or mistaken connection with the deities or spirits the clients wish to contact. Suspicions about practitioner fraudulence, though not unknown, are rare.[1]

Clients may consult two or three mediums and compare the results before settling on a course of action. They may do this because they are dissatisfied with the outcome of an earlier séance or because they wish to have additional spiritual endorsement of their intentions. Nowadays (as shown in *A Balinese Trance Séance*) clients often carry cassette recorders to record the medium's utterances, which they discuss with the practitioner after the séance or later with relatives at home. All mediums I encountered insisted that clients record only the speech of the possessing agents and not the discussion in between. They expressed the opinion that their own utterances as ordinary Balinese were not worth recording. Cassette recorders have been readily adopted to use at séances because the pronouncements of the deities and spirits are often obtuse and lists of offerings are long and difficult to remember. In cases in which the rituals to be performed are important and complicated, further discussion (of the utterances) at home is warranted before any decision is taken. It is possible that the use of cassette recorders may increase the tendency to consult more than one medium, as comparison of outcomes is facilitated. However, I have no evidence that this is in fact occurring.

When a séance has come to an unprofitable end, the clients sometimes suspect that they have mistaken the identity of the deity or spirit. This may be what is occurring, for example, in *A Balinese Trance Séance* when the chief petitioner asks of the possessing spirit, "Whose father is this, who is asking, who is speaking, so that I'm not confused?" (section 7G, speech 311). On other occasions clients conclude with resignation that the deities and spirits are not willing to speak on that day. These problems do not threaten the institution of mediumship even if they may weaken the standing

---

[1]  Belo, working in the 1930s in Bali, found the same limited doubt; see, e.g., Belo 1960, pp. 226–7.

of individuals within the profession. A medium's reputation suffers when clients consistently fail to gain satisfactory outcomes, but usually criticism is phrased in terms of weak inner spiritual forces mitigating against effective contact with the supernatural rather than in terms of the medium's being a charlatan.

Professional humility is a safeguard against the possibility of harsh judgment by clients and neighbors. It is from this perspective that Jero Tapakan's frequent protestations of ignorance and personal incompetence in *Jero on Jero* should be viewed. Stories abound of mediums who either became too greedy and eventually lost their clientele or became seduced into self-aggrandizement by the pursuit of spiritual power (*sakti*) for egotistical ends and thus lost the ability to communicate with the supernatural realm. These anecdotes foster an implicit code of ethics among balians and clients.

There is tension, however, between the expectation of humility and other demands of the profession: the necessity of displaying some virtuosity in the conduct of the séance, a facility for handling metaphorical language, astuteness in sensing mood and atmosphere during the séance, and the ability to make the most of the feedback that may be obtained from the clients. The tension between the expectation of humility and the strenuous efforts needed to attract a clientele is resolved by the commitment of participants to an ideology that spiritual agents rather than the medium are responsible for the practitioner's behavior. This is most evident in Jero's comments during *Jero on Jero*, for example: "I'm too ignorant. It's my 'siblings within' who pray and call the deity. I am ignorant about who should be addressed."

Although there are many perspectives from which the structure of the séance, the attitudes and behavior of participants, and the medium's functions can be analyzed, in the film *A Balinese Trance Séance* we have chosen to represent the situation as far as is possible in accordance with what we construe to be the participants' understanding of the event. In *Jero on Jero* we have tried to provide further insights into Jero Tapakan's view of the séance.

## B. Ritual possession

Since the 1930s scholars such as Gregory Bateson and Margaret Mead, Jane Belo, Beryl de Zoete, and Walter Spies have documented and analyzed the frequent and varied occurrences of ritual possession in Bali.[2] During possession, supernatural agents assume control over the persona of their human vehicle, who typically professes amnesia. Jane Belo's *Trance in Bali* (1960) is possibly the most exhaustive single ethnographic work on possession ever written. In the main body of the text she describes the various

---

[2] See, particularly, Belo 1960.

types of "trance practitioners" or "participants" in four districts in Bali. These types include spirit mediums like Jero Tapakan, as well as temple mediums who are the vehicles for deities and several types of ceremonial trance-dancers, including child dancers.

In the 1970s and 1980s a similar range and frequency of ritual possession can be found with the same positive evaluation by Balinese villagers as Belo found in the 1930s. There remains great variation from one village to another in the incidence of different types of ritual possession. In the district where I worked, several villages had integrated ritual possession into their cycle of temple ceremonies, though in many villages such events never occur. The region boasts large numbers of practicing spirit mediums; other areas have very few. Several customary-village communities stage public rituals of exorcism entailing dances involving possession, which recur over a period of days or weeks and in which many men and youths participate; neighboring communities may never perform such ceremonies. In one remote highland settlement male and female adolescents take part during important local temple anniversaries in ritual dances of possession. In some temples in mountain villages, groups of mediums consecrated to a particular deity become possessed and pronounce on the details of ritual, often effecting changes in the course of the proceedings. At many ceremonies, in both private houseyards and public temples, possession may overtake a number of the congregation in a seemingly unpredictable fashion. Variation from community to community is one of the most striking characteristics of ritual possession in Bali.

Since the 1930s and even earlier, several dance and drama forms incorporating episodes of possession have been performed for foreign and domestic visitors in numerous venues on the island. Today, with large numbers of tourists visiting the island, these commercial performances are a significant means of income for members of the many small dance clubs that abound on the island and function in more traditional contexts as well. But the impact of tourism and the doctrinal issues surrounding the "commercialization" of Bali's ritual arts, which are often debated in the provincial newspapers, have had little effect as yet on the beliefs and practices about possession in rural areas. Episodes of possession are usually accepted and welcomed and in many cases are considered crucial to the performance of a ceremony. There is often an element of fear and awe on the part of petitioners at a séance or members of a temple congregation drawn into close interaction with a supernatural agent acting through its earthly medium, but these emotions are mitigated by the rather stereotyped behavior of the spirits in any given context and by the set pattern of interaction with which people learn to deal with them. This is evident in *A Balinese Trance Séance* when the petitioners use polite gestures and formulaic phrases at key points in their interactions with the possessing agents, especially the more distant and imperious deity.

The three categories of supernatural agents that possess humans are demons (*buta* and *kala*), deities (*dewa*), and ancestors both uncremated (*sang mati, pirata*) and cremated (*pitra, hyang dewa*). The loftiest deities (*betara*) do not endanger their purity by possessing humans at all.[3] These deities (such as Betara Surya, Betara Siwa, and Betara Wisnu) may be approached only through offerings and prayer and, in the case of Brahmana high priests, through meditation. The possessing agent may be named (or proclaim itself through the medium, as in the séance on film) and may be associated with a particular temple, sacralized natural site, or descent group. In some cases, however, especially cases of possession by demons, the supernatural agent is not named or located, and only the category (deity, ancestor, demon) is known or inferred from the ceremonial context or the demeanor of the person possessed.

It is rare for someone possessed in a ritual context to lose complete control, although this is not the case in episodes of "deviant" behavior, which are attributed to demon possession. In cases of ceremonial possession by demons, when performers make dashes into watching crowds, they are restrained by onlookers. Damage to property, such as temple structures or refreshment stalls, is uncommon. During such volatile episodes, those possessed rarely make coherent utterances. The subjects (usually men) drink large quantities of rice whiskey and eat live chickens, the harsh food and drink the demons are believed to prefer. Those possessed by deities and ancestor spirits may often be impatient and angry, but they are also restrained and eloquent in their criticism of and comments on people and events. Deities are offered "pure" foods such as cooked poultry and coconut water. Their petitioners and congregation pay them deference by addressing them in particularly elevated language forms, as is evident in the filmed séance.

Balinese who are possessed usually report afterward that they cannot remember what they felt or did at the time. Indeed, the experience of possession is often referred to colloquially by the word *engsap*, "to forget" (see Jero's comments, section 6B). "Forgetting" may reflect a difficulty in talking about experience that is outside the context of everyday awareness or a reluctance to speak about behavior and feelings at odds with ordinary standards. Further questioning of possession subjects, however, usually elicits descriptive statements that are sometimes quite vivid. Subjects who are frequently possessed (such as spirit mediums) often describe the experience in considerable detail. This is the case when Jero Tapakan recounts her feelings and perceptions during a séance (see section 6B). She describes, for example, how she hears her own voice from afar, coming from above her head, as if it belonged to someone else. Jane Belo also records interesting

---

[3]  However, it is not unusual for deities who possess mediums to be referred to as *betara*. This happens in *A Balinese Trance Séance*, where "Betara Guru," a protective houseyard deity, speaks through Jero in the first episodes of possession in the film.

verbatim accounts of possession experiences from people she interviewed in the 1930s.[4]

Ritual possession, or what I have referred to less precisely as "trance" in the film *A Balinese Trance Séance*, is thus a highly differentiated sphere of behavior in Bali. The meaning of possession is constructed through a broadly based ideology that embraces many areas of Balinese culture. Balinese language does not contain within it a generic term for "trance" or even "ritual possession trance"; thus it is advisable to eschew the use of such terms as representative of primary analytical categories, or even as useful descriptive categories, except in the loosest sense.[5] In order to convey some information about the complex ways in which Balinese refer to experiences of possession, I have attempted to translate indigenous terms as literally as possible in the subtitles to *Jero on Jero*; for example, "forgetting" (*engsap*), "remembering" (*inget* ), "holding the brazier" (*ngisep*), and "entered" or "arrived" (*karauhan*).

The filmed séance conducted by Jero Tapakan has to be seen in the context of many similarly structured séances conducted frequently by hundreds of different spirit mediums over the island. It also has to be viewed against the background of the large repertoire of possession rituals and dance-dramas that Balinese villagers regularly participate in or observe, as well as a realm of ideas about possession available to explain much of human behavior.

## C. Spirit mediums' clientele

Clientele of spirit mediums differ from those of other balians because Balinese prefer to consult a medium whom they do not know personally if an important decision or problem is involved. Some people travel long distances across the island to find a medium of repute who is not acquainted with their affairs. This may seem to counter the widely stated assertion that those possessed cannot remember what was said or done during possession. However, clients do not seem to find this contradictory. I found little suspicion of fraud; perhaps people feel that consulting a balian whom they know well might tempt the balian to act beyond the role of passive medium because of an awareness of the petitioners' circumstances and a desire to be helpful or harmful. A more likely explanation is that people are embarrassed to discuss their affairs with a balian whom they know, when he or she is not possessed. Potential clients generally seem more willing to give credence to the great spiritual powers of distant balians than to rely on the readily observable powers of practitioners in their own neighborhood. For any or all of the above reasons, clients will rarely consult the same medium twice but will seek a new medium for each problem that arises. And if the

---

[4]  Belo 1960, pp. 219–25.
[5]  For further discussion of ritual possession, see Connor 1979.

first consultation is unclear in outcome, clients may consult other mediums about the same problem before weighing the results and acting accordingly. The family members who consulted Jero in *A Balinese Trance Séance* reported that they had been satisfied with the outcome of the séance and thus had consulted no other mediums. After the cremation of their son, they had consulted a different medium to learn whether the ceremony had been performed to the spirit's satisfaction. When asked why a different medium had been chosen, the father answered that it was always "clearer" to proceed that way.

If the clients' concerns are considered by them to be of minor importance,[6] they do not attempt to find a new balian far from their home but usually consult one close by. In these cases, only two or three members of the family attend, the offerings are simple, and the consultation is brief.

When the problem concerns a large group or community, such as a temple congregation, village council, or hamlet, all the members will be exhorted to attend the consultation and witness the speech of the medium. Thus groups of 20 or more petitioners occasionally pour into the houseyard of a spirit medium. On other occasions the medium may be asked to conduct the séance at the group's temple, so that it may be witnessed by the entire congregation.

The composition of the groups that arrive in the medium's houseyard varies according to the nature of the problem. Usually one sees groups of three, four, or five, including both males and females. Members of client groups are usually related (often members of the same patrilineally extended family) and often inhabit the same houseyard. These are people who co-operate most closely on ritual matters and in everyday economic affairs and thus are most likely to share the same problems. The groups often include senior female kin experienced in séances (as is the case with the group filmed in *A Balinese Trance Séance*). Each group has a chief petitioner (referred to as the *pangarep*, from *arep*: "front"), who may or may not be the chief spokesperson. The chief petitioner is the one who has primary responsibility for resolution of the problem in hand. Sometimes this person may be an older women, more often one of the senior males of the family. Other participants are not debarred from speaking. Clients dress in clothes appropriate for a ceremonial occasion, including the ceremonial sash without which one cannot enter temples or the medium's shrine house.

Illness is the most common problem brought to mediums. Other clients come to contact their dead relatives about instructions for cremation ceremonies and/or to discover the cause of death of a family member (as is the case in *A Balinese Trance Séance*). Clients also may seek instructions for building a new family temple or a new residential pavilion in their house-

---

[6] Minor matters include identifying the spirit of a newborn child (see Belo 1960, pp. 239–49) or the loss of a small piece of property.

yard; in such cases they need information about the form of the structure, its appropriate scale and orientation, and the necessary offerings for the blessing ceremony. Some groups come about family quarrels and tensions in the houseyard, suspecting that there is a spiritual origin for such events. They may come to learn more about a theft, although most balians will not divulge any information about the specific identity of a thief (or sorcerer; see Jero's comments in *Jero on Jero*, sections 6B, 6C) for fear of both police investigation and magical retaliation on the part of the accused party.

In my records of 79 séances with 11 different mediums in the Bangli district, the statistical breakdown of types of clients' problems is as follows:

1. illness of a relative (49 percent);
2. concern about the cause of a relative's death and/or instructions for mortuary rites (18 percent);
3. household strife and misfortune (10 percent);
4. identification of the reincarnating ancestor in a newborn child (6 percent);
5. other (16 percent).

## D. The clients in *A Balinese Trance Séance*

The séance we filmed in Jero Tapakan's houseyard was of average length and complexity,[7] and for the clients it reached a satisfactory outcome. These clients were farmers who lived in an outlying settlement of a small village about 20 kilometers to the northwest of Jero's home, in an area of nonirrigated fields planted with dry rice, sweet potato, corn, cassava, cloves, and citrus trees. The people involved in the filmed séance are all close relatives: the chief petitioner, his mother, his brother (or classificatory "brother"), and the brother's wife. Standing in the background, or sitting on the edge of the group, are neighbors and more distant relatives. This large group traveled together on the southbound bus that passes near their village in the early morning en route to market in the district town. Clients usually choose a market day because transport is easier to find. The day was also chosen because the clients considered it auspicious: *purnama*, the day of the full moon.

All of the members of this large group came about similar problems related to a collective cremation ceremony that they planned to perform about two weeks after the séance. Each person had one or more dead relatives (some deceased a number of years) who were to be cremated on the specified day. The clients had come to contact the spirits of these relatives in order to discover the spirits' wishes for their cremation rituals. On the morning we were filming, these petitioners rearranged themselves in Jero's shrine house three times, with different chief petitioners on each occasion. They told me that they had chosen Jero because she had been recommended to

---

[7] For information on the structure of séances, see Chapter 7.

them by other people in their village who had consulted her. Neither Jero nor I was acquainted with the clients previously, although, as Jero points out in *Jero on Jero*, between 1978 and 1980 the old women returned "about ten times" to assist other covillagers in their consultations. This woman would be considered valuable at a séance because of her command of the complicated forms of polite Balinese and because of her knowledge of offerings and ceremonies that are often requested in bewildering detail by deities and spirits.

The clients did not know that Timothy Asch and I would be filming on the day they chose, but they consented to participate after Jero explained that we were scholars interested in filming the séance in order to convey its significance to members of our own culture. The actual séance proceeded in much the same fashion as the many others I witnessed between 1976 and 1978.

A week later I visited the chief petitioner and his family in their "field cottage" (as it is referred to in the film). They received me warmly and were willing to speak about their response to the séance. I replayed my tape recording of the séance, which they already had heard several times because one of their neighbors (who appears on the film) had also recorded the proceedings with his own cassette recorder. The wife of the chief petitioner (who had been absent from the séance because she was menstruating and therefore "unclean") was particularly pleased to hear my recording because she said it was clearer than the one the neighbor had made.

The family members told me that they were satisfied with the information they had gained through Jero's séance, that it was very clear, and that they had felt no need to consult other mediums for a "second opinion." When asked if they had performed all the rituals according to the instructions of the dead son and his grandfather, they replied that they had done so, except for the offerings that were specifically requested for the day of the cremation, which was not to take place until a few days after my visit.

It was on this occasion that I obtained the information about the circumstances of the son's illness and death that is included in the film's narration. His symptoms (fever, vomiting, and a swollen stomach) had developed slowly. He had first been taken to a healer in the village, a man whom the family had often consulted about illnesses and problems. This healer had not said much about the nature of the boy's complaint or its causes but had given the parents some magically potent oil (*tutuh*) and some holy water with which to treat the child. When this had no effect and the child's condition worsened, they had made the difficult decision to take him to the district hospital. They traveled there by bus, an uncomfortable journey for a sick child. The bus trip took about 30 minutes, plus 30–60 minutes to carry the child up and down the three steep ravines between their house and the road. The father said the child died a few days after admittance to the hospital and that the doctors had told the parents the boy was suffering from typhoid and had been brought to the hospital too late for effective treatment. The séance we filmed was the first time since his death that his family had attempted to contact the boy's spirit.

In November 1980 I returned to the client's village with Tim and Patsy Asch to show the family the results of our filming in 1978. They showed little surprise when we arrived at their almost inaccessible dwelling (on foot, carrying heavy video equipment). Several members of the family and a large number of neighbors interrupted their preparation of offerings for a forthcoming ceremony to watch the videotape. They were excited to see themselves and identifiable objects and places on the videotape and in color. The arrival of the boy's spirit generated strong emotions among family members, especially the mother, who had not been present at the séance, and the father, who again wept. They seemed pleased with the videotape, expressed no objection to its contents, and insisted we show it a second time.

I also took the opportunity to ask them about the boy's cremation and any further contacts they had had with his spirit. The father told me that the cremation ceremonies had proceeded smoothly and that several weeks after their conclusion he had again consulted another medium to inquire if there had been any oversights or errors that might impede his son's path in the next world. The spirit had again spoken with the family, assuring them that its progress was satisfactory and that there were no major oversights during the cremation. The family's opinions about the fate of the sorceress referred to in *A Balinese Trance Séance* are discussed in the following section.

### E. Sorcery

Concern with sorcery is a strong undercurrent in Balinese social life. Unnatural or premature death, chronic or serious illness, and a host of other misfortunes are attributed to the malevolent intentions of those skilled in black magic or, to use the Balinese idiom, the powers of the left (*pangiwa*, from *kiwa*: "left"). In Bali, sorcery is construed to be the conscious and secret deployment of mystical powers by individuals with malign intent. Accusations of sorcery are seldom made publicly, but suspicions are widespread. Reprisals rarely take place through public, institutionalized means. The injured party who suspects sorcery as the cause of his or her troubles will privately seek countermagic from a balian. Those whose life-styles are sufficiently deviant or eccentric (often distinguished by living alone in mystically dangerous locations – near rivers, graveyards etc.) are commonly suspected of being "witches" or "sorcerers" (*leak*), but just as often the tensions among kin, affines, and neighbors are so great that the same sorts of suspicions and accusations arise within this intimate sphere. The provincial newspaper in Bali during the years 1977–8 contained several reports of assault or murder within families or hamlets – the motive cited was the murderer's belief that sorcery had led to the death or illness of a member of the murderer's family. Such motivations are by no means discounted in court during the trials, and the defendant can be sure to receive some popular sympathy. But these cases are the exceptions; suspicions are usually more diffuse and reprisals much less drastic, taking the form of defensive counter-magic or protective magic (*panengen*, from *tengen*: "right"), which balians of the "right" path can administer. These measures take the form of offerings and charms, to be worn on the body and placed around the house or in other threatened places.

It is revealed by the boy's spirit during the séance that the cause of his death was not typhoid, as the doctors diagnosed, but bewitchment by a female relative. The account of his death at her hands is stark and emotional: "I was pierced through the lungs!" The son is planning revenge, which requires his father's assistance. In the film the son says that he had been stabbed by a patrilateral female relative. In a society in which inheritance is patrilineal, women who marry out of their patrilineal descent group cannot expect an inheritance at their parents' death. Their alleged discontent with this situation is semiinstitutionalized by the common attribution of sorcery. The ascribed motive is envy of the good fortune experienced by the women's brothers, sisters-in-law, and their offspring, as well as discontent with the often difficult position of wives and daughters-in-law, particularly if they have no children. Anyone, male or female, old or young, relative or stranger, may be suspected of sorcery, although not with such regularly ascribed motivation.

The son does not expect that his grief-stricken father will take direct physical action against the female relative (whose exact identity, as opposed to structural position, is typically not mentioned). Rather, he expects the complicity of his father in the revenge plan that he, the son, is going to execute from his influential and relatively impervious position as a spirit in the afterworld. He enlists the father's cooperation by requesting that his living relatives make the necessary offerings to higher, otherworldly powers: a way of begging their permission for the spirit to undertake magical reprisals (see Jero's extensive discussion of these points in sections 6B and 6C). The father, at first carried away by his shock at discovering the cause of his son's death, agrees to the spirit's request, but later, when pressed further, he seems to try to evade the issue, changing the subject slightly ("What's this about sickness?") and seeming not to know what the son is talking about when he mentions the offerings that must be made. No doubt he feels that his son, as a spirit in the afterworld, is now powerful enough to carry out his revenge without implicating his parents. He refers to the spirit's advantages in this respect at another point in the dialogue when he says: "What has caused this to be so? Please try and speak of it a little to your father, as you already know about the 'great world' " (section 71, speech 450). To participate in a supernatural vendetta would place the father and his immediate family in a dangerous position over which they would have very little control. Later in the dialogue it seems as though the father has abnegated his authority over his small son, although his earlier spontaneous reaction was not to do so. Ultimate responsibility for the revenge is left with the spirit. Jero, however, does not agree with my interpretation of the chief petitioner's words at this point in the séance (see section 6C).

When I visited the family a week after the séance I learned that the parents had indeed made, or planned to make, *all* the offerings requested by the son. However, they were reluctant to discuss the offerings directed specifically toward the purpose of revenge, from which I gathered that they were not willing to involve themselves intentionally in the reprisals in any way.

During our visit to the client's house in 1980 I learned more details about the case of sorcery. In 1978 family members had declared that they knew the identity of the sorceress (although of course they declined to name her) and that the medium's utterances had only confirmed their suspicions. In 1980 I inquired whether they felt that any revenge had been perpetrated upon her. They agreed that it had and told me ill health had afflicted her for almost two years. First she had fallen down a ravine and broken her leg, which had prevented her from working for some months. Then she had suffered a severe respiratory and lung complaint, which had caused her discomfort for many months. The father stated that these afflictions were the proof he needed to confirm his suspicions that she had been instrumental in causing his son's death. At the same time her ill health was construed as just punishment for her behavior. The circumstances also vindicated the father's opinion that revenge could take place without his active participation. He attributed the woman's motivation to her envy of his household's economic position which, although by no means prosperous, had improved markedly in the last few years, whereas her household had declined somewhat.

## F. Offerings

Balinese religion, for most of its adherents, is elaborately ritualized; offerings form one of the main elements of worship and supplication, exorcism and propitiation. Offerings bind Balinese worshipers in a series of complex transactions with the forces of the supernatural world. The idiom of the marketplace is often used to describe the meaning of offerings in ritual. Offerings are a currency that is acceptable to spirits and deities. In the filmed séance, sins and omissions of petitioners are referred to as "debts" (*utang*). Petitioners who have not fulfilled past ritual obligations have to "redeem" (*nebus, nebas*) these debts with offerings.

Most women in rural households spend an hour or so each day making simple offerings. More complex constructions may take many hours, days, or weeks of preparation by women skilled in the art. Some women, especially those from the courtly and priestly families, spend their whole lives learning about offerings and acting on ceremonial occasions as consultants to those with lesser knowledge.

The basic components of offerings are plants, young coconut fronds (*busung*), the darker green leaves of a palm tree (*don ron*), flowers, leaves, and fruits; meats, especially chicken, duck, and pork; and rice, cooked or uncooked, ground or unground, often colored and molded into thousands of different shapes. Most of the elements of the natural world are at some time incorporated into offerings and form a link with corresponding supernatural forces. To take a simple example, two natural elements associated with the deity Brahma are the color red and fire. Thus, in household ceremonies, offerings to Brahma will be made at the hearth and will incorporate red rice, flowers, and leaves.

Completed offerings have a brief life. Women carry them on their heads to the place where the ceremony is held. There they are blessed by officiating priests and offered up to the supernatural beings concerned, although in simple everyday rituals the woman herself will recite a prayer of consecration. Offerings are prepared not only for the benevolent manifestations of divine forces and ancestors but also to propitiate potentially dangerous demonic manifestations. After the essence (*sari*) is consumed by the deities and spirits, offerings may be taken home where edible parts are eaten by household members. The remains of offerings made to deities are considered spiritually beneficial to their human petitioners.

Offerings carried to a séance are relatively simple and inexpensive. The exact form varies according to the petitioners' purpose in consulting the medium. If the matter is minor, they may carry only a simple *canang* offering, consisting of a small tray of cut and woven coconut leaves on which are placed perfumed flowers, betel nuts (see section 9D), and rice as well as the money to be donated to the medium in return for her services. In addition to the *canang*, many clients carry a *tapakan palinggih* offering, consisting of a round bamboo tray on which is placed a bed of rice, a length of cloth, and a string of Chinese coins (*kepeng*) with a *canang* atop. Clients endeavor to bring offerings as elaborate as their time and resources will allow when they consult about major problems, as they judge that the speech will not be edifying if their preparations are below what their means will reasonably permit.

In addition to the *tapakan palinggih*, many clients bring a large offering termed *banten apejatian*. This is a more elaborate version of the basic elements of rice, flowers, and delicately shaped woven coconut leaves, with the addition of some poultry and a coconut. Some clients bring the *banten apejatian* incorporated into the more complicated *banten asoroh* ("set of offerings"), which requires several baskets to contain similar ingredients in greater quantities and more elaborate arrangements. *Banten asoroh* and *banten apejatian* are common offerings on many ceremonial occasions. They are, so to speak, common currency, unlike *tapakan palinggih*, which is usually associated with séances.

Petitioners who wish to contact the spirits of dead relatives, both uncremated and already cremated, bring an additional offering called *rantasan*, which consists of clothes representing those of the dead person (or that person's actual clothes) folded decoratively on an ornate tray and capped with a *canang*. It is said that the spirit is attracted to these clothes. In the case of those already cremated (and thus in a purified state), the petitioners carry clothes of yellow and white, befitting the holy status of these spirits. (Yellow and white, symbolizing purity, are also worn by priests.)

The offerings seen in *A Balinese Trance Séance* are *banten asoroh, tapakan palinggih*, and *rantasan*. At the beginning of a day of séances, Jero also makes her own offerings, which she consecrates in her shrine house. These are usually very simple in form, just one or two *canang*, and are consecrated separately from the offerings the petitioners bring. The former are for the deity of Jero's shrine, who presides over the séances, whereas the clients' offerings are directed toward the deities and spirits whom they wish to contact, as well as the higher trinity of deities.

The deities and spirits who possess the medium may demand offerings in addition to those made by the clients and the medium. These offerings may be a means of easing spirits' paths in the afterworld, a way in which the petitioners can compensate for past mistakes, or a gesture intended to ensure success in a particular enterprise in which they are about to engage. The possessing agents often stipulate the day and the ceremonial occasion of which the offering is to be a part. In the séance filmed, for example, the deity in the first possession commands the petitioners to make some offerings in their houseyard on the day of the cremation so that household spirits will not be neglected when the family leaves for the ceremony in the village. In the second possession (the fourth in the full translation), when the chief petitioner's father possesses Jero, he chides his relatives for neglecting some important rituals at his own cremation (some years past) and requests that they make a compensatory offering called Guru Paduka (sections 6B, shot 29; 7G). The son's spirit in the third episode of possession (the fifth in the full translation) asks for a complex array of offerings, including one (to Brahma, Siwa, and Wisnu) that will enable him to take his revenge on the woman who bewitched him (see sections 6B, 7I) and a *durmanggala* offering to exorcise any evil influences that may prevent the smooth progress of his forthcoming cremation. Offerings requested in this manner demonstrate the dependence of the dead on their living relatives.

## G. Rituals of death

In the film, the petitioners have come to consult the spirits of their dead relatives through the medium. They have a specific purpose in mind: to learn the circumstances surrounding the death of their young son, for whom they are still grieving, and to elicit from him any special instructions he may have for the performance of his own cremation ceremony.

The latter is one of the main reasons that people consult mediums in Bali, especially at times of the year considered auspicious for the holding of mortuary rites (the dry months of July and August, when most harvesting is finished). As emphasized in the narration of the film, cremations are among the most complex and costly rituals in Bali. Mistakes may anger the spirits, which can only have ill effects on their living relatives. Often when kin consult a medium about the cause of some misfortune with which they are afflicted, it is revealed that they neglected some important component of a mortuary rite in the past, and this is put forward as the cause of their present suffering. In these circumstances, compensatory offerings are prescribed by the possessing spirit to remedy the oversight (which may be impeding its progress in the afterworld). These procedures may be more trouble and cost more than the original ritual that was overlooked or badly performed.

The process of purifying a dead person's spirit and liberating the soul is so expensive that poorer families have to wait many years before they are capable of carrying out this obligation to dead relatives.[8] Death rituals are composed of four basic stages, with elaborations depending on the wealth and status of the deceased. First, the body is washed and buried in the graveyard next to the village Death Temple (Pura Dalem), where the restless spirit may have to wait a long time while relatives prepare for the cremation. Consecrated persons (high priests, kings, village priests, balians, and others) may not be polluted by burial, however, and cremation ceremonies, usually with wide community support, are arranged soon after death for these people. The second stage in the death ritual is the cremation (*ngaben* or *pal-ebon*). Even the simplest ceremony takes many weeks of preparation, and some families place themselves in debt for generations (by pawning rice fields, for instance) to raise the necessary funds for the offerings and for food and payment for the necessary assistants. Stages three and four are further purification rituals. The first (commonly referred to as *roras* or *nyekah*) takes place 12 days after the cremation, or whenever the relatives can afford it. The second post cremation ceremony (often referred to as *nuntun*) achieves the final purification of the spirit (*hyang*) and the liberation of the soul (*atma*). This ceremony, which seats the now deified spirit in the ancestral shrine in

---

[8]  See Mershon 1971 for a discussion of mortuary rituals in Bali; see also Covarrubius 1973.

the house temple (usually referred to as Palinggih Betara Hyang Kompiang), may not occur until may years after the cremation, if at all.

Theoretically, once apotheosis has been achieved through these ceremonies, the spirit loses its individuality and merges with the divine. In practice, these spirits can be contacted to speak with their living descendants, especially when their separate personal identities are still remembered, as in the case of ancestors not more than two or three generations removed from the living. These deified spirits are addressed more formally and politely than recently dead and unpurified spirits.

The relationship between the living and the dead is one of mutual dependence. The living depend on the dead for their own well-being as the dead have the power to curse, whereas the dead rely on the living for their successful apotheosis through the cremation and post cremation ceremonies. In such a relationship there are many opportunities for error and oversight. Possession is the way in which communication is effected, to restore the balance that has been upset and to prevent further disruption. Usually, intervention of ancestors is deliberately sought through mediums because a specific problem has arisen. Sometimes, however, ancestral spirits are sufficiently provoked to spontaneously make their will known. This commonly happens at household and descent-group ceremonies when one of the group becomes possessed and speaks with the voice of an aggrieved ancestor.

In *A Balinese Trance Séance* two spirits are contacted. The first is the father of the main petitioner (the fourth possession of the actual event; see sections 6B, 7G). This spirit has already undergone a cremation and thus is well along the path to purification, but he chides the petitioners for overlooking some important rituals at the time of the ceremony. He is still awaiting the final post cremation ceremony for which his descendants (to judge by their replies) do not seem to have any immediate plans.

In the séance film the spirit of the recently dead son of the chief petitioner is the last to descend and speak. His relatives are concerned first and foremost to learn the cause of his death and then to receive his special instructions for his own cremation, as well as for other rites that may ease his path in the afterworld. It is for him that his living relatives brought the offering of clothes (*rantasan*), whereas the advent of his grandfather is unexpected but accepted as part of the order of events.

## H. Eka Dasa Rudra

At the time we filmed the séance (July 1978), Balinese throughout the whole island were involved in preparations for a centennial festival at their "mother temple," Pura Besakih, on the southern slope of the highest mountain on

Bali, Gunung Agung.[9] This temple, for which all Balinese are responsible, is a unifying symbol where homage is paid to the many manifestations of Sang Hyang Widi Wasa,the one God. It consists of hundreds of shrines, arranged in courts along the terraced sanctuary of the mountainside.[10] Different regions and groups of Balinese are responsible for the various complexes of shrines. Ceremonies are held throughout the year on the auspicious days of the lunar calendar and the *wuku* calendar, with different groups participating. The upkeep of the temple is financed by the government, by income from temple lands, and by contributions of the congregation. Caretaker priests and customary officials in the hamlets surrounding the temple complex have primary responsibility for the routine organization of the ceremonies that take place there, but on great religious occasions the whole Balinese community of worshipers is responsible for participation in the ceremonies.

In May 1979, Eka Dasa Rudra, a centennial festival of exorcism, propitiation, and purification, was performed.[11] This ceremony takes the form of a huge sacrifice (*taur agung*), followed by prayers of thanksgiving to Sang Hyang Widi Wasa. The sacrifice, an elaborate sequence of ceremonies lasting many weeks, is performed to appease the destructive aspect of supernatural forces that may otherwise vent their wrath on human beings and thereby to restore balance and harmony in the universe.

Preparations for the Eka Dasa Rudra of 1979 lasted more than a year. Not least of these was the ceremonial cleansing of polluting influences throughout the whole island. Most important, spirits of uncremated dead had to be released from their earthbound state. Thus for many months preceding the ceremony Balinese households, no matter how poor, were involved in organizing the cremation ceremonies that would ensure the purification of spirits of the dead and cleanse local communities of death pollution as well. Households that could not afford to stage the elaborate and costly cremation ceremonies separately joined together with others of their village, hamlet, or descent group to stage collective cremations whereby most of the cost could be shared. Without the pressure brought about by the forthcoming Eka Dasa Rudra, such households would have postponed these cremations for a few more years until they could muster the necessary resources.

During the weeks we were filming in Bali, the pace of life was transformed by frenetic preparations for the many collective cremations. Prices of commodities needed for such ceremonies rose steeply, and households placed

---

[9]  For further discussion, see Stuart-Fox 1982, and Lansing 1983b.
[10]  Goris (1969a, 1969b) describes Pura Besakih at some length.
[11]  The historical background to the Eka Dasa Rudra ceremony of 1979 and its regional political significance are discussed in Forge 1980a, the ceremony in Stuart-Fox 1982 and Lansing 1983b.

themselves in debt for many years to raise the necessary funds. For the weeks of preparation, and the many days it takes to perform a cremation correctly, work on everyday tasks slowed down as people's energies were directed toward the staging of these all-important events.

In the middle months of 1978, an unusually large number of clients consulted mediums to contact their dead relatives about their wishes for their cremation ceremonies. Jero Tapakan handled hundreds of such cases during the months from May to September 1978, the peak of the "cremation season." It is unlikely that this will occur again for many years.

## I. The language of the séance

Balinese is an Austronesian language (like most of the 300 languages in the Indonesian archipelago) and is of the Malay–Javanic subgroup. Inscriptional evidence from the eighth and ninth centuries A.D. indicates that from at least as early as this period there were Sanskrit influences on the island's language, and the scripts used derive from Indic origins. The integration of Sanskrit and Old Balinese linguistic forms (pre-11th century) was only one of a variety of Buddhist and Hindu influences on Balinese courtly culture, channeled through the Javanese kingdoms. After the 10th century, Javanese influence seems to have increased, for following this period (which corresponds with the marriage of the Balinese prince Udayana to the Javanese princess Mahendradatta and the reign of their son Airlangga in East Java) court inscriptions are written in Old Javanese. For many centuries classical manuscripts written in Old Javanese have been copied and adapted by Balinese scholars and communicated through art and ritual forms, thereby exercising a profound influence on ordinary spoken Balinese as well as on literary forms. Most Balinese, who are unschooled and illiterate in classical scripts, refer to any combination of Old Balinese, Sanskrit, and Old Javanese languages (often intermixed with modern Balinese) as "Kawi," although philologists usually identify Kawi with Old Javanese. For Balinese, Kawi is not just an archaic language but the vehicle by which sacred and powerful knowledge is imparted.

From the 14th century onward, the influence on Bali of the Javanese courts continued to increase. Part of this influence must have been the assimilation of spoken Javanese into the Balinese vernacular and the elaboration of the latter into different "levels" or "registers" according to status and intimacy. This is the language we find on Bali today. Refined language forms, influenced by the Javanese presence, must have developed among those in spatial or social proximity to the courts, and a more undifferentiated form of Balinese predominated in areas outside that sphere of influence. So we can conjecture, at least, by looking at patterns of language use in the 20th century.

Western commentators tend to overrigidify the conceptualization of levels in Balinese language. Balinese themselves refer to their language as having a "high" or "refined" form (*basa alus*) and a "low," "coarse," or "ordinary" form (*basa kasar* or *basa biasa*). Some Balinese and some linguists further subdivide the language into a "middle" form and into several subdivisions of the refined form. In fact, there are only about 600–1,000 words that vary (i.e. exist in two or more forms) according to the level of language used,[12] but as these words are among the most common (pronouns, tense markers, words describing parts of the body and bodily functions) they can make a considerable difference to the sound of any utterance. It is important to stress, however, that the attribution of levels to Balinese language is of limited usefulness as an analytical tool, because any utterance may contain a mixture of high and low words, depending on various characteristics of the speaker, the person spoken to, and the subject discussed. In general, those of low social rank speak high to and about those of high social rank, and the latter speak low to and about those beneath them. Formerly, inherited title in the traditional status system was one of the main indicators of social rank, but these days the situation is complicated by crosscutting factors such as wealth and modern occupational status. The social distance of the speakers, such as their relative age and sex, also affects the choice of language, as does the setting in which the interaction takes place.

In former times, if a low-ranking person spoke in a low Balinese form to someone with a high title, the punishment was exile or even death; even today (as some reports in the provincial newspapers reveal) such cases can be taken to a court of law, and the offender fined. Generally, however, especially in those areas of Bali where the traditional elite is still highly esteemed and enjoys some local power, such an infringement is unthinkable. It is not just a breach of manners but an offense against the moral order.

Many Balinese, especially those who never had any close ties with the traditional elite, are not eloquent or even fluent in high Balinese forms. The language of familiars is low Balinese, with minor modifications to take into account distinctions of age, wealth, and sex. Most Balinese are able to elevate their speech sufficiently to accommodate interactions with strangers and those of slightly higher status. When two strangers meet in the villages, if they are to carry on an extensive conversation the one initiating the interaction must ask the other, *Tiang nunasang antuk linggih?* ("May I ask your 'seat'?"), so that appropriate language may be used.

Modern life, with its increased social and geographic mobility and intermixing with other ethnic groups, has brought with it problems of status ambiguity and incongruity that are as difficult to resolve linguistically as they are any other way. Some of low birth have risen in the ranks of the bureaucracy or have attained wealth that outshines that of their titled neigh-

---

[12] For a detailed sociolinguistic analysis of Balinese language, see Zurbuchen 1981, chaps. 1 and 2.

bors. Women have married into descent groups previously considered beneath their status. For many who have received even an elementary education, the use of the more egalitarian national language, Bahasa Indonesia, provides a way around difficult status impasses. The public selection of a lexicon with which to address another person, or speak about a third, is one of the most potent indications of one's perceptions of the social status of self and other. Today mistakes, the social effects of which are difficult to remedy, can be avoided to a large extent by the use of Indonesian or by a mixture of Indonesian and some high Balinese key words.

The use of stratified speech extends into interactions with the supernatural world. Deities and spirits with whom humans converse during séances are generally of higher status than humans and must be addressed accordingly. Deities are addressed in a very high form, otherwise reserved for the highest-ranking humans. This usage reinforces the social distance between deities and humans, which is much greater than the distance between spirits and the humans with whom they once resided. Purified ancestral spirits who are long dead are addressed in high language, but not as high as that used with deities. The closest approximation to familiar everyday speech in this intercourse with the supernatural is in communications with spirits of recently dead relatives. These have the lowest spiritual status (if, as is usually the case, they have not yet been cremated), and the emotional bond of the living to such beings is strongest, creating pressure to speak intimately so that formal speech is an artificial constraint. Recently dead spirits are often addressed almost as they would have been in life by their emotionally distraught relatives at the séance.

Angry and imperious deities speak in an extremely low form to their petitioners. Spirits address their relatives in the colloquial low Balinese they would have used when alive, but often with a greater accentuation of anger (at petitioners' neglect of rituals) or grief (at parting from the petitioners), thus enhancing the emotional pitch of the whole interaction.

The linguistic interaction of séances brings into play many different levels and moods of speech. During a typical séance, language level and mood shift many times. As soon as the possessing agent leaves the medium, language forms are abruptly realigned with no apparent effort on the part of the participants. The medium, when not possessed, is addressed politely as a stranger of moderately high status. The vocabulary chosen depends on the rank of the petitioners as well as her own. Many nonverbal indicators of status also accompany language behavior. In the case of séances, the medium generally sits higher than her clients, both when possessed and when chatting with them conversationally. Relative head height is an important index of social status in Balinese culture, in this case reflecting both the medium's status as a consecrated practitioner and the status of the deities and spirits who possess her.

Brief summary of the language used in the film

During the interaction on film the clients speak fairly high Balinese to Jero; her speech to the clients is less high but still polite, as she is a consecrated person and they are commoners. Were they of higher rank than Jero (titled gentry), she would address them in high Balinese, and they would probably speak in a polite but less high form to her (if they thought their title prevailed over her consecrated status). The petitioners speak very high Balinese when addressing the houseyard deity. However, they are not fluent in the flowery phrases of this language, and the level of language occasionally drops. The deity speaks coarsely and imperiously to them. When conversing with the father's spirit the petitioners speak a lower, but still polite, form of Balinese. The spirit speaks low Balinese to them in return, but it is a more colloquial, familiar form of Balinese than the speech of the deity. To the spirit of their recently dead son, the petitioners speak more intimately when they are carried away by their emotions; at one point they forget to address him by the title befitting a spirit (Jero) and instead call him by his birth-order name (Nengah), a familiar form of address in Bali.

The mantras used by Jero

Preceding the séances Jero recites several mantras, and she repeats part of the longest one each time she seeks possession. These mantras are a mixture of high Balinese, Old Javanese, and Sanskrit, which Jero refers to as Kawi. As she is illiterate, it was impossible for her to obtain the mantras by consulting traditional palm-leaf (*lontar*) manuscripts. She learned the sacred phrases by rote from a ritual expert (*kelian adat*) in her hamlet, who is literate and owns several *lontar* manuscripts. The form and sequence of the words are in themselves powerful, and Jero does not make changes. The recitation, after more than 20 years, displays little variation in phrasing or pace. The first recitation of the séance is usually louder and a little slower than succeeding ones. The only other difference is a variation of several seconds in the point at which she becomes possessed and an attenuation of the mantra in succeeding recitations within a séance (see section 6B).

The early mantras are used by Jero to purify herself, her shrine house, and the offerings so they will all be fitting receptacles for the supernatural beings who are to descend. She also requests that her inner spiritual forces come to her aid in conducting a successful séance (see Jero's own exegesis of these mantras in section 6B). The last and longest mantra is an invocation to the deities of the Balinese pantheon to preside over the séance, bless the participants, and imbue the speech with clarity so that it will be successful. The powers of Brahma, Wisnu, and Siwa are invoked, but they are not expected to enter the medium, nor are other lofty deities such as Dewi Gangga (the goddess of the Ganges, or Gangga, and by association the deity of water) or Saraswati (the goddess of learning and thus of the spoken and written word). Most of the deities lend their powers in a generalized way without possessing the medium. It is a houseyard deity (Betara Guru) and the clients' dead relatives who possess the medium. Jero also invokes the Taksu deity (Bagawan Taksu), an interpreter or intermediary force whose power enables her to speak and be understood while possessed.

# SIX

## *The film and sound texts of* A Balinese Trance Séance *and* Jero on Jero

### A. Notes on *Jero on Jero*
### (Patsy Asch)

Background and filming

IN 1980 we — Timothy Asch, Linda Connor, and I — returned to Bali with two goals: to explore the value of showing people film of themselves in order to generate new data, and to fulfill a promise to show our footage to the people filmed. For these purposes, we transferred our footage to video-cassettes and took a color monitor to Bali. In the village where we had filmed in 1978, we played our videocassettes in houseyards, temples, and markets — wherever groups wanted to watch.

Approximately half the footage focuses on Jero Tapakan, the other half on the organization and performance of a collective cremation in Jero's hamlet. Before showing any of the footage of Jero to others in her village, we wanted her to have an opportunity to see it alone and to censor any material she did not want shown. Because a private showing in Jero's home was socially unacceptable, we invited her to a neighboring town, where a Balinese friend loaned us a large room.

We thought it might be valuable to film some of Jero's reactions, particularly to *A Balinese Trance Séance*, as data for Linda's research. Tim hoped that footage of Jero's reactions to the séance could also be shown to colleagues and students and that it would challenge some of their interpretations. We had very limited footage, however, and so we loaded only two 400-foot rolls of film — 22 minutes — although we intended showing Jero 105 minutes of videotape: the séance film (30 minutes), all the footage where Jero tells of her life before she became a medium (45 minutes), and a roughly edited version of a film of Jero giving a massage (30 minutes). Our plan was to tape-record all Jero's and Linda's comments and to film some segments if that seemed valuable, but as soon as the séance film began we realized that Tim was right: Jero's animated reactions could, and now do, form the basis of a short companion film: *Jero on Jero: "A Balinese Trance Séance" Observed.*

Editing

We began the editing process with an uninterrupted tape recording of Jero watching the séance film. I synchronized sound and film, putting in blank leader (spacing) whenever there was sound but no picture. Because the sound was continuously recorded while Jero watched the videotape, and because the film (with the added leader) was the same length, we were able to use the eight-plate Steenbeck editing table at the University of Sydney to look simultaneously at the séance film on one screen and Jero's reactions on the other, while listening to both sound tracks or to either one. In other words, we had a track for the original film of the séance, a track for its sync sound, a track for the film of Jero and Linda watching the video, and a track for that film's accompanying sound. All four tracks could be synchronized and run simultaneously. However, videotape physically expands and contracts, so the two sequences were not perfectly synchronized; the sound from the video tape heard below Jero's comments was not the same length as the original sound on the séance film. But by using this background sound I could synchronize any short segment fairly closely, and we were able to tell exactly what was on the screen as Jero commented.

Jero's and Linda's comments as they watched the film were transcribed in Bali by a native speaker. Using this transcription and Linda's running translation, the three of us selected a rough version based primarily on the sound track. There were certain points we thought important for Western audiences: Jero's account of the experience of possession, some of the cosmological details, information about sorcery, and something of the contrast between Jero's and Linda's viewing style – the one interactive and naive, the other goal oriented but more passive. We hoped that screenings of the séance film would raise issues problematic for Western audiences that could then be contrasted with the issues Jero felt compelled to address. Many Westerners have questioned the sincerity of Jero's practice, for example, and accused her of fraud, of consciously deceiving her clients. Jero does not defend herself against such charges, perhaps because it has never occurred to her that people would doubt her sincerity. What seems to worry Jero is that she will be accused of arrogance, that people will question her right, as an "ignorant commoner," to be a vehicle for the deities and spirits. Jero keeps addressing this point even when Linda seems to be expressing impatience or dismissing the issue.

Once we had settled on the dialogue we wanted to include, I used shots from the original séance film in two ways: as cutaways to fill in images either when we had no picture of Linda or Jero or when an image from the original film enriched Jero's comments, as, for example, when she explains the meaning of specific gestures. In either case I used the image that was on the video screen when the particular comment heard on the sound track was recorded (with the exception of the final departure shot).

Introductory stills

Three stills and shots of the television screen were added after the film was edited.

1.  *Title still of Jero*: This shot was recorded much later in the day when Jero was looking at the biography footage. Tim and I chose the shot without reference to the sound from the videotape, which we could not understand. It was only when we were mixing the sound tracks that Linda heard it. She felt it might embarrass Jero, who was laughing about an incident, discussed on the video-tape, when she had violent diarrhea. Therefore, we mixed the track with the sound very low, increasing the volume only on Jero's final comment.
2.  *Jero's houseyard*: This still was taken from a slide that Tim photographed from a tree in the street that runs along the eastern side of Jero's houseyard. The houseyard temple (*sanggah*) is in the foreground and most of the individual shrines are visible (see Diagrams 1 and 2). Behind, in the center of the frame, is the back wall of Jero's shrine house, in which she sits during a séance.
3.  *Filming*: This still is from a slide I took while Jero and Linda were looking at the biography footage on videocassette. Jero and Linda have changed seats at Tim's request, in order to have Jero turned more toward the camera when talking to Linda.

The shots of the television screen were filmed in Australia because the images on the screen recorded in Bali were not clear. In each case we made sure – by listening to the sound of the videotape in the background – that it was the image Jero would have been seeing. The television monitor and recorder are the ones actually used in Bali.

Translation of the dialogue

Linda has prepared a running translation of the entire recording that we made while she and Jero watched the séance film. All the comments re-corded while they were watching the film – those from which *Jero on Jero* were drawn – appear in the third column of the shot list and commentary in section 6B. Comments recorded after the film was over appear in section 6C.

Diagram 1. Jero's houseyard.

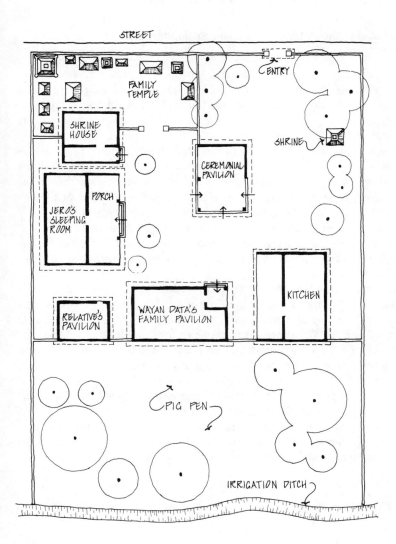

Diagram 2. Plan of Jero's houseyard.

## B. Shot list and commentary for *A Balinese Trance Séance* (Patsy Asch)

The following notes provide background information on each shot in the film. They are based on a taped discussion I had with Linda Connor and Timothy Asch as we looked at the footage before I began editing *A Balinese Trance Séance* and on our experiences creating and using our materials on Jero Tapakan.

My notes refer almost exclusively to the "film text" and not to what the participants experienced, each in her or his own way, at the time the film was being shot. Comparison of the film text with the text of Linda's translation of a continuous tape recording of the séance (Chapter 7)[1] shows the interpretive nature of film. The clearest illustration is the contrast of the compressed translation of dialogue, emphasizing clarity, that we used in the subtitles with the highly metaphorical and consequently ambiguous language of the fuller translation, which shows the way meaning is negotiated through discourse.

Each shot in the film is identified by number, by the film roll from which it came (FR), and by the footage count at the head and tail of the shot; for example, shot 1 begins at 1 foot, 8 frames (0001:08) and ends at 66 feet, 28 frames (0066:28). There are 40 frames per foot. To locate a particular frame number, the counter is placed at zero when the film is on "2" of the Academy leader, that is, 48 frames before the first image (to translate into seconds, the footage count is multiplied by five-thirds).

*Column 1* consists of my comments on the visual images, sound track, and editing of *A Balinese Trance Séance*.

*Column 2* is a written text of the narration and all the subtitles from *A Balinese Trance Séance*. The subtitles may be used to link comments to specific frames in the film. The initials preceding each subtitle identify the speaker:

|       |   |                         |
|-------|---|-------------------------|
| J     | = | Jero                    |
| M     | = | Man                     |
| W     | = | Woman                   |
| OW    | = | Old Woman               |
| D     | = | Deity                   |
| MS    | = | Mother's Spirit         |
| FS    | = | Father's Spirit         |
| BS    | = | Boy's Spirit            |
| A     | = | Timothy Asch            |
| N     | = | Narrator (Linda Connor) |

[1] Numbers used by Linda to identify each speech in her translation in Chapter 7 are given in the film text, in parentheses, alongside the speaker's initials.

Numbers placed between columns 1 and 2 (beginning at shot 17) are the reference numbers Linda used in her translation of the main séance (see Chapter 7). The beginning and ending shots of the film have no reference numbers because this footage comes from different séances.

*Column 3* is a free translation by Linda of Jero's and Linda's comments as they watched the séance film together for the first time. This column includes all their recorded comments, not just those in *Jero on Jero*. Each comment made while the videotape was running has been aligned with the subtitle that was on the screen when it was recorded. Some of the comments they made after the viewing appear at the end of this chapter.

| Comments | A Balinese Trance Séance (Subtitles and narration) | Recorded comments by Jero and Linda |
|---|---|---|
| FILM OPENS: JERO IS HOLDING THE BRAZIER | *Shot 1 FR4 (0001:08–0066:28)* | |
| Jero Tapakan, a Balinese healer, is seated in her shrine house talking with several clients. She is surrounded by the paraphernalia of a spirit medium (see shots 13–16). This shot was recorded toward the end of the filmed record but is included before the narration begins to give the viewer a sense of how a séance looks. Shots 1–16 are *not* linked to Linda's translation (Chapter 7) because they came from a different séance. | | L: It's just starting. [The television is switched on.] |
| Although Jero claims she cannot remember anything, in the sequence filmed and in many séances Linda observed she does remember a great deal, but it is likely that she needs some clue to trigger her memory. Perhaps it is because her experience is in a framework different from that of everyday experience, one that she may be unable to relate in an immediate, linear, and verbal way. She also may be influenced by the culturally accepted view that one is possessed by a supernatural being (see section 5B). In *Jero on Jero* we have used a more literal translation of Jero's words, referring to possession with her terms: "forgetting" (*engsap*) and "being entered" (*karauhan*). | J: When I come out of trance, I can't remember anything.  You have to tell me. | J: (*Laughs*) That's the shrine house. Oh, it's smoky [smoke from the brazier]. So it's like that . . . |
| When a client comes with a problem, Jero may be possessed by several ancestral spirits and/or deities in succession. Between each she usually talks with the clients, helping to clarify what has been said. | J: For me, speaking in trance is so complicated. | J: Crazy . . . I look a bit crazy. Look at that smoke. |

If people wish to undertake some important action or are experiencing misfortune, they will often consult a medium, such as Jero, in order to enlist the advice and support of ancestral spirits. What Jero may mean here is that other mediums are not possessed as many times as she is during a séance.

Jero appears to achieve a state of dissociation after chanting. It is as though she were concentrating so intently that she is oblivious to most external stimuli. This state is achieved through context and expectation rather than through somatic agents; Jero does not use drugs or hyperventilation, and it is unlikely that the aromatic smoke from her brazier has any physiological effect. Initially, possession is likely to be dramatic, but a practiced medium, such as Jero, appears to have control, moving in and out of a "possession state" many times in the course of a day. Were this the beginning of a séance (see shot 17) Jero would recite a long prayer, but here she only has to chant a few phrases before the spirit appears to enter.

Previously Jero had been possessed by a spirit who had called himself "father" (guru) and "grandfather" (pekak), depending on which of his descendants he was addressing. Grandfather's spirit had said "mother" would be coming. As it is less usual for the possessing spirit to be a woman, the clients discuss this development quietly among themselves. They decide that the fact that Grandfather had had no sons and his daughter had continued to live with him after she was married (her husband living uxorilocally) might explain it. Usually the identity of the possessing agent is problematic. Here is a good example of the process by which identification is determined.

J: I go into trance four or five times for each client.

J: Om, Gods on High, Lords of the Mountain.

J: O Heavenly Host…

J: Oh!
L: That's English at the bottom [referring to the subtitles].
J: Oh.
L: Now you've "forgotten."

| Comments | A Balinese Trance Séance (Subtitles and narration) | Recorded comments by Jero and Linda |
|---|---|---|
| The "mother" could stand in a maternal relationship to any of the petitioners, but they decide that she is the mother of the man seated in the middle. The petitioners respond in very respectful Balinese speech, but not at the highest level, which is reserved for deities and, on earth, for people of the highest status. | MS: I, Mother, have come. | J: "Mother has come." |
| | OW: Honourable spirit.... | I wasn't aware of that. |
| To avoid later confusion with a different "wife" we did not subtitle the spirit's question, "Is your wife here?" nor the answer, "Yes, she's here but she's too overwhelmed to speak." | MS: My child.<br>M: Yes.<br>MS: Mother is here. | L: Oh. |
| | I want you all to participate. Who will arrange the ceremonies for me? | |
| A common reason for attending a séance such as this one is to learn the spirits' wishes for their cremation and postcremation rituals. These rituals are so complicated and numerous that mistakes are inevitable. To avoid spiritual retribution, people seek guidance from the dead. | M: We will.... | |
| The camera pans to the clients who are seated on Jero's porch, just outside the door and window of her shrine house (see Diagrams 1 and 2). The younger man with the red sash is the central petitioner; the séance is concerned with his problem. His wife and mother are there, and the man to his left is his elder brother. The other two who accompanied him are more distantly related. | | |

MS: My purification rites are incomplete.

M: What do you require?

MS: My earthly sins have yet to be redeemed.

You have neglected the jauman offerings.

MS: What are my children going to do about my debts? My fate here is uncertain.

?: What do you want us to do about these debts?

J: Are they "asking for speech" [nunas raos]? [From deities and spirits, who speak through a medium.]

L: Yes.

J: The ones watching?

L: Yes.

J: That's English, is it?

J: "No pakidih ceremony; no peras offerings." [Pakidih is a ritual for deceased relatives, part of a cremation ceremony. Peras is a type of offering.]

That means, if there are no peras offerings, the ceremony isn't complete.

L: Yes.

J: The pakidih ceremony. In Bali, pakidih is a different type of thing. Peras are offerings. They're not finished. That's why there are problems.

"Purification rites" refers to the series of rituals that begin with washing and preparing a body immediately after death and include cremation and postcremation ceremonies, each an important step in purifying and releasing first the body and then the soul of the deceased. These rites usually take many years.

"Earthly sins" refers to sins committed while the spirit was alive. They include such things as neglecting to make correct or sufficient offerings. The presentation of offerings to deities, ancestral spirits, and demons is the major Balinese act of supplication and a central aspect of all ritual. It is easy to make mistakes or omit an offering because of their extensive elaboration. There are basic elements such as rice cakes, woven coconut leaves, and flowers, but each kind of offering is named, is unique, and has its particular place, be it in the daily offerings to the household spirits made in every family courtyard or in the intricate temple offerings.

We could not subtitle all the names of offerings mentioned, which is why the subtitles do not include the offerings that Jero comments on as she watches the videotape.

| Comments | A Balinese Trance Séance (Subtitles and narration) | Recorded comments by Jero and Linda |
|---|---|---|
| *Jauman* is a small, propitiatory offering made on a wide variety of occasions. In this context, "Betara Guru" refers to a protective houseyard deity, according to Jero, a manifestation of the Trimurti (Brahma, Siwa, and Wisnu; Indian: Brahma, Siva, and Vishnu). | MS: Those Jauman offerings must be dedicated to Betara Guru. | |
| Uncremated spirits are thought to be dependent on their living relatives for their purification and deification, but this dependency is mutual, for the deceased have the power to curse. Balinese perceive the relationship between the living and the dead as continuous, unbroken, and circular, since reincarnation is believed to occur within a descent group. (In this respect, their view of reincarnation differs from the more abstract conception of Indian Hindus.) | MS: I won't be pure until you make those offerings. | J: The *pakidih* ceremony had no *peras* offerings. "What are my children going to do about that?" [Paraphrasing the spirit's utterance.] |
| Throughout this exchange the voice of the spirit has sounded angry and imperious, but the voices of the petitioners have remained restrained and formal. | M: We are distressed at your situation. Please instruct us . . . | The spirit of the dead doesn't have a smooth path. |
| | *Shot 2 (0066:29–0076:04)* | |
| FILM TITLE: FREEZE OF JERO HOLDING THE BRAZIER | A BALINESE TRANCE SÉANCE © 1979. Timothy Asch, Linda Connor, and Documentary Educational Resources. | L: This is the real beginning. That was just an introduction. That's the name of the film. |
| In this freeze frame Jero has already been possessed. She holds a flower from the offerings in her right hand and a brazier of fragrant, burning incense in her left. I chose the chant for its sound; it is one Jero uses to dedicate herself and her offerings (see shot 16). Thus sound does not match picture. | | |

## FREEZE: JERO HOLDING THE BRAZIER

Jero Tapakan is not a personal name. Jero is an achieved, honorific title applied to a person with recognized spiritual power, such as a local priest; a *tapakan* is a vessel in which the deities may reside. In this case it refers to a type of *balian* (healer) in whom the deities and spirits reside during a séance. To protect her privacy, we have not identified Jero or her village. She lives north of Klungkung, not far from Besakih. This close-up was taken during a later possession.

## FREEZE: LINDA WORKING WITH JERO

Between October 1976 and October 1978, Linda Connor lived in Central Bali. During that time she studied traditional healers, many of whom lived in remote villages. During the latter half of her fieldwork she also worked with the staff and families of patients at the mental hospital in Bangli. Timothy Asch joined Linda for two months of filming in July and August of 1978. In 1980, after the séance film was finished, we (Linda, Tim, and I) returned to Jero's hamlet and spent six weeks showing our 1978 footage to the participants.

This color slide is the only visual material in the séance film that was not recorded on the morning of 24 July 1978.

## FREEZE: OLD WOMAN PAYING JERO

This freeze comes from a shot recorded near the end of our filming when the old woman gave Jero 200 rupiah for conducting the séance. Jero is putting the offerings back into her clients' baskets for them to take home to eat, now that the

*Shot 3 (0076:05–0084:32)*

N: Jero Tapakan lives in a small village in Central Bali. She is esteemed for her ability while in a trance to contact the many deities and spirits who influence day-to-day affairs in Bali.

L: That's my voice.
J: You're explaining in English?
L: Yes.

*Shot 4 from a slide (0084:33–0092:06)*

N: I met Jero at the beginning of a two-year period of fieldwork, while studying some aspects of trance, magic, and curing. During that time I worked closely with her.

J: You're asking me questions?

We're not at all alike.
L: Yes we are. (*Both laugh*)

J: Are we alike there?

*Shot 5 (0092:07–0101:04)*

N: Over the past 20 years Jero has built up a practice as a spirit medium. She provides the main source

L: What do you mean?
J: We're sitting like sisters, but one dark, one light face.

| Comments | A Balinese Trance Séance (Subtitles and narration) | Recorded comments by Jero and Linda |
|---|---|---|
| essence has been consumed by supernatural beings. Jero usually receives about 150 to 200 rupiah (about 30 cents) for a séance that may last an hour or more. She charges according to what she thinks a client can afford – Linda has seen her return money if she feels it is too much. It is exceptional for her to earn more than 1,200 rupiah (two dollars) in a day. | of economic support for her family with the money earned by holding trance séances. | L: We're alike in spirit. (*Both laugh*) |
| Jero, like many other healers, holds séances only on two days out of every three. On the third day (*pasah*), which is not considered an auspicious day to contact spirits, she dispenses medicines and gives therapeutic massage (see *The Medium Is the Masseuse: A Balinese Massage*). Certain days, such as *kajeng-kliwon* (the intersection of the day *kajeng* in the Balinese three-day week and *kliwon* in the five-day week), are important for calling down deities and spirits. On auspicious days, including the full and new moon, Jero may have clients from early morning to late afternoon. On these occasions, she may work ten hours or more without resting or eating, because she feels a responsibility toward her clients, who are often very demanding. Jero's work is exhausting, mentally and physically. She complains that she often has a stiff neck from sitting cross-legged on a hard bench, hunched over the smoking brazier. Many mediums have to sleep after a few hours. | | |

## FREEZE: JERO'S FACE

In this close-up Jero's face is contorted as she approaches the transition to a state of possession.

In the film *Jero Tapakan: Stories from the Life of a Balinese Healer*, Jero describes her illness, poverty, and suffering, including some of the visionary experiences that led to her decision to hold a consecration ceremony – with the help of a local ritual expert – and to become a healer (see section 10D).

## FREEZE: THE PETITIONERS

This shot of the main petitioner was taken while Jero was possessed by Betara Guru, the household deity. The petitioner's gestures and speech are extremely deferential. Unlike the other freezes, this frame was taken from a shot used in the film.

Since most of the people who visit Jero to "ask for speech"

J: Alike in spirit.

My clothes keep changing.

L: This is just the explanation. In a moment there will be the complete one [séance]; it's cut only a little.

J: If something sad is told, we'll see people crying there, shall we?

L: Yes, there is that too.

J: There is?

L: Yes, there are people crying.

*Shot 6 (0101:05–0119:32)*

N: She became a spirit medium after suffering a series of mental and physical illnesses which could not be cured by ordinary medicine. Finally she was told at a trance séance that these illnesses were a sign from her guardian deity that she had been chosen to become a spirit medium. She underwent an elaborate consecration ceremony which enabled her to practice her vocation, after which the symptoms disappeared.

*Shot 7 (0119:33–0132:12)*

N: Because deities and spirits are closely concerned with human affairs, skills such as Jero's are highly valued in Bali. Balinese petitioners seek the guidance of these supernatural beings in carrying out the many

J: The ones crying, they remember, like you, their mother, their father, they feel upset, they cry.
The spirit tells of how things were when it was alive. They [the relatives] recall the death; they cry.

| Comments | A Balinese Trance Séance (Subtitles and narration) | Recorded comments by Jero and Linda |
|---|---|---|
| have no other contact with her, we have used "client" when referring to the relationship these people have with Jero and "petitioner" when referring to their relationship to the deities and spirits. | rituals which are an important part of everyday life. | Where are they [the clients] from?<br>L: From Bucaman.<br>J: Bucaman. He's the head of the hamlet.<br>L: The head of the hamlet. |
| FREEZE: JERO'S FACE<br>The spirit is speaking through Jero. Now that the spirit is in full possession, Jero's face looks relaxed. Her eyes remain closed. This freeze is part of the same shot used in Shots 2 and 6.<br><br>"Forgetting" (engsap) is a word Jero often uses to refer to the change in herself while she is possessed. | Shot 8 (0132:13–0139:24)<br>N: Protective village and houseyard deities, as well as the spirits of dead relatives, speak directly through the medium to their earthly petitioners. | J: When I "hold the brazier," I close my eyes. (Laughs) I wasn't "remembering" there.<br>L: (Overlap) You had already "forgotten."<br>J: Yes, when I "forget" it's like that. |
| FREEZE: PETITIONERS IN THE STREET OUTSIDE<br>This shot was taken when the people we had filmed were leaving. The man on the right is carrying a tape recorder, which he used to tape the séance (see Shot 44). The women are carrying baskets of spent offerings, which will be taken home and eaten by their families. Every group arrives with offerings. These six people, wearing ceremonial clothes appropriate for a religious occasion, come from the same | Shot 9 (0139:25–0147:14)<br>N: Petitioners come to the house of the spirit medium, often from towns or villages some distance away. The problems which have prompted | L: Now I'm explaining about people coming....<br>J: (Overlap) People coming, people going home. |

village and are related to each other. But they came with several distinct problems about which different people took a central role in communicating with the deities and spirits. In this picture their backs are to Jero's gate: They are walking toward the bus (*bemo*). Although they came when it was market day in the nearby town to ensure transportation, they traveled for at least two hours to reach Jero's and will probably take even longer getting home. They have chosen Jero because of her reputation, even though there are mediums who live closer to their village.

## FREEZE: MAIN PETITIONER

This man, in his late thirties, is the main petitioner in the detailed sequence that follows. He farms nonirrigated land in an area 20 kilometers northwest of Jero's hamlet. Many people from his village have consulted Jero. The man behind him is not related and came in a different group. Possibly he is a neighbor, for they seem to know one another.

## FREEZE: OLD WOMAN

This old woman is the mother of the man in the previous shot and is related to all the people who came together. She may have been asked to accompany them because of her knowledge of ritual and her ability to speak formal Balinese to the deities and ancestors. Throughout the filming it is she who arranges the offerings and helps with the ritual. She takes an active part in each verbal exchange with the spirits and deities. During the next two years she brought other

them to consult a medium are diverse.

*Shot 10 (0147:15–0154:34)*

N: Sometimes they seek advice about illness and accidents, wanting both information on medicine and on the supernatural causes of these misfortunes.

*Shot 11 (0154:35–0163:10)*

N: At other times, they may want to find out about the correct place to build a new house or temple, ways to resolve family quarrels or local political disputes, or instructions for undertaking a major ritual.

That's in the yard, in the street.

L: Yes, in the street.

J: It's the old lady!

L: Has she come since then?

J: She's come about ten times.

L: Recently?

J: Whenever people finish a cremation, they "ask for

| Comments | *A Balinese Trance Séance* (Subtitles and narration) | Recorded comments by Jero and Linda |
|---|---|---|
| people to Jero. Old women frequently perform ritual actions – once past childbearing and menstruation they are less affected by pollution restrictions. | | speech" [*nunas raos*] again.<br>L: Oh, really.<br>J: When they want to have a post-cremation ceremony [*ngroras*], they "ask for speech." After the postcremation ceremony, they "ask for speech" again. |
| | *Shot 12 (0163:11–0172:06)* | |
| FREEZE: WOMAN RECEIVING HOLY WATER<br><br>The woman receiving holy water is the sister-in-law of the main petitioner. This holy water, *tirta empul*, probably comes from the sacred springs at Tampaksiring. Unlike many Balinese, the people in Jero's hamlet do not obtain holy water from a *pedanda* (a high priest). Flowers are floating in the water, and another flower is used by the old woman as a sprinkler. Three handfuls of water are sipped and three used to wipe the hair and face. Receiving holy water is a blessing, a purification, and is part of all Balinese ritual. A brief prayer follows.<br><br>We would have liked to commence filming as the petitioners approached Jero's compound, but we did not feel we could film without their permission. Jero, acting on our behalf, asked these strangers if they would participate in the film. She explained that she had known Linda for almost | N: Misfortunes arise from such things as neglect of important ritual, the ill-omened positioning of a house or temple, witchcraft and supernatural revenge. | J: And then when they are going to have the final purification [*nuntun*], they "ask for speech" again. At the "seating of the ancestors" in the family temple [*malinggih*], again they "ask for speech." That's the end of it.<br>L: [Was she] with the head of the hamlet?<br>J: No, she accompanied others.<br>L: Oh, with others.<br>J: With others. |

two years, that Linda was a student interested in Balinese culture, and that the films would be used in universities. In Balinese, Linda also told them a little about her background. They agreed to be in the film without apparent reluctance. Then they waited about 20 minutes while Tim set up his equipment.

## FILM RESUMES: TIM WALKS PAST JERO'S PORCH

At approximately 8:10 a.m. Tim began filming in the street outside Jero's compound. As he filmed, he walked up the steps and through her gate, past a building used for family rituals and guests, past the kitchen and Jero's son's house, and toward the porch. We decided not to use the beginning of this shot because it was so long. The film begins as Tim approaches the clients who are waiting on Jero's verandah and continues as he walks up the steps into Jero's shrine house, from where most of the film was taken (see Diagram 2).

The blue doors behind the people on the porch lead into the room where Jero sleeps and keeps her personal belongings. She sleeps alone because her husband died 16 years earlier and her two living children are married with children of their own. Her son, with his wife and children, share her compound; Jero's daughter lives on the other side of the village with her husband and children. The bed on the right, on which several clients are seated, is used every third day when Jero gives massage; the table, to the left, is used to serve coffee to patients waiting their turn for a massage.

*Shot 13 FR1 (0172:07–0234:00)*

N: The clients await their turn on the verandah before being received in the medium's shrine house, which is usually erected next to the family temple.

L: Now, this is the beginning.

J: Here is the ceremony.
L: Yes, here.
J: They're beginning by putting their baskets down. That's my house.

| Comments | A Balinese Trance Séance (Subtitles and narration) | Recorded comments by Jero and Linda |
|---|---|---|
| The household temple is behind the pillared gate in the northeast corner, the most sacred of their houseyard, closest to Gunung Agung, the mountain home of the gods. The temple consists of a series of small shrines dedicated to local houseyard deities, the spirits of purified ancestors, and higher deities, including a shrine dedicated to Betara Surya. This temple is the responsibility of relatives of Jero's husband who live in North Bali near Singaraja. They come on each anniversary of the temple. Jero's family temple is in her husband's elder brother's compound, in the same village where Jero and her husband were born. At marriage women become affiliated with their husband's family temple, where it is usually their responsibility to make the daily offerings. Because many marriages, including Jero's, are between patriparallel cousins, a woman's natal ancestors may well be those of her husband. |  | L: Yes.<br>J: Is that the shrine house?<br>L: Yes.<br>J: Yes, it is the shrine house. |
| TIM WALKS INTO THE SHRINE HOUSE | | |
| The man in the center is holding a flower. This probably means he will say a private prayer before the séance begins. | N: On the day we were filming this group of relatives arrived from an isolated village twenty kilometers to the northwest. | |
| Jero has been talking with the petitioners at greater length than usual, as we asked if we could begin with a few informal shots. Jero, like the petitioners, is wearing ceremonial clothes, though not her best. In order to contact the spirits she must be pure. For example, were she | | L: Tim is walking with the camera.<br>J: My house looks well on film, but it's shabby really.<br><br>L: No it isn't. And on a big screen it looks even better! This is small, but it can go on a big screen. |

100

"polluted" by menstruation or by a recent death in her family or hamlet she would not be able to hold a séance. She must be cleansed both spiritually and physically. Behind Jero is a large, covered ceramic pot used for storing rice. Jero is sitting on a raised platform that places her above the clients. Elevation is extremely important in Bali: Not only do consecrated people and those of high rank sit higher than others, but effigies and offerings are carried on the head and petitioners kneel before the shrines of the deities. In this case, Jero, as a consecrated person and an intermediary, should be spatially closer to the supernatural beings than are her clients.

Jero's shrine house is approximately six feet by eight feet. It was very dark inside, so Tim opened a side window and used a 100-watt lamp run by a 12-volt car battery to light Jero's face and the bottles and other paraphernalia. Throughout most of the filming Tim stood or sat inside the shrine house. Behind him was a bed, never seen in the film, where Jero sometimes sleeps when seeking a visionary experience, or if she is depressed or does not know the answer to a question, perhaps about a personal problem or a difficult cure. She says many significant dreams and visions have come to her while sleeping in her shrine house.

As the camera zooms back one can see the offerings placed beside Jero by the petitioners. One of their baskets has been placed near Jero's own offerings because this has been prepared for the deity Surya. This can be interpreted as an offering to the general pantheon of important deities, whereas the offerings placed on the lower table are for the

J: (*Laughing and pointing, speaks over Linda*) I'm turning around.

| Comments | A Balinese Trance Séance (Subtitles and narration) | Recorded comments by Jero and Linda |
|---|---|---|
| ancestral spirits that the people wish to attract. Offerings to the manifestations of the higher deities should be placed higher than those to ancestors, for just as there is social rank on earth, there is hierarchy in the supernatural realm. | | |
| Jero is preparing to light the aromatic wood in her brazier. Balinese try to stimulate all the senses in order to tempt supernatural beings to descend to the world of the living. Behind Jero are bottles, collected wherever she can find them, filled with medicines: remedies for all sorts of illnesses. Each medicine has its own history and is sacred: It may have "dropped out of the sky," "come whistling through the air," "been found in an unusual place" or when she was "bathing in a sacred spring." Jero has a story about each one that usually reveals its anomalous characteristics. Discoveries often were accompanied by dreams outlining their curative properties: This one is particularly useful for massaging people with rheumatism, this one for swelling under the skin, and so on. (See the film *The Medium Is the Masseuse*.) During a séance, possessing spirits may direct Jero to a particular potion, which she then gives to the client to take home. In making medicines, Jero often uses traditional recipes, but it is thought that they are lent potency by the sacred ingredients that she adds. Medicine, however, is thought to treat only the symptoms; the main purpose of holding a séance is to get information about the | J: I'll light the incense brazier, then we'll begin. | J: I've got callouses from sitting cross-legged. There's no more feeling – right here. <br> L: Oh. <br> J: There's no more feeling – just sitting cross-legged! |
| | J: How many are in your group? <br> OW: Let's see . . . | J: It's been twenty-four years since I began as a medium. <br> L: Yes. |

primary cause of illness, which is likely to be the neglect of specific ritual obligations.

Jero is just making conversation. She does not ask, indeed she never asks, about the purpose of a visit. "Four" may refer to the number of people involved in the subgrouping concerned with the first problem. A group of six actually arrived and left together; the old woman participated in séances concerning all six.

As the narration resumes, Tim stands up in order to see the brazier more clearly.

Balinese told Linda that for serious problems they preferred to consult a medium whom they did not know rather than one with whom they were acquainted. To us this may seem illogical in light of their stated belief that a medium is simply a vehicle for the spirits and deities, but Linda could find no evidence that the Balinese she worked with found this a contradiction. People may feel that it is more professional, perhaps even less embarrassing, to go to a stranger. Since people usually consult strangers, and for important matters rarely return to the same medium, word of mouth is very important in building up a medium's clientele. Jero has had many clients from the village in which this group lives.

THE CLIENTS, SITTING IN A ROW

This shot is a continuation of the previous one, but we cut a slow, distracting pan from Jero to the petitioners, who are waiting while Jero completes her preparations.

J: How many did you say?
OW: There are four of us.
J: Oh, four.

N: They told me Jero had been recommended by neighbors in their village who had previously consulted her. Clients usually choose to consult a medium whom they don't know personally.

Shot 14 FR1 (0234:01–0291:32)

N: Before the trance these clients would not discuss the purpose of their visit with me

J: That's how long I've sat cross-legged.

L: I'm explaining again.

J: Do any other mediums appear in this film?
L: No, it's just you "asking for speech."
J: So there's nobody else . . .
L: Not in the film.
J: You mean you went around to see who would agree and who would not?
L: Yes.

J: And my guardian deity agreed [sasuunan, a powerful ancestor or deity who presides

| Comments | A Balinese Trance Séance (Subtitles and narration) | Recorded comments by Jero and Linda |
| --- | --- | --- |
| In order to know what form of address is appropriate, Jero, like all Balinese, must ascertain the status of another person before conversing. Were these clients from a high-ranking group they would have to be addressed in high, formal Balinese, but since they are commoners she can address them as she would her neighbors; they, on the other hand, must use a more polite form to address Jero, since she is a consecrated person, even though a commoner. (See section 51 and shot 17.) Inherited rank does not determine who may become a healer or restrict the status of a healer's clientele. Thus Jero has many titled clients, as well as clients who are commoners. Not all healers are commoners; members of the gentry (*triwangsa*) may become spirit mediums, and it is possible for commoners (*jaba*, "outsiders," as Jero calls herself, or *sudra*) to be among their clientele. | or with Jero. As she begins, the only information Jero has about them is their village of origin, and the fact that they are of commoner, not aristocratic, family. | over human beings; here a being who has power over Jero's profession). But I'm the most ignorant.<br>L: No. |
| The name of this group's village, which is in an area with widely dispersed, dry fields, indicates they are probably poor farmers who are likely to have a small field cottage as well as their main home. Their offerings include the usual *tapakan palinggih* of rice, coconut, and Chinese coins, an offering that induces the spirit to come down, plus a set of offerings called *banten asoroh*, as well as clothes the deceased wore in life, to attract him (*rantasan*). These offerings indicate that the clients wish to contact a dead but as yet uncremated relative rather than other spirits or deities from the higher pantheon. | N: Also, the offerings for the spirits, which they bring and place beside Jero, give some clues about the purpose of their visit. These offerings – woven coconut leaves, flowers, rice, small colored cakes – vary according to the particular ritual occasion. | J: Others are literate and can do anything.<br>L: ?<br>J: Incense. . . .<br>L: Incense. |

Jero is chipping an incense stone in order to add fragments to the wood burning in her brazier. This stone, fragrant when burned, is often used in these ceremonies. It is not found locally; Jero probably bought it in a market. She calls it *menyan Arab* (Arabian incense).

As Tim walks back into the shrine house, Jero is reaching for one of her bottles of holy water, essential in all Balinese ritual. Jero sprinkles holy water at the beginning of the séance, when she dedicates herself and the offerings, and after each possession. At the end of each séance, she gives holy water to those petitioners most closely involved. Jero's holy water comes from a variety of sites, frequently temples and springs where she has had spiritual insights. Jero reconsecrates the water by reciting a short, traditional prayer (*mantra*).

## JERO POURS HOLY WATER

Jero pours water into a bowl. The smaller vessel is used for sprinkling and dispensing the water.

Behind Jero can be seen a black and white cloth, a cloth common in adorning religious statues and certain performers in ritual dramas. Here it indicates the shrine where Jero's

Jero prepares the incense brazier, holy water and offerings in readiness for the séance.

J: I'm pounding it. (*Laughs*) Bang, bang, like that. Incense. Kindling. The fragrant smoke reaches the heavens to call down the deity. It reaches the heavens; it reaches the deity.

L: How's that?

J: So the deity descends. To bring down the deity.

L: You've just begun here.

J: (*Interrupts*) Yes, I'm taking down the holy water. After lighting the incense brazier.

But I find the container is empty.

L: Mmm.

J: Look, you can see the offerings.

J: That's what I'm doing. Look, the coal burns

105

| Comments | A Balinese Trance Séance (Subtitles and narration) | Recorded comments by Jero and Linda |
|---|---|---|
| sacred objects are kept, objects associated with the visionary experiences she had during the period of fasting and meditating that followed her consecration as a medium. Since this is a sacred area, no one may approach it except Jero. In the shrine Jero keeps a gold ring with a red stone considered auspicious in Bali. Some mediums have little figurines. These are not idols but, like the medium, are *tapakan*, receptacles in which the gods may reside when they descend to earth. On a small, elevated wooden tray can be seen Jero's daily offering – a coconut, some rice, some rice cakes, incense, and woven coconut leaves – a *canang palinggih*. Here is the resting place of the guardian deity that enables her to contact supernatural beings. Jero might be able to dispense with a lot of the other paraphernalia, but in the context of a séance this offering is essential; in other contexts, such as during a cremation, Jero has been possessed without its presence. | | me [when the coal falls off the brazier and Jero picks it up]. <br><br> L: Oh. <br><br> J: Mmm. Before, before I "got burnt" wandering around in the mountains, when things were bad. [See *Jero Tapakan: Stories from the Life of a Balinese Healer.*] Now I "get burnt" from just sitting. (*Laughs*) <br><br> L: It was so. |
| CLOSE-UP: BRAZIER, FRAGRANT WOOD, AND INCENSE <br><br> A zoom to a close-up of the brazier (1.5 seconds) was cut. | *Shot 15 FR1 (0291:33–0293:17)* <br><br> N: The petitioners are not sure which deity or spirit is going to speak through | |

# JERO CLEANSING HER HANDS IN SMOKE

Jero must purify herself before she may begin the séance. A three-second zoom was cut as Jero put her hands into the smoke. This movement is a form of cleansing: Fire and water are both considered cleansing agents. The Balinese view of fire as both destructive and creative or purifying is typical of their general view of balanced opposition. Fire, water, and flowers are a part of all Balinese ritual.

Jero requests that Siwa and Surya witness the event, although these paramount deities never possess a medium. She then turns to those spirits closest to her, her "siblings within," for guidance and assistance. Here Jero refers to them as *nyamane ane ajak* ("siblings who are with me"). The common literary reference for these siblings, said to be born with each Balinese, is *kanda mpat*, the four elder siblings who provide support throughout one's life, linking one to larger, cosmic forces. They can also be malevolent if neglected in ritual (see section 3B). It is Jero's "siblings" who invite her guardian deity to participate and to choose the deity or spirit who will "take possession." The chain from medium to spiritual siblings, to guardian deity, and finally to the possessing spirit or deity is one example of the way in which the medium remains free of responsibility for what happens while possessed: She is not even responsible for choosing the possessing agent.

*Shot 16 FR1 (0293:18–0376:07)*

N: the medium but usually they are seeking information from a particular spirit. Jero is able to contact a large number of supernatural beings on behalf of her clients. In achieving a state of light trance by praying and chanting, her personality is transformed. A supernatural being takes possession and converses with the petitioner. Jero often goes into trance four or five times at the request of one of her clients.

N: Each time she is entered by a separate deity or spirit.

J: Oh, the flame looks so big [the close-up of the brazier]. Now, that's the blessing [just after her hands are cleansed in the smoke]. Are you saying it's about to begin, Linda?

L: Yes.

J: It's up to that part.

L: Yes.

J: Praying to Siwa. Asking Surya and Siwa to witness. [Jero is praying silently. Her hands, while holding a flower, are held together above her head.] Then asking blessing from my "siblings within."

L: Now?

J: Yes, from the "siblings within" and from "Those Above" [*leluur*, purified spirits or deities].

L: Ah.

J: The "siblings within" invite my guardian deity [*betara*]. The "siblings who are not seen" [visibly]. They invite.

| Comments | A Balinese Trance Séance (Subtitles and narration) | Recorded comments by Jero and Linda |
|---|---|---|
| Jero picks up a red flower, wafts it in the smoke, and prays silently. This is repeated with a second red flower, which she then places in her hair. Next she chooses a red and a yellow flower and begins her first audible prayer, one to her guardian deity. | N: At the beginning of the séance, Jero prays to her guardian deity, asking that she be blessed with the ability to go into trance on behalf of her clients. | L: (*Jero starts to speak, too*) To make contact? J: They call down the deity. I'm too ignorant. It's my "siblings within" who pray and call the deity. I am ignorant about who should be addressed, who is to be addressed now. |
| The language of Jero's prayer is a mixture of archaic Balinese and Javanese, both influenced by Sanskrit. Jero memorized these prayers many years ago when they were given to her by a ritual expert in her village (*kelian adat*). | | This is the Balinese meaning. |
| "Gangga" (the Hindu name for the Ganges River), is used by Balinese to refer both to the river and to the goddess of water. Gangga is invoked whenever holy water is used for purification. It is the spiritual essence of the holy water that purifies, not the physical properties of water. Siwa, Brahma, and Wisnu represent the trinity (of Hindu origin), manifestations of the one great God. They are commonly invoked in ritual. Usually Jero refers to the one great God as Ida Sang Hyang Widi Wasa, or more colloquially as "Widi." | J: O Gods of the Gangga River, Siwa, Brahma, Wisnu, we worship Thee in Thy many manifestations. Imbue the holy water with Thy spiritual essence, purify Thy lowly medium. | L: Oh, yes. J: Now I ask for purification. Here I remove impurities. Wherever they are, whatever they are, impurities of the body. |
| Jero sprinkles herself three times with holy water and again places a flower in her hair. She chooses a red, a yellow, and a white flower and continues her prayers. | N: During the prayers, she purifies herself with holy water. | To cleanse. Now, only after cleansing myself, may I cleanse the offerings. L: Oh, after cleansing the body |

J: (*Interrupts*) Then I cleanse the offerings. That's how it starts, the beginning.

L: And now . . . [as Jero places her hands in the smoke].

J: That bird! (*Laughs*) [She could hear a chick chirping.]

The offerings are cleansed. They may have been in contact with ritually unclean people or with chickens, dust, hair.

J: All sorts of impurities are dissolved. So the two things are cleansed: me and the offerings. Only now can the deity be brought down.

J: Thou with no impurities

Gods of the Wind, Sea, Sky, of the points of the compass.

Bestow Thy blessing upon us.

N: In the following segment, Jero goes into trance three times at the request of one of the petitioners from this family group.

Because we did not have space to subtitle the whole list of gods mentioned, we combined the elements of each prayer.

The cardinal points are essential references in all Balinese ritual. They are linked to the deities and the demons, to colors and elements, in a system of correspondences. On completing her dedication, Jero sprinkles the brazier and the offerings with holy water: three times for the brazier, three for the offerings. As she does so, the camera pans to the clients to show that they are waiting their turn, not yet taking an active role in the ritual.

PAN TO THE PETITIONERS

Jero was possessed five times for this grouping (i.e., in relationship to a single problem): three times by an abstract deity, once by a father's spirit (*guru*), and once by a child's spirit. As we had little footage of the second and third possessions, we combined them with the first so that they appear as one in the film. Tim had only 45 minutes of film, and he had no idea which sequences might prove most revealing for foreign audiences or how long this séance would last. Linda was taking sound from the steps outside the shrine house, so they could not see one another or communicate during the filming. They filmed only about 15 minutes of the séance, which lasted 38 minutes, but they made a complete tape recording. A translation of the recorded dialogue comprises Chapter 7.

| Comments | A Balinese Trance Séance (Subtitles and narration) | Recorded comments by Jero and Linda |
|---|---|---|
| As the camera pans back to Jero she says, *"sira marep?"* (lit.: to face the front), "Which person is going to take responsibility to answer the spirits when they come down?" We did not subtitle this. The man seated in the middle of the front row answers, *"Titiang,"* "I [am going to do that]." | N: She begins by intoning the long chant that will take her into trance. | J: If there's firewood, put it down below so things are right. |
| Again Jero sprinkles the brazier with holy water. | | |
| CLOSE-UP OF BRAZIER, THEN ZOOM TO IN-CLUDE JERO | *Shot 17 FR1 (0376:08–0435:15)* | |
| Tim turned off the camera momentarily and then realized that Jero was about to begin: He began filming as he focused on the brazier. Therefore the prayer begins with this slightly shaky close-up. | | |
| Jero uses the same prayer at the beginning of each séance but thereafter uses an abbreviated form. When this prayer began, Linda was changing her tape, so we had no sound until the final subtitle. Linda recorded two later versions at the beginning of other séances. I was able to use one of these prayers to create the illusion of synchronized sound. | | |
| The only major difference occurred at the very end. In this version and in one of the others Jero's transition appears to be on the word *dalem,* but in the third version it is on *pertiwi.* In order to make the sound appear synchronized with Jero's lips, I had only to lengthen or shorten the spaces | | |

110

where she paused. Her pauses relate not to normal speech phrasing but rather to breathing.

In this context, Jero uses a stereotyped chant as a means of achieving a withdrawn state. The familiar pattern seems to create the context in which Jero "forgets," withdraws. The chant is not long enough to create a deep physiological change (as hyperventilation or prolonged dancing might do). Jero's rocking motion is another way of limiting her awareness of external stimuli.

In this context the prayer means, "Descend and possess the medium." Much Balinese ritual is concerned with attracting the attention of the deities so that they will descend either to possess a person or to reside in an effigy or a particular place, there to attend for a time to the affairs of human beings. This is an incantation to the many deities and spirits whose names and locations are chanted. In the film we have shortened the prayer to fit in the subtitles.

Note that although Jero is not yet possessed her attention is sufficiently withdrawn from common concerns so that when she drops an ember on the floor, an ember that continues to burn, she only glances at it; she does not pick it up as she did earlier. While Jero continues her prayer, one can see the smoke rising from the floor to her left, until the chief petitioner reaches in to remove the ember.

(3) J: O Noble Gods on High, Guardians of the Heavens, we, Thy lowly servants, humbly beseech Thee,

Descend
to the earthly regions.

Speak with divine voice.

Take Thy seats,

Heavenly Host, amongst Thy servants.

Partake of the offerings we have prepared.

O Sublime Goddess of Wisdom, inspire Thy lowly medium.

J: Now [the deity] is brought down.
L: Yes.
J: We can begin. When I reach the deity who will speak, that's when I "forget."

That's who comes down. Sometimes from the Pura Dalem [Death or graveyard temple].

I ask that they be brought down, that it not be a long time.

I feel confused. I "forget" for a moment, I "remember" for a moment.

What's that writing?
L: English [subtitles].

J: See how it smokes! [Probably refers to the brazier, since the ember on the floor has not begun to smoke visibly.]

| Comments | A Balinese Trance Séance (Subtitles and narration) | Recorded comments by Jero and Linda |
|---|---|---|
| Male and female are commonly paired in Bali. They contrast with one another and yet form a unity. | Descend in Thy male and female manifestations. | My rocking makes a noise. (*Laughs*) |
| | | L: Does it? |
| Synchronized sound resumes now that Linda has changed her sound roll. In all our footage, at the moment Jero is thought to be "entered" or "possessed," she leans forward, strikes the brazier against the vessel containing holy water, and then, her face gradually relaxing, continues to rock back and forth, eyes closed. Her first utterance is a stereo-typed laugh. | Come down, O Mighty Lords, | J: I'm still "remembering." He [the chief petitioner] is removing the ember. (*Laughs*) |
| | we implore Thee, speak. | L: Oh. |
| | We have waited long for Thy words. | |
| POSSESSION OCCURS | Descend, Gods of the Seas and Gods of the Nether Regions. . . . | J: That was quick. It's quick. (*Laughs*) I've never known how I looked. Only now do I know. I'm game to have this shown, Linda. I'm game to have this shown [brave enough]. |
| Jero has been possessed by an imperious deity who speaks low, coarse Balinese to the petitioners, whereas they are re-quired to respond in the most deferential language of which they are capable. For more information on speech levels, see section 5I. Since these people are from an isolated mountain village, they are probably not practiced in speak- | D: My loyal servants. | |

112

ing refined Balinese. This inexperience adds to the formality and stiffness of the exchange. Unfortunately, in order to fit in the subtitles we have had to take out many of the flowery, more deferential forms of address such as, "Oh, Exalted One"; but, then, standard English is not a language in which differences in social status are clearly marked. The deferential gestures of the petitioners parallel the formality of their speech. At first the man seems to find it difficult to speak; the old woman takes over. During this exchange the deity expresses considerable irritation and anger, far more than is proper in conversation between human beings, in which restraint and control are highly valued.

## THE PETITIONERS IN DEFERENTIAL POSTURES

A few seconds are missing between shots 17 and 18. "Impure spirits" refers to uncremated dead. Until the proper purification rituals are performed, including cremation, spirits of the dead cannot join the deities. Instead, they are said to remain within the earthly realm, in limbo, where they may well bring misfortune to the living.

Even the simplest Balinese cremation is an elaborate ceremony involving days of preparation and extensive resources. Few Balinese can afford such rituals, so when a commoner dies he or she is generally buried in a "temporary" resting place. Frequently a poor family will wait to cremate their relatives until wealthy relatives organize a cremation, but as even this is expensive, many corpses remain uncremated.

My servants seek divine mediation in their affairs.

(5) OW: Yes, O Mighty One.

(6) D: Your affairs are in disorder, your Lord is angry.

*Shot 18 FR1 (0435:16–0478:11)*

(8) D: Are you performing the rituals for impure spirits?

(10) D: Your Lord will show the way.

(11) OW: Speak, O Lord.

(12) D: Is it your intention to perform a cremation ritual?

(14) M: That is our intention, Lord.

(18) D: Are you planning a collective or a private cremation?

J: My lips are speaking. I'm not aware of it.

J: Yet I hear.
It's dark. There's "speech," but I'm not taking it in and it's dark.

J: Yet I hear.

J: I feel like this – just still and quiet.

When I'm already "entered," it feels this way (*sits motionless with eyes closed*). My ears hear. I sense the voice up here (*points above her head*).

| Comments | A Balinese Trance Séance (Subtitles and narration) | Recorded comments by Jero and Linda |
|---|---|---|
| | (19) OW: A collective. | |
| | (20) D: I'm filled with anger and misgivings at your past incompetence. | L: Really? Is the voice clear? |
| In order to purify the island in preparation for Eka Dasa Rudra (see section 5H), many poor Balinese performed collective ceremonies, in which hamlets or large kin groups cooperated to cremate all their dead at one ceremony. | (22) M: A thousand apologies. | J: If there's a voice, I hear it, as do the people who've come. I hear, they hear . . . |
| | D: Which type of ceremony do you intend to perform? | |
| The deity is referring to this type of cremation, the likely option for peasant families. | (26) OW: Speak, O Lord. | J: I speak, yet I don't understand. |
| | (27) D: Now, heed my words! | It's like this, like that, like this . . . I'm in a daze. |
| | Where will you hold the cremation? | |
| | (28) M: We desire to perform the cremation in the village. | I can't open my eyes. |
| In a *ngrintes* ceremony [*ngerintes* in subtitle] the bones of the deceased are dug up, carried back to the house, and treated as though they were a whole corpse. In a *nyekah* ceremony no bones are actually dug up. Symbolic earth is taken from the cemetery, and effigies are constructed to represent the body. | (29) D: With a ngerintes ceremony? | When the voice has finished – emptiness. Only then is it bright. |
| | (30) M: No, a nyekah ceremony. | |
| | (31) D: Nyekah. | |

An empty place is a dangerous place. The deity is saying that, if everyone has gone to the cremation, offerings should be left behind in the houseyard to signify to the household spirits that they have not been forgotten and that the house has not been abandoned. This particular offering is not common; many people may well have overlooked its performance. It seems to be the kind of oversight that people can readily understand; that is, that the spirits should be upset at being neglected, even forgotten.

(31) D: Don't leave the houseyard empty of offerings.

(33) M: Yes, Lord.

(34) D: The household spirits must be propitiated.

(36) D: Will the procession pass through your houseyard?

L: You feel yourself again?

J: We discuss it. "How did it go?" "Did you get what you wanted?" "Yes."
Then we go on:
"What did you learn?"
"What did you hear?"
"What was the medicine?"
"Was there a paste for the forehead?"
"Was it like this?"
"Was this said?" – "It was."

## THE PETITIONERS, STILL USING DEFERENTIAL GESTURES

Because the film roll was almost finished, Tim turned off his camera while the deity outlined the required offerings (see the translation of the missing dialogue, section 7A, speeches 38–82). In order to include the dialogue, we use a shot of the clients taken the second time the deity "came down." Since the possessing agent was the same deity, the clients' posture and speech level remained extremely formal.

*Shot 19 FR2 (0478:12–0481:16)*

(37) M: Only through the village.
(38) D: Remember these offerings.

J: "Was that said?" – "It was."
"Was *don pinis* mentioned?" – "It was."

## CLOSE-UP OF JERO; FREEZES AFTER TWO SECONDS

This is a very short shot because the film ran out. The freeze is of a very simple image, not only because it is the last

*Shot 20 FR1 (0481:17–0482:31)*

(83) D: Your Lord has spoken.

J: "Was garlic included?" – "It was."

| Comments | A Balinese Trance Séance (Subtitles and narration) | Recorded comments by Jero and Linda |
|---|---|---|
| | Freeze (0482:32–0493:09) | J: If there was a lack, they ask me about it. "It seems as if there might have been this." "Yes, there was." |
| | N: While we were putting on a new roll of film, Jero came out of trance and turned to ask what had been said. By discussing the "trance speech" with her clients, she helps them to interpret the often ambiguous pronouncements of the deities and spirits. | |

frame of picture on the roll and shows Jero returning to a normal state of awareness (shifting to her left and setting down the brazier) but also because we wanted the audience to concentrate on the narration and not a complex visual image.

Jero usually takes an active role in explaining exactly what should be done. She seems to need to have her memory jogged about what was said, but after that she often knows more than her clients about how a particular ritual should be performed and is able to outline the details. She does not consider herself a ritual expert, although in her own hamlet's affairs Jero often plays an active role. In these discussions Jero stresses that she is trying to help her clients understand what the deity or spirit meant and that she, personally, has no responsibility: She is simply a "medium for others." It is this aspect that has led some Westerners to feel Jero is a fraud. We are convinced she is acting honestly in accordance with her professed beliefs and that belief in possession is so fundamental to her world view that Jero has not questioned the validity of this perspective. This does not mean one need accept her explanation about what occurs during a séance. Her experience, skill, and sensitivity to the needs of her clients are immense.

The second and third conversations with the deity, not included in this film, were elaborations of the points raised in the first exchange and consisted primarily of detailed lists of offerings to be left in the houseyard (see sections 7C, 7E).

JERO, NO LONGER POSSESSED, IS CONVERSING WITH HER CLIENTS

Time: approximately 8:30 a.m.
The only footage cut at the head of this roll is a quick shot of Linda to identify the film roll, a pan from her past the clients, and a close-up of Jero in order to focus. The sound recorded while Tim changed his film roll had to be cut.

CAMERA PANS FROM JERO TO HER CLIENTS

The clients are now speaking with Jero in a relaxed manner. Explicating the ambiguities of the speech of the deities and spirits is extremely important in helping the clients feel confident that they know how to proceed. It is precisely because there are ambiguities that interpretation is necessary and that people often go to several mediums before undertaking a major ritual. They do so to ensure that they understand, in detail, all that is required. Perhaps it was because there was so much confusion over the ritual that Jero was again possessed by the same deity.

*Shot 21 FR2 (0493:10–0519:24)*

(88) J: Do you understand about that ritual?

L: That one [the speech] is finished – almost finished.

(99) M: When did HE mean we should perform it?

(100) J: You neglected that ritual. You mustn't forget again.

(101–3) M: Should it be held in our main houseyard or our cottage in the fields?

J: Ah, that's Grandmother Sayang. (*Laughs*) Grandmother Sayang. They're from Kayukapas. From Kayukapas.

(104) J: In the cottage.

(105) M: Please go into trance again, Jero. We need more details.

(106) J: That was just a preliminary. We will get more details.

(107) M: But it is still unclear when we should hold this ritual.

J: "It's entered a little." They mean that they understand a little.

(108) J: Only on the main day of the cremation.

So there's no mistakes, we discuss it together.

| Comments | A Balinese Trance Séance (Subtitles and narration) | Recorded comments by Jero and Linda |
|---|---|---|
| | There must be offerings for the guardian spirits. | J: Their situation and the speech.<br><br>Fit it together first. So that I am not mistaken. |
| JERO IS PREPARING THE BRAZIER, AS THE OLD WOMAN ARRANGES OFFERINGS | Shot 22 FR5 (0519:25–0533:10) | [It is unclear whether Jero is quoting the clients or referring to her own, imperfect knowledge of what was said.] |
| While the camera was off, Linda asked Jero if she would move the basket on the high table because it was blocking Tim's view. Jero agreed and put it on the lower table but closer to the shrine than the other offerings. Since we had no footage of that incident, I selected a shot taken toward the end of the morning, to create a smooth transition. This shot shows Jero's preparation clearly, but the clients are in a different seating arrangement discussing a similar problem about where to make the appropriate offerings. (The next two subtitles do not appear in Linda's translation.) The offerings the old woman is arranging are different from those in the previous shots, because each new séance requires a new set of offerings. | | |
| It is common for people from the region to erect small houses near their fields. Population density is lower in these areas, and people often live permanently or semipermanently away from the main village. Since offerings are expensive, if only in time, people often neglect those in their field houses while they participate in ceremonies in the main village. | M: But where should we make them?<br><br>J: The Deity said "branch"; that must mean at your cottage. | J: It's bright, isn't it?<br>L: There's a lamp [Tim's lamp].<br>J: Oh, I forgot, there was a lamp.<br>I look a bit crazy. What do you think, Linda? |

L: No, on the screen it doesn't look like that. This is too small.

J: Wherever; I still look like that, a bit crazy. (*Laughs*) Before I became a healer, everyone said I acted crazy. [Jero is referring to the period of "madness" that preceded her consecration as a healer. See *Jero Tapakan: Stories from the Life of a Balinese Healer.*]

The children's voices in the background are probably those of Jero's grandchildren, neighboring children, and perhaps clients' children. Several of these children can be seen at the end of the film.

JERO LIGHTS FRAGRANT WOOD AND INCENSE

This shot follows shot 22 and shows Jero preparing to be "entered." The objects on her table are clearly visible.

*Shot 23 FR5 (0533:11–0542:39)*

J: I still look a bit crazy. Now people don't say it. They offer respect.
They don't think I'm a commoner.

CUTAWAY OF A MAN WHO HAS BEEN LISTENING

All the close-ups of clients' faces were taken after the main sequence was filmed and were intended as cutaways to be used when we wanted to continue dialogue but had no picture. This man listened throughout but was not from the same group.

*Shot 24 FR3 (0543:00–0545:26)*

(295) J: Om, Noble Gods, Lords
. . .

L: (*Interrupts*) This time you forget quickly.

119

| Comments | A Balinese Trance Séance (Subtitles and narration) | Recorded comments by Jero and Linda |
|---|---|---|
| AS HER CHANT ENDS, JERO IS POSSESSED BY "FATHER" | *Shot 25 FR2 (0545:27–0573:09)* | |
| This shot followed shot 21, although missing from it are several minutes in which Jero prepared her brazier. Note that her chant, included in full, is brief, because the clients are concerned with a continuing problem. However, the transformation, seen when she strikes the brazier against the water vessel, is similar to the transformation that followed the much longer chant. The offerings are again those seen when Jero was first possessed. | | J: It's the second time – the beginning of the second. |
| This time an ancestral spirit "descends" rather than a deity. The posture of the clients is more relaxed. They are able to address the spirit less formally. The old woman replies in what seems to be a wheedling tone of voice, probably hoping that "Father" will help them and not create difficulties. She appears to identify the spirit as that of her husband. Since he is dead and already cremated, he must be addressed with respect, and yet something of their previous marital familiarity is expressed in her words and tone. | FS: I, Father, have come. <br><br>(296) OW: If it pleases you, Honourable Father, speak clearly to us. <br><br>(297) FS: What do you want to ask of me? <br><br>(298) M: Forgive me my ignorance. <br><br> I must hold a ritual for your grandchild, my child. | Only the first is difficult because then I'm like this, like that . . . Now it's just like that. <br><br> It's quicker. |
| Mention of the child is the first direct indication we have had about the clients' purpose. We also get some indication of the assumed relationship between the central petitioner and the spirit, "Father." | (299) FS: A child? <br><br>(301) M: Your grandchild, Honourable Father. | His grandchild. |

(305, FS: 307) You have completed my ceremonies, but there are details you overlooked.

The spirit begins to talk about his own rituals. Probably his postcremation ceremonies have not been completed.

(308) M: What is your request?

## CLOSE-UP OF THE BRAZIER

Again we wished to continue the dialogue but had no picture, so this and the next two shots came from later footage. The brazier shot had to be cut in two because Jero's mouth was visible as she rocked back and forth, which would have been distracting because it would not have appeared in sync with the sound. We wanted to include this close-up to show the way Jero balanced the brazier and held the flowers.

*Shot 26 FR4 (0573:10–0574:36)*

(309) FS: You forgot some propitiatory rituals.

## CLOSE-UP OF JERO'S FACE

Note the difference in the brazier, flowers, and offerings in this later shot.

*Shot 27 FR3 (0574:37–0578:14)*

(311) M: Whose father is this?

The spirit's comments about propitiatory rituals have confused the clients, and they are suddenly uncertain of his identity. The ambiguity in the classificatory kinship terminology leaves considerable room for differing assumptions. Perhaps they thought they had completed his mortuary rites satisfactorily.

*Shot 28 FR4 (0578:15–0579:29)*

(312) FS: Your own father.

## CLOSE-UP OF THE BRAZIER

Continuation of shot 26. "Father" could be a classificatory term; the spirit could stand in a "father" relationship to several of the people present.

| Comments | A Balinese Trance Séance (Subtitles and narration) | Recorded comments by Jero and Linda |
|---|---|---|
| **THE PETITIONERS** | Shot 29 FR2 (0579:30–0624:14) | |
| This shot followed 25 and is a return to the chronological film sequence. In the missing dialogue the spirit of the father outlined the offerings that he still required (see section 7G, speeches 33–69). The exchange between spirit father and son highlights the complexity of Balinese ritual practice: Each ceremony has many different offerings, and the correct time and placement of each ritual action is vital. Elaborations are endless. People come to Jero with specific problems, but in the course of a séance other issues become important in their interpretation of past misfortune. When we visited the clients, they said they had performed each of the rituals mentioned, not just the ones for the spirit of the young child, which had been their initial concern. | (370) M: Forgive us if we are ignorant in these matters. <br><br> (371) FS: You must make the correct mortuary offerings for me. <br><br> (372) M: Of course we'll hold the ceremonies. | J: What's he saying? "*Mangiris*"? What's that? "*Maleteh*"? [Words apparently unfamiliar to Jero.] <br><br> My breasts are prominent, Linda. [*Laughs at the close-up of herself*] |
| Guru Paduka is a propitiatory offering to Siwa; each component – cakes, fruit, rice, side dishes, cloth – is replicated in four colors: red, white, black, and yellow. | (375) FS: You haven't made the Guru Paduka offerings | |
| The vocabulary used parallels that of a Balinese market exchange with reference to "sins" as debts and to "redeeming debts" with offerings. | to redeem my sins. | |
| The man on the floor who taps the main petitioner's knee is tape-recording the possession utterances (see Comments, shot 44). It is common for petitioners to confer in private tones in order to decide how best to proceed. | (378) M: Where should we make these offerings? <br><br> (379) FS: At the main shrine in the house temple. | J: "Wrong. Wrong" [*Salah, salah*]. |

J: If I were "remembering" could I speak as quickly as that, Linda?
If I myself speak, I'm slow.
Aren't – I – like – this?
You've often heard me, Linda.

L: Yes, yes.
J: I don't know....

I don't know anything. In truth, it's "Those Above" who are wise.

Ask forgiveness from the God of the sky, from Lord Siwa,

and from the Protective Lord of your family.

(380) OW: Yes, Honourable One.

(381) FS: In that way all sins will be redeemed.
If you can't afford it now, make future offerings.

(384) OW: As you wish.

(385) FS: Do you understand my words?

(386) M: Should I make offerings in the main house temple?

Or in the cottage shrine?

Forgive me my ignorance.

The list of deities was longer than subtitling permitted.

As in the dialogue accompanying shot 1, "sins" or "wrongs" (salah) refers to sins against the spiritual realm, such as neglect of ritual obligations.
Here the spirit asks that the petitioners promise to make offerings at a future date.

Here the petitioners converse among themselves.

The man is probably concerned because of the prior discussion with the deity, in which the location was stressed. The spirit's response, which appears to contradict the earlier emphasis on location, highlights the complexity: The redemption of his sins is not the same as the neglect of a houseyard ritual; one deals with the whole pantheon of deities, the other with specific spirits related to a specific location.

123

| Comments | A Balinese Trance Séance (Subtitles and narration) | Recorded comments by Jero and Linda |
|---|---|---|
| | (387) FS: Fools! Wherever you invoke Deities, it's all the same. | |
| CLOSE-UP OF JERO WITH THE BRAZIER | *Shot 30 FR3 (0624:15–0628:16)* | |
| Sound and image appear synchronized in order to continue the dialogue, but the image was actually recorded later. A few seconds of dialogue were cut (see section 7G). The spirit seems to be making the kind of personal request an older man might make of his son or wife. | (399) FS: Before I go, (401) give me some rice whisky. (402) M: Forgive us, Honourable Father. (403) OW: There is no whisky. | L: ? J: Like that, [I look] crazy. *[Laughs at a close-up of herself with eyes closed while she holds the brazier]* |
| CUTAWAY OF A WOMAN | *Shot 31 FR3 (0628:17–0633:05)* | |
| This cutaway was made in order to complete "Father"'s speech. The woman in this shot is the main petitioner's sister-in-law. By leaning forward in that way, she may be removing herself from the interaction. Even in earlier exchanges with the deity she did not adopt the deferential hand position but kept her gaze averted. | | |

The spirit now demands money, the old Chinese coins (*ke-peng*) used in many offerings.

## JERO, JUST AFTER THE SPIRIT HAS LEFT

We cut part of a long pause because we had no picture. Whenever the spirit "departs" Jero prays briefly and wipes her face before turning around. This face wiping is a charac-teristic action following possession (see film by Bateson and Mead, 1951).

This money is for the spirits (not for Jero) and will be re-trieved by the clients, along with the bulk of their offerings. Since it is intended for the spirits, it must be wrapped in an offering, which is the reason the man asked about the offer-ing flowers (*kewangen*).

The man starts to place the money on the high table, but Jero indicates it should be placed with the other offerings for the spirits. There are already several bills there, the money they will give to Jero. Possibly the man exhibits slight em-barrassment because of the camera.

The main petitioner may have looked at his watch because he still had not spoken with the spirit he sought. The group had come with several other problems as well, and they

---

(405) FS: Well, give me some money. I'm leaving now.

*Shot 32 FR2 (0633:06–0697:37)*

(406) M: Where's the money?

Where are offering flowers?

(407) ? Here's some money.

M: We don't have the cere-monial coins he asked for.

(410) M: Please Jero, can you go into trance again?

---

J: Who is that? He's crying.
L: Not yet.

J: It is so. If not, then his expression would not look so guarded. Closed.

If he were happy there would be no tears.

Have the gentry seen this film yet? [Probably referring to the people who owned the house where we were watching.]
L: No. You are the first. Then others may look at it.

| Comments | A Balinese Trance Séance (Subtitles and narration) | Recorded comments by Jero and Linda |
|---|---|---|
| probably wanted to reach town before the last market-day bus left for their village. There was no discussion of what "Father" said. Jero did not ask how it went, as she normally did, and the clients sought no clarification. Everyone was waiting for the next spirit "to enter," each spirit coming "one by one." | (412) J:   Yes, the spirits want to speak again. | J:   So you're asking me to say whether it may be shown or not, is that it? |
| | (413) OW: I didn't understand it all. | L:   Yes |
| The young man seated behind hands the old woman tobacco to add to the offering. | | J:   Then it can be shown anywhere. |
| | (414) J:   Om, Noble Gods, Lords . . . | J:   Seven times I "hold the brazier." If many spirits come, they come one by one. If seven come, seven times I "hold the brazier." If five , then five times. |
| There has been no cut since "Father" departed, so this exchange, real time, has lasted about three and a half minutes. | | |
| | | L:   [In English] Get this Tim, if you can. |
| JERO IS POSSESSED BY THE CHIEF PETITIONER'S SON | | |
| The words used for father, *bapa teka*, are informal. The statement is ambiguous: It may mean "Daddy has come," or "Has Daddy come?" Since the man answers "Yes" it is clear he interprets it as "Has Daddy come?" thus identifying the spirit as his son. The exchange is now in a lower form of Balinese, except for formal terms of address, although as the father becomes more emotional these, too, are dropped and, | BS:   Is Daddy here? | J:   "Is Daddy here?" |
| | (415) M:   Yes. | |
| | (416) BS:   It's me. I've come down here. | |
| | (417) M:   Yes. | |
| | (418) BS:   Grandma? | |

126

(419) M: She's here. She's come to speak with you.

(420) BS: Mummy?

(421) OW: Mummy couldn't come today.

(422) BS: Why not?

(423) M: She's ritually unclean today.

(424) BS: Do you want to know about the cause of my death? Or my wishes for my cremation?

(426) M: Where are you now? Are you suffering? Why did you die?

*Shot 33 FR3 (0697:38–0702:25)*

(428) M: Now's your chance to tell us how you died.

(429) BS: I was pierced through the lungs!

J: He's calling his grandmother. He's calling his mother.

L: Oh.

J: Do you know "*nelahin*"? [To purify a spirit through cremation.]

L: Yes.

J: Oh, I'm crying. [Her sobbing and sniffling can be heard on the sound track.]

instead of continuing to use an honorific title appropriate to a spirit, he calls the boy familiarly by his birth-order name. Later the boy refers to himself by name. The earlier imperious tones of the deity contrast with the gentler voice of the son. The son speaks low Balinese, not as a mark of superiority as the deity did but because it is the language he used when alive.

Literally, "she's dirty" (*kotor*) or, as in this context, unclean because she is in a state of ritual pollution (*sebel*). (The mother was menstruating.) A séance is regarded as a ritual event; the same pollution restrictions would apply to going into a temple, for example.

Balinese do not emphasize the physiological causes of death, particularly of unnatural or premature death. A premature death such as the boy's is generally attributed to sorcery or supernatural revenge (see shots 42–3 and Jero's comments, sections 6B, C). They all know that the boy is not talking about the physical symptoms of his illness in the Western sense.

CUTAWAY TO THE WOMAN SEEN IN SHOT 31

We had to use another cutaway to avoid cutting the dialogue. "Pierced through the lungs" does not mean that someone literally came and pierced him with a visible object. Rather, it means that a magical object was introduced into his lungs by supernatural means.

127

| Comments | A Balinese Trance Séance (Subtitles and narration) | Recorded comments by Jero and Linda |
|---|---|---|
| JERO IS ROCKING VIGOROUSLY AND CRYING | Shot 34 FR2 (0702:26–0719:09)<br>(431) M: Please tell us. | J: The spirit is crying, but it's me you see.<br>L: Yes.<br>J: He's crying the way [your friend] Douglas showed me. [When Douglas Miles went to visit Jero, he must have rubbed his eyes in dramatizing his description of this scene.] |
| | (433) M: Who is that evil person who took you away so young? | |
| Literally, "It's your relative, a female, uncle's relative. I'm not game to say who, I'm not allowed, so that I won't make a mistake." If we assume nothing could be said that Jero did not herself know, then as these were strangers she could not have identified a specific person. Nor would she want to, because she might be associated with trouble (see Jero's comments, section 6C). But, likewise, if we accept that the spirit does know, he is placing the father in an awkward position: It would be better for everyone if the spirit sought his own revenge and did not create tension within his family. Belief that spiritual revenge requires the participation, and thus the sanction, of the living is an aspect of countersorcery, one emphasized by Jero, that may heighten interpersonal distrust. | (434) BS: It is a female relative, but I must not say who. | |
| We cut out a rather blurred zoom to the father, which followed this shot. | (434) BS: Daddy?<br>(435) M: Yes?<br>(436) BS: Don't bother about me. | |

CLOSE-UP OF THE CHIEF PETITIONER CRYING

The living know that the dead are dependent on them in order to become pure and to move from the earthly to the heavenly realm. How could his relatives possibly abandon the dead boy? Such a statement is bound to upset them, to increase the emotional tension; indeed, many of them begin to cry – unusual public behavior in Bali.

The younger woman finally becomes involved and explains why they have come. As the camera pans back, one can see not only the men wiping their eyes but the woman sitting up and directing her gaze toward Jero. She, too, is deeply moved. She speaks in fairly high Balinese because the boy is now closer to the deities than those still living.

ALL THE PETITIONERS ARE CRYING

*Durmanggala* [durmangala in subtitle] are offerings of exorcism and propitiation.

(In Jero's comments, notice the matter-of-fact reference to conversations between the living and the dead.)

*Shot 35 FR2 (0719:10–0771:19)*

(437) M: Oh, my son, how can you say that?

You know we want to hold your cremation.

J: This is the one from Bucaman, isn't it? He's trying to control his tears. They remember the child and that someone caused his death. They're not afraid to ask about it here.

(438) W: That's the reason we asked you down to talk with us. We only want to know what you want.

(439) BS: When is the cremation?

They're crying at the back.

(440) M: We want to have it as soon as possible,

so you won't suffer and your mother will not grieve so. Please tell us your wishes for the ritual.

L: Yes. Wouldn't they be ashamed to cry elsewhere?
J: It's like this, Linda. Say you die and you tell about it through a medium [*balian*].

(441) BS: First I want some durmangala offerings.

(442) M: When? Now?

(443) BS: Whenever you can afford it.

Relatives are reminded of the cause of your illness. You talk as if still alive: "Mother, give me money..." "Mother, give me rice...."

| Comments | A Balinese Trance Séance (Subtitles and narration) | Recorded comments by Jero and Linda |
|---|---|---|
| | Please make offerings for me to Brahma, Siwa and Wisnu. Daddy, I want to curse the person who killed me. | You ask, like that. You ask like that here. "Mother, give me rice, give me rice. Mother, give me money, give me money." They recall when the spirit was alive. |
| The boy returns to the theme of revenge and begins to describe what the father should do. Crossroads are important in Balinese ritual; they are places where offerings or payments to the demonic forces (kala, buta) are made. All forces in the world must be kept in balance: There could be no deities without demons, no good without evil. Each deity, in each of the cardinal directions, also has a demonic manifestation, and offerings must be laid out in the proper orientation. Offerings to the demons are made on the ground. Those to the deities are elevated. People would not dare to forget the demons. (During the séance, shot 44, Jero, too, makes an offering to the demons.) | (444) M: I agree, if it will ease . . .<br><br>(445) BS: Well, in that case make a payment at the crossroads, three mounds of rice: a red, a yellow, and a white one.<br><br>(446) M: At the crossroads?<br><br>(449) BS: Now, heed what I say! Don't cross that evil person. | So they cry.<br><br>J: The spirit asks their consent to cause illness [by a curse]. L: Illness against whom? J: Suppose, Linda, that you make me ill and I die. Now, to my mother I say: "Mother, make offerings for me to Brahma, Wisnu, and Siwa. |

CUTAWAY OF A MAN, FROM ANOTHER GROUP, LISTENING

"She'll bewitch you," just as the boy was bewitched.

The boy's spirit adds, "and when you're wrong, she'll say you're right."

This cutaway, recorded later, was used to replace a distracting zoom. The sound track is continuous.

CLOSE-UP OF JERO

The son, who is closer to the deities, is now thought to be wiser than his father. Again the boy suggests revenge, but now by direct action and with the cooperation of his father. Perhaps because he has had time to consider the consequences, the father backs off, sounding surprised, and then changes the subject. Were he to agree, and were a woman in his family to get sick – a likely event in an extended family – he might be thought responsible. In a tightly knit group, suspicions of sorcery are a source of tension. Balinese regard deliberate violence by mystical means as evil or immoral when performed by a living being (pangiwa, "black magic") but not when initiated by a spirit, as punishment. Although the father seemed afraid to retaliate, two years later he reported that they had made all the offerings their son requested (thereby consenting to revenge). Some months later a woman whom they suspected fell, injuring herself seriously. This they interpreted as a sign that she had been the guilty one and was suffering spiritual punishment.

*Shot 36 FR3 (0771:20–0775:32)*

She'll bewitch you with her magic needles. When you're right, she'll say you're wrong.

J: I want to make Linda ill." It's like that.

*Shot 37 FR2 (0775:33–0802:17)*

(450) M: What has made her like this? Tell me, my son.

(451 –3) BS: I'm not allowed to say.

These things can be brought into the open. Only if names are mentioned is there fear. "Those Above" do not allow names to be mentioned, only relationships: "My relatives," "mother's relatives," "in-laws."

L: Oh.

If you agree, Daddy, I'll get my revenge.

I'll make her sick. But if you are against it, I won't.

J: If relatives don't make offerings, the spirit can't get consent to cause illness.

(454) M: What's this about sickness?

(456) M: What sort of durmangala offerings shall we make?

(457) BS: First make offerings to Brahma, Siwa, and Wisnu.

L: Whose consent? The father's?
J: No, God's [Widi's] consent.

| Comments | A Balinese Trance Séance (Subtitles and narration) | Recorded comments by Jero and Linda |
|---|---|---|
| | (459) BS: I also want durmangala offerings for my cremation. | L: Oh, God's.<br>J: By making offerings the father gives his own consent. |
| CUTAWAY OF A YOUNGER MAN<br><br>Again we do not have film of the "departure" of the spirit. This shot was taken much later, shortly before the shot used to introduce the film. The sound is continuous. | Shot 38 FR4 (0802:18–0807:05)<br><br>(459) BS: Don't be unhappy on my behalf.<br><br>(461) BS: That's all I have to say. | J: Suppose Linda, that you die; your younger sister or brother has made you ill. You tell your mother: |
| JERO, JUST AFTER THE BOY'S SPIRIT HAS DEPARTED<br><br>The emergence from possession, beginning when Jero leans forward to put down the brazier, appears so casual that the petitioner is not aware of it and asks another question. Because the spirit has departed, it is ignored. The stereotyped movements of Jero's transition are clearly shown: a quick prayer, cleansing her hands in the smoke, wiping her face, and sprinkling herself three times with holy water. This shot follows shot 37. | Shot 39 FR2 (0807:06–0857:31)<br><br>(462) M: Will we make offerings with the village group? | J: "Mother, because someone made me ill, give offerings for me so I can make a request to the deity of the Death Temple [Pura Dalem] because my death was not a right one. Now, mother, if you give offerings, I can cause illness. |
| "How did it go?" is characteristic of the type of question Linda observed Jero asking each time a spirit or deity "departed" and she turned to converse with her clients. | (463) J: How did it go?<br><br>(464) M: My little boy was crying. | "If you don't, I can't. It's up to you. If you consent, I'll cause illness. |

(465) J: What happened? Was he stabbed?

Hey! Fix those baskets, they'll fall off.

If not, I won't."

Although the clients continue to explain what was said, Jero may have felt she had spoken rudely to the basket owners or, perhaps, that her responsibility in this problem was fulfilled. She twice addresses the new group from Bakas.

(466) M: Yes, he said he was pierced through the lungs with. . . .

No names are mentioned. Linda, I'm game to have this shown.

(467) J: Where have you come from? Bakas?

(468) M: His stomach was swollen. He died in the hospital.

L: Yes, yes.

Jero returns to the Balinese cause rather than the medical symptoms (see shots 41–3).

(469) J: The real trouble was, he was pierced through the lungs.

J: Oh, illness of the lungs. Here we're clarifying it.

(470) M: The doctor couldn't do anything for him.

I ask questions like: "Was it really an illness of the lungs?"

(471) J: That's all for now, is it?

I've gone into trance several times for you.

It's finished. "Yes, we obtained [what we wanted]," [they say].

Normally there would be more discussion, but in this case there did not seem to be many ambiguities and Jero may have felt pressed for time because many people were waiting. Before dealing with another problem, even one brought by the same group of relatives, as happened in this case, Jero recites a closing prayer. The clients pray and are blessed with holy water, the offerings are changed, Jero begins her long introductory prayer; and a new séance begins.

133

| Comments | A Balinese Trance Séance (Subtitles and narration) | Recorded comments by Jero and Linda |
|---|---|---|
| Misfortune is frequently caused by the anger of ancestral spirits whose death rituals are still incomplete. These ceremonies affect everyone in Bali. Belief in reincarnation within a family further ties the living and the dead in an endless cycle of obligation and support, a cycle dependent on the proper performance of ritual. | N: After this consultation the family regrouped to consult other spirits about their wishes for their cremation ceremonies. These ceremonies are the most important ritual events in Bali. | J: There's crying. L: No, it's Toko [Jero's eldest grandchild] crying. J: Oh, Toko crying. |
| Time: approximately 8:50 a.m. This séance was completed with prayer and the dispensing of holy water, while Tim was changing his film roll. The remaining footage is of the two séances that followed. | | Even striking a match can be heard. |
| A NEW SÉANCE INVOLVING THE SAME PEOPLE | *Shot 40 FR3 (0857:32–0864:22)* | |
| Before performing a costly ritual, or after having experienced misfortune, a family may consult several mediums. Linda found no indication that this was because people suspected a particular medium of being a fraud. Rather, they want to be sure they get the clearest instructions possible, so that nothing important is overlooked. | N: People consult mediums to avoid making mistakes in complex and costly ritual. Mistakes may provoke ancestral anger | |
| This shot shows the same clients in a new grouping, the second grouping of the morning. | | |

134

## CLOSE-UP OF CHIEF PETITIONER OF THE NEXT SÉANCE

This shot came just before the previous one. We wanted to give a quick sense of the repeating process and then show the conclusion of a séance.

*Shot 41 FR3 (0864:23–0869:27)*

N: which is manifested in misfortune for living descendants.

J: When you explain it there you use "Jero."
L: Yes.

## JERO RECITING PRAYERS AT THE END OF THE SÉANCE

In another variation, the spirit in this footage has requested that the petitioners pray, that they ask for blessing while the spirit is present. Those not involved appear quite unconcerned. This shot was included as background for the narration.

*Shot 42 FR3 (0869:28–0884:09)*

N: Unnatural or premature death is normally attributed to supernatural causes. I later visited the family filmed and discovered that their seven-year-old son had died two months earlier. He had been diagnosed as a typhoid case but according to the doctors, had been brought for treatment too late.
The fact that

L: Did you hear it?
J: Yes, just then.
L: Yes, then.

J: There's praying [the clients after the séance].
The flowers fell down. [The old woman drops the flowers as she prays.]

## JERO CHANTING A CLOSING PRAYER

Suspicions of sorcery are readily accepted if there appears to be some evidence, as in this case. Because Tim was changing film rolls at the end of the first séance, we have no footage of the older man receiving holy water or praying. We have substituted this shot from the second séance.

*Shot 43 FR3 (0884:10–0914:06)*

N: the doctors were unable to save him, together with the medium's utterances, confirmed the family's suspicion that his death had been caused by witchcraft.

L: And now?
J: That's offerings at the side, is it?

| Comments | A Balinese Trance Séance (Subtitles and narration) | Recorded comments by Jero and Linda |
|---|---|---|
| A *rantasan* offering (see Jero's comments) is a pyramid of folded clothes, necessary in this context to invoke spirits of the dead. *Segehan* are small offerings of food and flowers on woven trays laid on the ground to propitiate demonic forces. | | J: *Rantasan, Segehan.*<br>L: Now?<br>J: Now I'm offering holy water to "wash the hands" of the deity.<br>It means that after the speech is finished, as in everyday life, the deity partakes of food.<br>L: What's it called?<br>J: "Washing the hands." Just like when you are going to eat.<br>L: And what are those offerings?<br>J: That's *tehenan* and *pabuat.* Containing flour [small offerings of rice flour and flowers on a coconut leaf, used to purify]. So that when the deity descends there are no impurities. |
| As Jero sprinkles the offerings three times with holy water, one can hear a recording of the séance in the background. The clients are obviously amused and probably embarrassed by the overt attention when Tim moves over to show the film viewer the source of the recording. Jero continues unperturbed; she still has ritual duties to perform, but others are free to relax and need not pay attention to all the proceedings. This is characteristic of all Balinese ritual: The participation of nonexperts has its place, but attention is not required throughout. | A: Again! Again! | |
| JERO PREPARING OFFERINGS | *Shot 44 FR3 (0914:07–1005:26)* | |
| A pan to Jero has been cut to shorten the ending. Jero offers rice to the deities and spirits and then prepares the offering flowers for the clients' final prayer. A bright cloth is visible | J: Put the offering flowers on the sill. | J: My voice is harsh as I give them the offering flowers. *(Laughs as she speaks)* |

as part of the clients' offerings. The tape recorder is turned on, then off, then on again, at Jero's request.

Jero is preparing a small offering – Chinese coins, rice, and flowers on a mat of woven coconut leaves – to be thrown onto the ground for the demons. Demons do not play a central role in these séances but are never completely neglected. (A similar offering is made when Jero prepares for a day of massage.)

Linda found no evidence that tape recorders were used to test the integrity of a medium; such an idea does not seem to be part of the clients' thinking. Much of the speech of the deities and spirits is ambiguous. (The metaphorical style is not evident in the subtitles that are of necessity a simplification.) People want to be able to think about and discuss what was said. In some of the segments, not included in the film, there were long directions for preparing offerings, details that might be hard to remember. If people go to several mediums they want to be able to compare what is said in order to have a full understanding of the wishes of the spirits and deities. In the dialogue we missed while we were changing film rolls, Jero asked the clients if they had turned off the recorder. She accepts the fact that people will want to record the words of supernatural beings, but she always asks them to turn the recorders off between each possession. This does not seem to be because she feels she is vulnerable that she will contradict herself or make some slip.

J: Play back the recording so we can hear it.

N: Whenever possible, the clients bring a tape recorder and record the trance speech. The tape is sometimes played back and unclear points are discussed with the medium. But more importantly, members of the family who are not present, such as the mother in this case, can later hear the proceedings at home and give their opinions.

"I haven't prayed yet, Jero. Get the flowers first."
My pavilion isn't visible, Linda.
L: No, it's not.
J: You didn't want it in, I suppose.
L: No.
J: Because it was shabby.

L: No, not because of that. It's in the life-story film.
J: That one's pretty, isn't she [of the woman on the screen]? There are the offerings. (Camera pans to offerings.) I'm going to ngluarang. I take rice and flowers.
L: What's ngluarang?
J: Making offerings to demons below to appease them.

That one behind the wall is watching.
L: That's the one with the tape recorder.
J: Do they play the tape later?
L: Yes.

| Comments | A Balinese Trance Séance (Subtitles and narration) | Recorded comments by Jero and Linda |
|---|---|---|
| When Linda first asked Jero if she could record all the dialogue at a séance, Jero told her that what people had to say was valueless, that human comments are not relevant to the communications of supernatural beings. People should not be interested, they should not waste their tapes. Furthermore, she is embarrassed to have her voice recorded, although she did permit Linda to tape many séances. The only things she considered worthy of recording are performances, like *topeng* (a form of masked, musical drama). People go to a *topeng* and tape it; they might tape music, but they would usually not want to tape an ordinary person giving some imperfect opinion in ordinary Balinese speech. | | J: So we can hear the words? <br> L: There's music on it too [as the music starts]. |
| On all ritual occasions Balinese must wear a sash; the old woman was using a towel. This reflects the relaxation of standards of elegance in favor of comfort and practicality as one gets older. She has taken the towel from around her waist, perhaps thinking her part in the ritual is over. Apparently she does not remember and receives holy water with the towel over her shoulder, but then, just before praying, she puts it around her waist again. She will use this towel as a cushion to carry her basket on her head. The man operating the tape recorder may have felt it inappropriate to continue the music during the blessing. First Jero sprinkles the group with holy water, using a flower. Next she gives each of them three handfuls to drink, then three to wipe their hair and faces. Finally, she gives them each a flower to use for | N: At the end of the séance, the family prays and is blessed with holy water. | J: What am I pointing to? <br> L: Where to kneel. <br> J: I look strange there [while dispensing holy water], but it is me. When people come they don't think I'm a commoner. They pay their respects. "Excuse me," I say. "I'm a medium. Just an ignorant commoner. God directs me. I'm a medium for others." <br> I always say that I'm a commoner because they think |

prayers. Jero begins to pray aloud; the old woman makes three quick prayer gestures.

The clients are using old tapes, so when their recording of the séance ends one can hear the music that remains. Linda misunderstood "gong" in her original translation, as there is an offering called gong. Gong also refers to the gamelan heard on the cassette music. Jero suggests that the music itself is an offering.

## THE CHIEF PETITIONER

Although we did not try to subtitle the snatches of conversation in these shots, we included this comment to convey the idea that they were reusing tapes.

## JERO TAKING SOME OF THE RICE FROM THE OFFERINGS

Here we have switched to several shots from our final roll, which show people leaving. Jero is arranging the offerings so the clients can take them home. We can see clearly that the rice she has taken (about a cup for each séance) is added to the pile already there. In general, people pay little attention to what she takes for that would be considered rude. She chooses according to the needs of her family and what she thinks the clients can afford.

## THE CHIEF PETITIONER BEATING TIME TO THE MUSIC

We have used this shot to indicate the transformation in the man's behavior – formal when he first arrives, deeply disturbed when talking with his son, and, finally, smiling and

---

I am of high rank. I'm just a medium for [others].

L: What do the next words mean? (The music starts; they listen.)

J: It means that it's finished, so it's proper to play the music as an offering to the deity.

L: Gong offering?

J: You should have brought some gong offerings, too . . .

*Shot 45 FR3 (1005:27–1010:18)*

M: Look how many cassettes we've taped over.

J: The music on the tape.

L: Oh really? (Laughs) So that's it. Yes, of course.

*Shot 46 FR5 (1010:19–1015:08)*

N: Jero receives a small payment of cash for her services. She also may take some of the rice and other foodstuffs from the offerings.

J: The proper thing is to play the music, just one piece, as a means of bidding farewell.

L: Yes, I see.

J: Here, it's music on the cassette.

*Shot 47 FR3 (1015:09–1025:18)*

J: What's happening there? [The man is beating time on his knee.]

| Comments | A Balinese Trance Séance (Subtitles and narration) | Recorded comments by Jero and Linda |
|---|---|---|
| beating time to the music. Preparation for the first séance began just after 8:00 a.m. It is now 9:20. The spirit of the boy departed about half an hour earlier. Linda thought the group was about to depart, but then they brought forth another set of offerings and a new problem. | | L: He's dancing. (*Jero laughs*) J: He's joining in, I guess. |
| The material remains of the offering are taken home and eaten. | N: The deities and spirits consume only the essence of the offerings. The remainder, including the money requested by the spirit, is taken home by the clients. | |
| TWO CLIENTS PREPARING TO DEPART | *Shot 48 FR5 (1025:19–1040:28)* | |
| The family that was the focus of the film has departed. The people in this shot came from the same village. We included this shot because it was the only good one we had of people packing up and departing and the only good shot of Jero's houseyard. The people standing around are Jero's neighbors and relatives. | | J: That's the pavilion to the north. It's really broken down, Linda. It's embarrassing to have it on the film. There's the western one [her son's]. |
| The small house beyond Jero's porch is used by the widow of Jero's deceased husband's brother. She has lived there for several years. The western building with the blue shutters is used by Jero's son. He sleeps there with his wife and three children (four in 1980). Beyond that is Jero's kitchen. It is slightly better than most of the kitchens in her village, primarily because it has a concrete floor and tiled roof. The open pavilion is used on ceremonial occasions. (By the time we returned in 1980, Jero had replaced this pavilion with a | | And there's the open pavilion. It looks good even though it's broken down. |

more elaborate one, built from the proceeds of her practice and donations from grateful clients.) The roosters (heard throughout the film) belong to Jero's son. Like most Balinese men, he has fighting cocks that are specially fed and handled in hopes of victory in the cockfights that are often part of temple festivals. (See Diagrams 1 and 2.)

## CLIENTS LEAVING THROUGH JERO'S GATE

These last two shots were taken almost two hours after the main sequence, at the conclusion of Jero's morning. The gate is typical of many Balinese houseyard entrances. Families live behind high walls. Within are their living quarters, their family temple, usually a few banana, coconut, and papaya trees, and a pigpen. Often a single courtyard houses a patrilineally extended family. (See Diagram 3.)

*Shot 49 FR5 (1040:29–1044:27)*

24 July 1978
8 a.m. to 11 a.m.

J: There's the street.
L: That's the end. (*Jero laughs*)

*CREDITS*
A Film by
TIMOTHY ASCH
Department of Anthropology
The Australian National
University
&
LINDA CONNOR
Department of Anthropology
University of Sydney

\*

| Comments | A Balinese Trance Séance (Subtitles and narration) | Recorded comments by Jero and Linda |
|---|---|---|
| Jero had attended a literacy course in her village and could read a little, although she needed to wear glasses. Linda had also helped her to learn to read. | This film was made possible through the cooperation of JERO TAPAKAN her family and her clients | L: Your name is there too. J: Yes, I see it, "Jero Tapakan." L: Can you see it? J: Now it's gone. "Linda" L: And "Patsy" at the bottom. J: "Linda Connor" "Linda Connor" |
| | * | |
| We turned off the videotape, as the credits continued. | PATSY ASCH: EDITOR Co-Producer TIMOTHY ASCH: ETHNOGRAPHIC FILMMAKER, Co-Producer LINDA CONNOR: ANTHROPOLOGIST Soundperson, Narrator, Translator | |

| *Remaining credits* | *Remaining Conversation included in* Jero on Jero |
|---|---|
| Produced by DOCUMENTARY EDUCATIONAL RESOURCES & The HUMAN ETHOLOGY AND ETHNOGRAPHIC FILM LABORATORY of The Department of Anthropology at the Research School of Pacific Studies, The Australian National University with assistance from The Department of Anthropology University of Sydney | L: Is it good or not? (*Laughs*) J: Yes. It's fine to show it. L: (*In English*) She thinks it's really good and we should show it to everybody. J: Is there one with massage? L: Yes. And your life story. J: Let's look at that now. L: All right. (*In English*) She wants to move on to the biography. (*Laughs*) |

142

\*

The support of the Lembaga Ilmu Pengetahuan Indonesia (L.I.P.I.) is gratefully acknowledged.

\*

We are particularly thankful for the assistance of the
Australian National University's
INSTRUCTIONAL RESOURCES UNIT
The Research School of Physical Sciences Mechanical Workshop,
Graphic Design & Central Printing,
James J. Fox, Komang Suweta, Ian Matters, Darien Rossiter
Tony Jurd, Ann Buller, Judith Wilson, Sue Ann Marshall-Cabezas
Ria van de Zandt, Ita Pead,
Staff of Bali Beach Hotel Freezer,
QANTAS Airlines, Customs at Ngurah Rai Airport
and
Film Australia, Chris Rowell Productions,
Optical & Graphic Pty. Ltd., Acme Opticals,
Arriflex SR, Angenieux 10/150, Kodak 7250, Nagra IV.2, MKH 416 TU,
Syntec Rycote, Scotch AV 177, MAGNA-TECH Electronics 63b,
Agfa-Gevaert MF5PE, Steenbeck ST 1900.
LAB SERVICE BY COLOUR TRANSCRIPTIONS

(*Continues in English*) That was just fantastic. It was amazing the way . . . [tape turned off momentarily] just incredible.

J: It brings it all back.

L: Did you enjoy it?

J: Yes.

L: So did I.
It takes a lot of time to finish a film properly. Some of it is cut.

J: Where it's damaged.

L: Yes, damaged or too dark, or where I didn't get sound. But could you understand it?

J: I could.
It would have been a shame to cut out the crying. When it came on, it touched me. People watching will be drawn in and feel sad.

L: That happened in Australia.

J: Did they cry?

L: They were sad because the child was still young.

## C. Further comments made by Jero and Linda after viewing *A Balinese Trance Séance* (Linda Connor)

When the videotape of *A Balinese Trance Séance* had finished, Jero and I continued to talk about the film for another 20 minutes. Jero discussed in more detail several of the issues raised when she was watching the videotape. Two particularly interesting segments of this discussion are translated and annotated below. In the first, Jero spontaneously raises again the issue of balians' ethics; in the second, introduced by my question, discussion concerns the dynamics of revenge by sorcery and the etiology of the boy's disease. (My annotations are bracketed and in italics.)

**J:**   Some balians pray in order to become sorcerers. There are balians who are blessed by the deity of the Death Temple. But those who use poison don't get blessed from anywhere. They are like thieves.

*[Jero means that these balians — adherents of the destructive "path of the left" — are furtive in their operations.]*

Nonetheless, the deity does not choose to expose them. So there is no trouble, so there are no quarrels.

*[The deity referred to here is the one who speaks through a medium at a séance. It is unclear whether Jero is referring to the deities who speak through her, in particular, or deities in séances in general. It is probably the former, given the specificity of her next remark.]*

**L:**   Where? In the village?

**J:**   Yes — in the village. That's the wish of my guardian deity, although there are other balians who will expose them [the sorcerers]. Then there are all sorts of quarrels, it's a lot of trouble.

**L:**   But your guardian deity

**J:**   My guardian deity does not allow it. I'm not allowed to get angry at people, not allowed to be mean to people. That's what was decreed. If anyone accuses me of anything, or swears at me, I'm not allowed to challenge them. I just have to concentrate on God, and keep my silence. No matter what's going on around me, it's just voices trying to make trouble. That's called "the sound of frogs," that's all.

*["The sound of frogs" is a common Balinese phrase often used to describe empty talk or gossip.]*

If one challenges it, then that's [the work of] demons. Just keep quiet. If it's proper, go to the north; if it's proper, go to the south. In fact it's God who witnesses [all].

*[I interpret this to mean that spiritually pure people should not allow themselves to become distracted from their honorable concerns by idle gossip with malign intent. To respond in kind may be to succumb to demonic forces that tempt honorable people to betray their goals.]*

**L:**   Is there trouble when other balians reveal names?

**J:**    There's trouble — a court case, a summons, all that. All sorts of wrongs are imputed. The balian is blamed by the person [culprit] named.

**L:**    The balian is summoned too?

**J:**    Yes, they [the police] go after the balian. Just recently they say that happened at Lekedbatu.

**L:**    Really? What happened?

**J:**    It's said he [the balian at Lekedbatu] revealed names. "I accuse in this way, in that way," about poisoning and all that.

**L:**    And the thieves? Can [their identity] be revealed?

**J:**    No, it's not permissible. If people "ask for speech" over something that's missing it's not permissible to mention names. It's like: "If you encourage a flea in your blanket, it's sure to bite you."

*[A proverb]*

It has to be worked out with the clients. But the name can't be given:

"Male or female?"
"Male."
"And he looks . . ."
"A man with a heavy frame, coarse hair, quietly spoken."

That's the way it's revealed, not by saying Mr. X, Mr. Y. That's not allowed, so there's no trouble. In this film there are no names.

**L:**    Yes, yes.

* * *

**L:**    What about when the child presents offerings to the deities Iswara and Wisnu?

*[The deceased child presents the offerings that are made in his name by his living relatives.]*

If it's agreed to, agreed to by the deity, the child may cause illness?

**J:**    Well, just suppose you are innocent. You are innocent but you are bewitched by someone; you get sick. Do you know *perentah*?

*[An illness caused by sorcery]*

**L:**    Yes.

**J:**    Then you die. You are angry. Say you kill me. I die. I die but I'm innocent. You curse me. Then my mother asks for speech.

*[Through a medium]*

I ask to be made offerings to present to Brahma, Wisnu, Iswara — propitiatory offerings [*tebasan*] for Brahma, Wisnu, and Iswara. The type of offering is named, not just the deities who receive it.

*[Jero is explaining that the instructions for the offerings are very detailed and specific, as are the instructions for who must receive them.]*

"If you agree, mother, I'll make a request to the deity of the Death Temple."

If those offerings are not given, it's not permissible no matter how much anger there is.

**L:**   Not permissible to . . .

**J:**   Not permissible to cause illness. No matter how much anger there is, it's not possible to cause illness.

"If you make the offerings for me, I will request a blessing, because I am not in the wrong."

If there is indeed no guilt but the victim has been cursed, then the deity of the Death Temple agrees:

"Go ahead and cause illness. You are not in the wrong, so get on with it."

That's why the offerings are used to petition the deity of the spirit of the deceased.

**L:**   If offerings are not made on his behalf by his father here, then he can't make a request to the deity of the Death Temple.

**J:**   No, [because] there's nothing.

**L:**   So that's the speech:

"If Daddy agrees . . ."

**J:**   "Give me the offerings, so I can make a request."

**L:**   "If not, then I won't."

If his father doesn't agree, then it won't come off. He asks for offerings from his father first, then asks permission from the deity of the Death Temple, to cause illness.

**J:**   Yes. That's why he asks permission from his relatives.

Say I have a mother. And you're her child, or my cousin or second cousin. But there are no names. Say I'm also a child of hers. Now, if I'm the child, I make a request to my father. If my request to my father is granted, I will make a petition. If not, I will die.

"Don't be lazy about it." [I say to my father.] If father is prepared to give the offerings on my behalf, I will make a request like this:

"If you agree, I will cause illness, father."

Later, after the illness is caused, [they] will look for a cure. It's so that [they] can't be cured again.

*[I have translated this passage as literally as I could because the meaning is unclear to me. The last sentence may refer to the fact that the illnesses of sorcerers are difficult if not impossible to cure when their perpetrator was motivated by revenge and the deity had consented.]*

**L:**   It seems that in the film the father wasn't game to do it.

**J:**   He was.

"Whoever has committed the wrong, whether it's a relative or someone else, I will give [the offerings], why should I not? So that revenge may be carried out."

*[In my opinion, the father displayed much more ambivalence about complying in the revenge tactics than is indicated in this speech. Jero attributes these words to him, but they were not recorded during the séance. See discussion of this point, section 5E.]*

**L:** So the father felt sorry for him?

**J:** Yes, the Balinese way is that offerings may be asked for at the séance as long as they are not too expensive. A person, or a pig, or a buffalo. That's not allowed. The limits are from five cents to the largest, ten thousand rupiah, that's what can be given. That's the Balinese way. After they have promised to make the offerings, then the intent to cause illness is mentioned.

"I wish to cause lameness, Daddy. Whoever gets the lameness, that is the one who made me ill."

"But I'll wait a little while; I won't do it right now." [Father's response.]

*[The delay is probably preferred so that no direct connection will be made between the information the relatives obtained at the séance and any possible repercussions to the sorcerer as a result of ceremonies the victim's relatives agree to perform.]*

"When are you going to make the offerings for me? Make them for me in another six months."

And then a month after that, the second cousin may become ill. Then the father will say:

"So that's the one who did it."

*[This is the way it worked out in the séance film (see section 5 E).]*

That's how it goes.

**L:** The doctor's explanation was different than the explanation . . .

**J:** Yes, different.

**L:** The doctor said it was typhoid, but the boy's father said the doctor couldn't cure him. Really he was made ill through sorcery.

**J:** Yes, somebody made him ill.

**L:** Is that the reason the doctor couldn't do anything?

**J:** The doctor didn't have the means to vanquish the disease. There's a disease and there's a cure. If you don't have the right cure, nobody will be able to do anything.

*[The implication here is that modern medical methods will not be adequate to cure an illness that is caused by sorcery. And, as Jero goes on to explain, not all balians will be able to prescribe the correct treatment for the illness.]*

"Daddy, if I had had that treatment then I wouldn't have died."

That's what's meant by the means to vanquish the disease.

**L:** Would a balian have been able to cure him if he had been taken there before he died?

**J:** If the right cure had been found! Say, if the sickness needed the seed of a coconut – do you know *tombong*?

**L:** Ah . . .

**J:** You've often seen the white seed-bud of a coconut tree.

**L:** Oh, yes.

**J:**    So he's given medicine, like tonics, eggs, coconut, honey, all sorts of things — but they're not appropriate. So he died.
The correct cure is the seed-bud of a coconut tree.

"If I had obtained a coconut seed-bud I would have recovered. You didn't want to find a seed-bud, Daddy. That's what I needed to recover. That was the precise cure."

Then his insides were quickly destroyed, so he died.

*[His insides were destroyed by the potent magic of the sorcerer.]*

**L:**    Do you mean in the case in the film or in another case?

**J:**    Another case. It's just an example. It's different. There are lots of different ways — for instance, the mother may be the object of anger, and the child is the one who is cursed.

# SEVEN

## *An annotated translation of the main séance in* A Balinese Trance Séance

### LINDA CONNOR

I have used "séance" to refer to the social interactions that occur among a medium, one or more possessing agents, and a group of petitioners for the purpose of resolving a specific problem. The medium may be possessed once or up to five or more times, with each episode of possession lasting from about 30 seconds to 15 minutes, with equally variable pauses in between each episode for discussion between medium and clients. Thus any particular séance may last from a few minutes to a couple of hours. The length of the séance depends on the complexity of the clients' problem, the skill of the medium in handling it, and the individual style of each medium.

The core of the film *A Balinese Trance Séance* (that footage dealing specifically with one séance) – approximately 13.5 minutes – was edited from an uninterrupted, 38-minute sound recording. Two tape recorders were used during the séance. I recorded sound to be used in the film on a Nagra 4.2. Each Nagra reel of tape had to be changed every 15 minutes. On a portable cassette machine I recorded the complete séance, without interruption, on a 90-minute cassette. The clients also used their own cassette recorder.

During the séance, which is conducted entirely in Balinese, Jero is possessed five times, with discussion after each possession. The first three times a deity descends and converses with the petitioners (these three episodes have been condensed into one in the film version); in the fourth possession, the spirit of the chief petitioner's dead father descends; in the fifth, the spirit of the petitioner's recently dead son.

Each speech is numbered. In section 6B of this book, corresponding numbers have been placed to the left of the second column, in order to link subtitles to the full translation. In the body of the translation, annotations for my translation occur in italics. The initials introducing each speech refer to the identity of the speaker and are abbreviated as follows:

| | | |
|---|---|---|
| J | = | Jero Tapakan |
| L | = | Linda Connor |
| P(M) | = | Petitioner (Male) |
| P(F) | = | Petitioner (Female) |
| P(W) | = | Petitioner (Younger Woman) |

P(M) is the *pangarep*, which I translate as "chief petitioner." (The role of this person, and of other petitioners in the séance, is discussed in section 5C.) In this case, the chief petitioner is the male head of the household concerned with the séance. P(F), the chief petioner's mother, also particpates actively in the dialogue with deities and spirits, as well as the discussion with the medium. One speech (438) is by the younger woman, P(W).

The translation is a free rendering into English. Where, as frequently occurs, the pronouncements are ambiguous or unclear, I have not attempted to create an artificial clarity in the translation. The reader may find these as cryptic in translation as they appeared to the participants at the time (and to Jero upon hearing the recording played back). Where pronouncements that are potentially ambiguous or otherwise unclear have been interpreted in a specific way by clients or medium (as evidenced by subsequent utterances), it is this meaning that I have rendered into English. Some words and phrases, such as the names of deities, ceremonies, and offerings, proved impossible to gloss in English, and I have dealt with as many of these as possible in the annotations. In these cases I have retained the Balinese term in italics in the English translation. Where I found it impossible to arrive at a satisfactory translation, either because of the quality of the tape recording or because of the limitations of my own knowledge of Balinese, I have inserted a question mark in the translation. Occasional minor clarifications appear in brackets in the translation.

Absent from the transcript is an indication of the language level of each word or utterance. Such indication, important to any detailed sociolinguistic understanding of the séance, is beyond our purposes here. There is some discussion of language levels in section 5I.

## A. First Possession (deity)

**1. J:**   Who is the chief petitioner?

**2. P(M):**   I am.

**3. J:**   Oh, Holy deities, Ye are all asked to be seated, to be seated, to be seated in the shrine house, Holy Deities descend, Holy Iswara, Thou art invited to be seated in the assembly. Descend Holy Taksu in the company of the Yudadara and Yudadari, be seated in the pure offerings, descend.

Holy and learned Goddess Saraswati, be pleased to assemble all thy brothers and sisters. We request Thee to reside together in the *tapakan palinggih.*

Descend Holy Deities of Mount Lebah, Mount Agung, and Suluk Peak, all Ye deities. Most Holy Dalem Taruk, we await Thy wisdom, we ask that speech be granted.

We have long awaited Thee to be seated in the shrine house. Holy Earth Goddess, Nusa Ped amidst the ocean . . . ah ha ha ha . . .

*[This* mantra, *in the most general terms, is a request that the deities bestow their blessing on the séance and enable the communication to proceed smoothly.*

*Jero asks that the petitioners be given the information they desire. Invocations are addressed to major deities of the pantheon (such as Ida Betara Sakti Iswara, of the Trinity Brahma, Wisnu, Iswara (or Siwa) and to Ida Betara Sakti Ibu Pertiwi, the earth goddess), although these are not deities who possess the medium. All the deities who reside on Bali's most sacred mountains (Mount Agung, Mount Lebah, Suluk Peak) are asked to descend and preside over the séance. The deity Saraswati — the guardian of knowledge and the arts and therefore of the spoken and written word — is also invoked. The deities who have inspired Jero in her calling, specifically Dalem Pajanengan Dalem Taruk, are also invited; likewise Ida Bagawan Taksu, the deified form of taksu ("interpreter" or "intermediary" spirit or force), which facilitates Jero's communications as a medium.*

*All these beings and more are beseeched to descend and seat themselves on the offerings to witness the séance. Their realm is firmly located above, part of a cosmos that is clearly stratified as well as spatially tiered. The deities are asked to speak (raos, baos, babaosan) on behalf of their petitioners.]*

My servant?
My servants seek my instruction in their affairs?

**4. P(M):**   Yes, Lord.

**5. P(F):**   Yes.

**6. J:**   I have been brought down below to the emptiness. I am angry.

**7. P(F):**   Yes, I . . .

**8. J:**   What is the reason my servants have summoned me? Is it about a ceremony for impure spirits?

*["Impure spirits" (lit.: "those below") refers to the spirits of uncremated dead.]*

**9. P(F):**   Yes, I beg forgiveness. I have a request.

**10. J:**   Now petitioner. Don't get into confusion like you did before. I will show you the path.

**11. P(F):**   Yes, tell us, O Lord.

**12. J:**   What is your task? Are you "grinding the flour"?

*[Holding a cremation ceremony]*

**13. P(F):**   Yes.

**14. P(M):**   Yes, O Lord.

**15. J:**   Well?

**16. P(M):**   Yes.

**17. P(F):**   Yes.

**18. J:**   Do my servants intend to have a collective or a private cremation?

*[See section 5G for a discussion of collective cremations.]*

**19. P(F):**   I will have a collective cremation.

**20. J:**   If you have a private cremation, I will show you the way. If a collective cremation, I will show you the way. So you aren't confused like you have been in the past. I'll show you the way. My responsibilities are heavy!

**21. P(F):**   Yes.

**22. P(M):**   Yes, O Lord. I wish to have a collective cremation.

**23. J:**   Now you must obey my words.

**24. P(F):**   Yes, tell us now, Lord. I . . .

**25. J:**   Now, so you'll know . . . well?

**26. P(F):**   I am your servant, O Lord.

**27. J:**   What type of collective cremation will my servants have? The burning of an effigy at the cemetery?

[*There are many different ways in which cremation ceremonies can be performed in Bali, as this and the following speeches reveal. The variation chosen depends on the status of the deceased, the status and resources of the group holding the ceremony, and the amount of time that has elapsed since the death, as well as the constraints of local custom. In Jero Tapakan's village, people commonly discuss several different sorts of ceremonies, namely:* nyawa preteka *(or, as it is referred to in the séance,* ngrintes*), where a buried corpse is exhumed for cremation in the graveyard;* nyawa resi *(otherwise referred to as* nyawa wedana*), in which symbolic earth is dug up from the graveyard, where burning takes place;* nyawa geni *(there are two meanings attached to this phrase, the first referring to the burning of a corpse at the graveyard soon after death, without burial – it is unlikely that this meaning would have prevailed in the séance because theirs was a collective cremation, which would have been planned by all concerned months ahead of time – and the second referring to the burning of an effigy of the deceased in a ceremony at the graveyard);* newasta *(what is referred to here, in the deity's idiom, as* nyekah*), the burning of effigies at home or in the village, with symbolic earth dug up from the cemetery.]*

**28. P(M):**   Forgive me, Lord, I will not burn an effigy at the cemetery. It will be the usual collective cremation.

**29. J:**   Burning a corpse?

**30. P(M):**   Burning effigies in the village.

**31. J:**   Burning effigies in the village. If that's the case, heed me so you'll know! Don't leave the houseyard empty!

**32. P(F):**   Yes.

**33. P(M):**   Yes, yes.

**34. J:**   At the time of the burning make sure there are offerings at home.

**35. P(M):**   Yes.

**36. J:**   Do my servants plan to call in at the houseyard or to finish all the ceremonies with the group?

**37. P(M):**   We will finish the ceremonies with the group . . .

**38. J:**   If it's finished with the group, make sure there is a *dapetan* offering [made at home], [like] the *dapetan* offering of birth. Well?

[*Dapetan lekad is an offering made to a newborn child, to welcome the spirit reincarnated in the infant. Here it probably relates to the rebirth aspects of cremation.]*

**39. P(F):** Yes.

**40. J:** Do you understand *dapetan lekad*? Well?

**41. P(F):** Yes, I understand.

**42. J:** Below, make "filling up" (*pangebek*) offerings, so you'll know.

*[The request for "filling up" offerings alludes again to the theme that the house-yard should not be left empty when its inhabitants are away at the cremation in the village. These offerings are to be made "below," that is, to appease demons.]*

**43. P(M):** Yes.

**44. P(F):** Yes.

**45. J:** Make *pejati* offerings so the place is not empty of sustenance. Well?

*[Pejati offerings (or* banten apejatian*) are discussed in section 5F. Offerings are frequently used as a way of making one's intentions known to the deities (in this case, the intention to hold the cremation in the village), as is indicated in speech 48.]*

**46. P(F):** Yes.

**47. P(M):** Yes.

**48. J:** Make *pejati* offerings as a sign of your intentions to the Sacred Earth Goddess, the "World Sweeper."

**49. P(F):** Yes, I comply with Thy wishes.

**50. J:** *Tangkeb* rice, *kawisan* rice, *ibungan*, with a covering. Offer it to the demons of the womb, the five-colored demons. Well?

*[These are small offerings of rice and meat to be made on the ground to the "demons of the womb": The demonic manifestation of the* kanda mpat *or spiritual siblings who are born with every human being as a source of protection throughout life. They are referred to be many designations, as is evident in this utterance, where they have two names. There are four spiritual siblings, who with their human sibling number five.]*

**51. P(M):** Yes.

**52. P(F):** Yes.

**53. J:** Five-colored *segehan* offerings. After that, the *peras sesantun* offering, for the siblings who are buried. For the demons of the womb. So that they cause no trouble. That's the instruction. A bee has entered, a wasp has entered. Have my servants ever uttered the prayers? Well?

*[The offerings listed are for the spiritual siblings, called here "the siblings who are buried," referring to the ceremonial burial of the afterbirth in the houseyard soon after a child is born. The fifth sibling has as its manifestation the human form; the other four siblings are manifest in the amniotic sac, amniotic fluid, blood, and placenta.*

*The theme of the bee or the wasp occurs in this and the next few speeches and is brought up again in the first discussion between clients and medium. It foreshadows discussion about the petitioner's neglect of their house temple. In the first discussion, Jero explains that the bee or wasp (which the chief petitioner acknowledges he has indeed seen hovering in his house temple) is probably the spirit siblings of an ancestor who has been denied appropriate offerings and who thus "takes essence" (speech 57) at the shrines in this way (see speeches 89–96). Thus in speech 57 the deity is painting a picture of angry, vengeful spiritual forces around the petitioners, of which they are not aware. In speech 60 the deity again returns to the many forms that angry spirit siblings may take (i.e., not only a bee or a wasp but caterpillars, demons, or thieves) in their attempts to extract the "sustenance" (offerings) that is their due but which is denied them by neglectful householders.]*

**54. P(M):**   My apologies. I don't know. Because I am ignorant.

**55. P(F):**   Yes, tell us, O Lord.

**56. P(M):**   Tell us now.

**57. J:**   So, petitioner, if you don't wish to carry sustenance, the essence will be taken, so you'll know. It's like that, so you'll know. All is confusion, some enter my shrine, some enter my servants' houseyard. My servants are not aware of anything. Well?

**58. P(F):**   Yes, tell us, O Lord.

**59. P(M):**   Yes, it's true, O Lord. I . . .

**60. J:**   It's about the siblings who are buried. The demons of the womb. They can become caterpillars. They can become demons, they can become thieves. They challenge me. It is difficult. It must be stopped, do you understand?

**61. P(F):**   Yes, I beg forgiveness, O Lord. Inform us now, O Lord. I am in ignorance.

**62. P(M):**   Well . . .

**63. J:**   So now the "sky" is going to join you.

*[Ancestral spirit]*

**64. P(M):**   Yes.

**65. J:**   But don't throw that away.

*[Don't ignore my words.]*

Buy a place with the group. Pay little by little and it's inexpensive. [Otherwise] pay twice as much, whatever you pay it will be expensive, it will never end. So you'll know.

*[The deity is admonishing the petitioners not to ignore its words. They are being advised to be meticulous in making all the little offerings that go into the collective cremation, with the warning that to be neglectful at this stage will have greater consequences later on, when they may have to make twice as many propitiatory offerings to compensate for their mistakes.]*

**66. P(F):**   Yes.

**67. J:**   So that I'm not going up and down every day.

*[This means that if the petitioners do not do things correctly now they will have to keep calling the deity down for further consultation.]*

**68. P(F):**   I comply with thy wishes, O Lord.

**69. J:**   Well?

**70. P(M):**   Yes.

**71. J:**   So it will be enough to make a "filling up" offering as a notice of your intentions, but don't discard the most important part. I will explain.

**72. P(F):**   Yes.

**73. P(M):**   Yes, O Lord.

**74. J:**   Well, so now on the day of the cremation buy a place with one set of *peras* offerings and fifty-four coins. It is difficult . . .

**75. P(M):**   At – at – the collective ceremony?

**76. J:**   That's right. Well?

**77. P(M):**   Yes.

**78. J:**   Well, think on that, think, my servants, [and] are you able to perform the postcremation ceremony?

**79. P(F):**   How is the group doing it – I . . .

**80. P(M):**   I will perform the postcremation ceremony with the group, it will be finished with the group. I ask for blessing, O Lord, who gives speech.

**81. J:**   In a moment the "sky" will converse with you.

**82. P(M):**   Yes.

**83. J:**   That is all I have to say.


## B. First discussion (between the medium and her clients)

**84. J:**   How did it go?

**85. P(F):**   [We] obtained some speech . . .

**86. J:**   Is that [the clients' tape recorder] turned off?

**87. P(M):**   Yes.

**88. J:**   This is about a ceremony for impure spirits, a cremation, according to the speech of the deity.

**89. P(M):**   Yes, there was discussion about a bee, a wasp. I accept that, according to the speech of the deity. It's true, at my home there was [a bee, a wasp] in the shrine of my house temple. What was it doing there?

   *[See speech 53.]*

**90. J:**   "Nobody has uttered the prayers." Who is that?

**91. P(M):**   According to the speech just then.

**92. J:**   Possibly the essence is being carried away. Someone is taking the essence from the ancestor shrine.

**93. P(F):**   He – he . . . [indistinct].

**94. J:**   Such was the speech. Now so that it doesn't happen again. The siblings who are buried, isn't that what the utterance was about? There were no *peras sesantun* offerings. It can turn into a caterpillar, it can become a caterpillar. It can become all sorts of things.

**95. P(F):**   So that is doing the stealing?

**96. J:**   Yes, the siblings who are buried can turn into a thief, into all sorts of things.

**97. P(F):**   Those who are buried . . .

**98. J:**   It's the siblings of the afterbirth that are buried. They didn't get the "adoption" ceremony [*pamerasan*] [so that their souls may be purified by cremation also], that's what it means. It's not just *anybody's* siblings.

> [Here "siblings of the afterbirth" refers to the physical manifestations at birth of the four spiritual siblings.
> The "adoption" ceremony (pamerasan) referred to here is a small ceremony prior to the cremation, which is similar in form to the actual adoption of a child. It is performed in this context to ensure that the deceased's four spiritual siblings accompany him or her on the path of purification by cremation.]

**99. P(M):**   Should that ceremony now be at the ritual, is that it?

**100. J:**   Previously there wasn't one; now there should be. You're not permitted to have the house empty of offerings, it must be gone through with . . .

**101. P(M):**   Meaning that it's empty at – at, at my field cottage, is that the case?

**102. J:**   Yes.

**103. P(M):**   I'm having the ceremony in the village; isn't it [empty] at the field cottage?

**104. J:**   Yes, that's it. The house must not be empty of offerings. There must be some "filling-up" offerings.

**105. P(M):**   Just to make certain, Jero Tapakan, could you ask [for speech] again? The speech just then needs clarification.

**106. J:**   Yes, it's like that. The meaning of the deity's speech has to be explained first, so that there are no mistakes later.

**107. P(M):**   Yes, that is my intention, to make sure what is given is certain.

**108. J:**   Begin on the day of the cremation, make sure there is an offering as notice of your intention at home – just once, on the day of the cremation.

**109. P(M):**   Yes.

**110. J:**   Make sure there is a *dapetan lekad* offering.

**111. P(M):**   I understand.

**112. J:**   Now the "sky" will converse with you. Isn't that what was said?

**113. L:**   Jero, can this [offering basket] be moved?

> [Jero at first refuses to move the offering basket but later (unrecorded on the sound track) moved it herself when she realized it was obstructing the camera's view.]

**114. J:**   No, these are offerings to God. These are for the ancestors; these are for God.

**115. P(M):**    Well, he – he . . . So that's what appears [on the camera].

**116. P(M):**    Jero Tapakan. Can the offerings [be mentioned] just one more time? I'm still not clear about it, because I'm ignorant.

**117. J:**    This is still the deity.

**118. P(M):**    Yes.

**119. J:**    This is still the deity. You can ask about these matters in a moment. The deity's speech comes first.

**120. P(M):**    Yes.

## C. Second possession (same deity)

**121. J:**    Holy deities of Mount Lebah, Mount Agung, Suluk Peak, Most Holy Dalem Taruk, Nusa Ped amidst the ocean, Holy Aji Sakti, we seek Thy blessing, bring down the deity of the séance, all Ye deities . . . eh, ha ha . . . Petitioner?

**122. P(M):**    Yes?

**123. J:**    Do my servants not yet understand?

**124. P(M):**    Forgive me, I'm still . . .

**125. P(F):**    Forgive me . . .

**126. J:**    It was just mentioned about the offerings at the field cottage. I'll finish telling about that first.

**127. P(M):**    Yes.

**128. J:**    I'm confused. For a long time my servants have been making promises that my shrine will be consecrated. The "core" one, so you'll know.

*[This long dialogue (speeches 128–70) between the petitioners and the deity centers around the question of the house temple in their field cottage. Families who live for part of the year in field cottages away from the main village may erect a makeshift set of shrines in their yards (usually of rough bamboo and thatch construction) at which to make the necessary daily offerings while they are in residence. Often, as in the case of these petitioners, demographic pressures and convenience of locale induce the family to make the field cottage their main residence. In these cases the temporary shrines should be replaced by a permanent house temple, but often residents understandably postpone the lengthy and expensive proceedings as long as possible. It is this the deity is alluding to when it says, "For a long time my servants have been making promises that my shrine will be consecrated." According to the deity, the main house temple (or the "core") is now in the petitioners' field cottage, not in the village.*

*The petitioners are somewhat flustered and indignant (in as respectful a manner as possible) because they strongly assert that they have performed the appropriate consecration ceremonies for their field cottage shrines. They debate this point for as long as possible with the deity (speeches 131–49). But the deity asserts that they have only made part of the offerings (the "base," speech 149) and that they have not yet performed the main offerings (the "center" including the "opening ceremony," (speech 149). In speech 153, the deity implies that it can protect the petitioners ("I can carry my servants") from malevolent incursions such as the "bee" or "wasp" only if they comply with its wishes for the ceremony. In speech 161, the deity suggests that making the offerings is like "planting a seed" and that the inevitable good fortune that will result is the "harvest." Speech 163 contains a reference to opening the shrine and buying it with earth. This is a way of speaking about the ceremony, that the deity wants the petitioners to perform: A hole is dug at the base of a shrine, and offerings are buried there. It is a way of spiritually purifying and strengthening the shrine and thus "opening it up" as a seat of deities.]*

**129. P(M):**   O Lord, which shrine is that, O Lord?

**130. J:**   The core one at the field cottage.

**131. P(M):**   I have already completed that shrine at the time of the house-blessing ceremony, O Lord. I have already bought that shrine.

**132. J:**   It's already finished?

**133. P(M):**   I don't yet understand. Now, forgive us and speak so that all is clear, because I am ignorant.

**134. J:**   Now, so you'll know, my servants!

**135. P(M):**   Yes.

**136. J:**   Perform the opening ceremony, my servants.

**137. P(M):**   Yes.

**138. J:**   Now buy the main offerings for the opening of my shrine. Who said they were already bought? I'm constantly giving reprimands.

**139. P(F):**   Yes, speak, O Lord. I . . .

**140. J:**   Well?

**141. P(M):**   The purchase, what am I to buy?

**142. J:**   Buy offerings, buy the opening path. Buy for me, buy the offerings, don't buy this at the market!

**143. P(M):**   How much should I buy the ceremony for thy shrine, O Lord?

**144. J:**   Now remember to finish it, my servants, the opening offerings for my shrine.

**145. P(M):**   Yes.

**146. P(F):**   Yes.

**147. J:**   Well, is it done?

**148. P(M):**   I feel that it is finished, but because I am stupid, now O Lord . . .

**149. J:**   That's the "base" of the shrine. Then buy the center. Then have the opening ceremony, the *pancer*, so you'll know.

**150. P(M):**   Yes, speak as it pleases you, O Lord. I am ignorant.

**151. J:**   Now just go slowly. Do my servants wish to carry me?

**152. P(M):**   Yes.

**153. J:**   I can carry my servants, because there is a bee, a wasp, which has entered. What is "riding" there? A deity? A demon?

**154. P(M):**   I don't know what it is.

**155. P(F):** Inform me now.

**156. P(M):** Inform me now so that I will know. So that I can comply with thy wishes, O Lord.

**157. J:** Now, so you'll know, my servants.

**158. P(M):** Yes.

**159. J:** Have the opening of my shrine. Buy a set of offerings for me. Finish that first, [with] a "base" of holy water, thoughts, energy, life essence.

**160. P(F):** Yes.

**161. J:** Do you understand? That's what's called planting the seed so that there is a harvest. It's not just something you buy at the market.

**162. P(M):** Yes.

**163. J:** What's more, my shrine is strengthened, a place of worship. It's opened, bought with earth.

**164. P(M):** Yes.

**165. J:** Give notice of your intentions at the northeast . . . [?] that's why I'm adrift [floating].

**166. P(F):** Yes, speak . . .

**167. P(M):** Yes, it is true, O Lord.

**168. J:** Now, a set of offerings, well?

**169. P(M):** Yes.

**170. J:** Ask blessing with *pejati* offerings, with redemptive offerings to Brahma, Wisnu, Iswara. That will be all. I will be pleased.

**171. P(M):** Yes.

**172. J:** So that my servants are not just plucked, carried away, in constant sickness, that is the message. Isn't it understood?

**173. P(F):** Yes, I beg forgiveness.

**174. J:** Well?

**175. P(F):** Thou speakest well, O Lord. I am ignorant.

**176. J:** Do you understand *sabda*?

**177. P(M):** What is the *sabda*, O Lord? I do not understand.

**178. J:** A dream — is it not a dream? — that's *sabda*, so you'll know. Someone was chased. Do you understand?

**179. P(M):** True, if that's it, it's true.

**180. J:** What is that? That, so you'll know, is the Sacred Lord "World Sweeper." If my servants are swept up, how will it be? I am sick at heart all the time.

*[The image here is that a powerful deity will annihilate the petitioners if they do not fulfill their ceremonial obligations.]*

**181. P(F):** Yes.

**182. P(M):** Yes, I ask blessing, O Lord, in order that I not be swept away. If it pleasest Thou, O Lord, in order that I not.

**183. J:**    If that's the case, my servants, then truly promise to comply.

**184. P(M):**    Yes.

**185. J:**    Slowly. Listen first.

**186. P(M):**    I am prepared, O Lord.

**187. J:**    Complete [the ceremonies] for me first. Then the lower ones [for ancestors]. Well?

**188. P(M):**    Yes.

**189. J:**    That's called the foundation of holy water. Petitioner?

**190. P(M):**    Yes?

**191. J:**    A set of offerings, with redemptive offerings to Brahma, Wisnu, Iswara . . .

**192. P(M):**    Yes.

**193. J:**    How much will be paid for my ceremony, the lowest [price], the medium, or the highest? Which one?

**194. P(M):**    I ask to pay the medium price.

**195. J:**    The medium? Five hundred [Chinese coins]. One hundred and twenty seven. One hundred and eighteen, and eleven.

**196. P(M):**    Yes.

**197. J:**    Well?

**198. P(M):**    Five hundred, twenty seven, eleven.

**199. J:**    Five hundred, one hundred and twenty seven, one hundred and eighteen, eleven. There must be that amount. It will be enough to bury. There must be that amount.

**200. P(M):**    Yes . . . Lord.

**201. J:**    Well?

**202. P(F):**    Yes.

**203. J:**    Ask witness of the Lord of the Sun, with a *pejati* offering. And purchase [offerings] for Betara Sakti Ibu Pertiwi, Empu Bradah, Sapu Jagat Panca Bumi, Ratu Sakti Tangkeb Langit. Remember?

**204. P(M):**    Yes.

**205. J:**    When that's finished, bury the *pejati* offering with money, [and] the redemptive offering to Brahma, Wisnu, Iswara, my servants. Ask for the essence, ask for the strengthener, for energy, for life force. Well?

*[This and the preceding speeches of the deity contain the specific instructions for the ceremony referred to in speech 163.]*

**206. P(M):**    Yes.

**207. J:**    That's all, my servants. Are you prepared [to do it]?

**208. P(M):**    I am prepared.

**209. J:**    Don't just make promises. If really willing, give me a purification ceremony first, because I am in confusion. I'm not able to tell my servants anything.

**210. P(M):**    Yes, I am willing, on Landep Sunday, I will carry out these arrangements, but I ask of Thee, O Lord, should I or should I not send offerings to all the village temples on Landep Sunday? The reason I ask is because there is a cremation in progress at Kayukapas. Wilt Thou, O Lord, wish to descend?

*[He means that the village is polluted during a cremation, an unfit place for deities to descend and partake of offerings. Kayukapas is a pseudonym for the petitioner's village, where the collective cremation will be held.]*

**211. J:** Why do you use a *palebon* [the high Balinese word for "cremation"]? *Palebon* [is a word] of the higher level.

*[This quibble over the petitioner's use of a high Balinese word for "cremation" could indicate that the petitioner's former question is difficult for the deity to respond to. Although it is not acceptable for commoners to refer to their own cremation ceremonies (i.e., those they are organizing) by the high word, it could be argued that it is acceptable in this context as the petitioner is attempting to address the deity in as high language as possible. That the chief petitioner does not respond to the deity's reprimand about the use of the word may indicate that he feels it is unreasonable. In the following speeches the deity advises the petitioners to postpone the offerings in the village temples, which it had previously recommended.]*

**212. P(M):** If, O Lord, I make offerings at the temples, dost Thou, O Lord, agree?

**213. J:** Leave them empty [of offerings] first.

**214. P(M):** If empty, then when should I make the offerings to purchase Thy shrine, O Lord?

**215. J:** Now, if you are able, just purchase the shrine first. Well?

**216. P(M):** Yes. When?

**217. J:** Are you able to on the Wednesday?

**218. P(M):** Which Wednesday?

**219. J:** On Landep Wednesday.

**220. P(M):** Yes, I can do it.

**221. J:** Just buy that first. Finish that first. Don't make all the arrangements yet.

**221. P(M):** To make things shorter, O Lord, please instruct Thy servants [about the offerings] to prevent enemies from entering.

**222. J:** Yes. Just have a *pejati* offering first. A set of offerings outside the temple [i.e., in their houseyard] is adequate. In the future you can make offerings at the shrine to Brahma.

**223. P(M):** Should the purchase of the shrine be inside [the house temple]?

**224. J:** That's at the opening ceremony for my shrine.

**225. P(M):** Yes, so that it's clear, so that I don't make mistakes.

**226. J:** Just make a round of offerings [in the houseyard]. Don't be concerned about whether it is Sunday or not. Make the round of offerings, give notice of your intention. Well?

*[The reference to Sunday here (the seventh day of the Balinese seven-day calendar – thus the vernacular can be translated as "Sunday") alludes back to the*

*petitioner's query about the date on which he should make the offerings (speech 210).]*

**227. P(M):**  Yes.

**228. J:**  Are you prepared [to do it]?

**229. P(M):**  Yes.

**230. J:**  As preparation for the round of offerings, make *pejati* offerings. Leave it empty for the time being.

**231. P(M):**  Yes.

## D. Second discussion

**232. J:**  How did it go?

**233. P(F):**  We obtained speech.

**234. P(M):**  We obtained speech. It's startling. My wife is always dreaming. Being chased by someone.

*[The petitioner is alluding back to the deity's speech (178), where someone's dream of being chased was interpreted as an inauspicious omen. The dreamer was not specified by the deity, but now the chief petitioner in some amazement provides the clarification that his wife has often had that sort of dream.]*

**235. J:**  That's called "encircled."

**236. P(M):**  Yes, it's true.

**237. P(F):**  Yes, that's it. We haven't bought [the ceremony for] the deity yet.

**238. P(M):**  But in accordance with the instructions of the temple caretaker priest – I'm ignorant, but the reason I denied it – I have already properly carried out the foundation ceremony above and below. I've already done it twice.

*[Here the chief petitioner is initiating discussion about the deity's utterances that most disturbed him: the accusation that he had not properly completed the consecration of his house temple (speeches 128–70). He asserts that he has already carried out both parts of the ceremony alluded to by the deity – the offerings made above ground and those made below the ground in a hole in the earth.]*

**239. J:**  The foundation ceremony is finished?

**240. P(M):**  Yes.

**241. J:**  Even the closing ceremony, the notice of your intentions, everything?

**242. P(M):**  Well, at the opening, I didn't perform the *ajuman* ceremony, so it's not yet complete, isn't that so?

*[In this speech the chief petitioner admits that he did overlook one small ritual (the* ajuman*). In speech 245 Jero explains that to the deities it seemed as though the ceremonies weren't finished, because of these small oversights.]*

**243. J:**  There was just the ceremony as notice of your intentions?

**244. P(M):**  Yes.

**245. J:**   Wasn't the purchase made, and the notice of intentions, so the ceremony was finished, but from above [the deity] it was perceived as though it wasn't?

**246. P(F):**   Yes. That's true.

**247. P(M):**   Yes, but which one? . . . [?] It's finished.

**248. J:**   You have to make a purification offering for the deity first. You will be told how many offerings to make in a moment.

**249. P(M):**   The purification ceremony has not yet been mentioned.

**250. J:**   Did you request it [of the deity]? If you ask about the offerings, the instructions will come to me [while possessed].

**251. P(M):**   Wasn't it a *pejati* offering?

**252. P(F):**   A *pejati* offering.

**253. J:**   Buy offerings of witness, for the purification ceremony; have that first. Who is that? [To new clients just walking into the yard.] Put the offerings there.

**254. P(F):**   Excuse me, but we weren't told how much.

**255. P(M):**   Can you repeat it again in a moment, the offerings, so that I don't make a mistake later? Ask for blessing from Those Above.

**256. J:**   You haven't yet been told the offerings?

**257. P(F):**   No.

**258. L:**   Is this the deity coming down?

**259. P(F):**   The deity.

**260. J:**   The deity is repeating the offerings.

**261. P(F):**   Yes, it will be repeated.

**262. J:**   In a moment. The speech will tell us how much.

## E. Third possession (same deity)

**263. J:**   [Prayer repeated.] Petitioner?

**264. P(M):**   Yes?

**265. J:**   You don't yet understand [what was said]?

**266. P(M):**   I don't yet understand about those offerings. Please inform me so I don't make any mistakes.

**267. J:**   Now, buy the foundation for the purification ceremony first. Then give notice of your intentions. My servants must perform the purification ceremony so that you are not troubled by demons. Well?

**268. P(M):**   Yes.

**269. J:**   A white redemptive offering.

**270. P(M):**   Yes.

**271. J:**   A redemptive *durmanggala* offering, to purify everything, for my servants to begin the foundation of my shrine.

**272. P(M):**   Yes.

**273. J:**   A *pejati* offering. Well?

**274. P(M):**   Yes.

**275. J:**   Cleanse everything. Cleanse, my servants, so you'll know, all at once.

**276. P(M):**   Yes.

**277. J:**   Do you understand that?

**278. P(M):**   The cleansing ceremony, what do I use for that?

**279. J:**   Well, complete it with a *durmanggala* offering, and with water.

**280. P(M):**   Yes.

**281. J:**   The fluid from a young coconut, whatever you use for a cleansing ceremony.

**282. P(M):**   Yes, so it's clear, because I am ignorant.

**283. J:**   Then, after that, have the strengthening ceremony there, so that it's all at the same time. Well?

**284. P(M):**   Yes.

**285. J:**   Do you understand that much?

**286. P(M):**   Yes.

**287. J:**   Now Father will talk with you.

**288. P(M):**   Yes.

**289. J:**   That's all.

**290. P(M):**   Yes.


## F. Third discussion

**291. J:**   How did it go?

**292. P(M):**   That's all. We have it there [on tape].

**293. J:**   Now Father will talk with you, is that it?

**294. P(M):**   Yes.


## G. Fourth possession (father's spirit)

**295. J:**   [Prayer repeated.] Father has come.

**296. P(M):**   Honorable One, you've come, please speak well to us.

**297. J:**   Why did you call me down? Why?

**298. P(M):**   I ask forgiveness, Honorable One. I have asked you down because I am making some arrangements for your grandchild.

**299. J:**   A child?

**300. P(F):**   Yes.

**301. P(M):**   Your grandchild, my child.

**302. J:**   A child.

**303. P(F):**   You're here now . . .

**304. P(M):** Yes, please tell us . . .

**305. J:** So this is to be arranged. Mine are already finished.

*[Here the father's spirit is referring to his own cremation ceremonies as being "finished."]*

**306. P(M):** Yes.

**307. J:** They just appear as if they are finished.

**308. P(M):** Well, what is lacking?

**309. J:** Now, do you want to comply?

**310. P(F):** Father, Father . . .

**311. P(M):** Whose father is this, who is asking, who is speaking, so that I'm not confused?

*[Again, the chief petitioner is confused about ceremonies he thought he had finished but which it is asserted are still incomplete (in this case, the father's cremation). It is this confusion (and possibly feelings of irritation) that prompts him to check on the identity of the possessing agent.]*

**312. J:** Your own father.

**313. P(M):** Well, if it's my own father, my intention is that I mean to send your descendant. What is lacking now? Tell us.

*[The reference here to "sending a descendant" is an allusion to the forthcoming cremation of the chief petitioner's child, when he will be sent to the world of purified spirits where his grandfather's spirit is thought to reside.]*

**314. J:** It's like this, my child. Do you remember the ceremony of casting the ashes into the sea [at the end of a cremation]?

**315. P(F):** No. [He] was still small.

**316. J:** Well?

**317. J:** So that you don't make your errors worse.

**318. P(M):** Yes.

**319. J:** Now my children, you mustn't keep going in different directions, so that you won't make any mistakes.

*["Going in different directions" is a metaphorical way of referring to the confusion the petitioners will experience if they do not focus their energies on the correct ceremonies.]*

**320. P(M):** Yes.

**321. J:** Well?

**322. P(F):** Yes. Speak well to us.

**323. P(M):** Speak well to us.

**324. J:** Now my children, you have to pay a debt. Are you prepared [to pay it] Redeem the wrongs first, my wrongs, and all your wrongs!

**325. P(F):** Yes, your children were small at that time, Honorable One. Speak truly to us now, you know everything, ask from the deity, Honorable One.

**326. J:** Well, my children, can you perform the postcremation ceremony?

**327. P(M):**   The postcremation ceremony for whom?

**328. J:**   The child.

**329. P(F):**   Well, if we are able to.

**330. J:**   Well?

**331. P(F):**   Your grandchild.

**332. P(M):**   Do you mean that if I have the collective cremation for your grandchild, that I should proceed with the group and have the postcremation ceremony?

**333. J:**   It's like this. If you wish to have the postcremation ceremony, then you must be rid of all your wrongs first, so that there are no mistakes. Are you willing?

**334. P(F):**   Yes, speak so that I will know.

**335. P(M):**   What wrongs are these, Honorable One? This is the first time you have mentioned wrongs.

**336. J:**   These are the wrongs, so you'll know.

**337. P(M):**   Yes.

**338. J:**   You were wrong at the earlier cremation, so you'll know. Do you remember? I will show you where you went wrong.

**339. P(F):**   Yes.

**340. P(M):**   Yes.

**341. J:**   It was wrong to leave the place empty. Do you understand "to leave the place empty"?

**342. P(F):**   Indeed.

**343. J:**   Well, why did you leave the place empty?

**344. P(F):**   Am I not very ignorant? When I joined the work with the group, where was it? . . . I don't know. Where was the place left empty?

**345. J:**   Well, you rushed out, just rushed out. At home you'd just wake up and go, just wake up and go; it was left empty.

**346. P(M):**   Indeed.

**347. J:**   Nobody uttered any prayers. Nobody came home, nobody did anything. I was so unfortunate, I had nothing.

**348. P(M):**   Yes, indeed.

**349. P(F):**   It was all so that we were able to pay your debts, to purify you. We left because we were all busy. Who could stay at home?

**350. J:**   Don't say things were busy! Why, if things were busy, could you not just make some "filling-up" offerings? But none of you did that!

**351. P(F):**   Yes, speak to us now.

**352. P(M):**   I ask forgiveness. Because I'm ignorant, I was still small.

**353. J:**   Because you didn't make the "filling-up" offerings, you still have debts up to the present, you still have debts up to the present.

**354. P(F):**   No.

*[This is one of several occasions when the old woman petitioner adopts an overtly challenging or placating tone toward her husband's spirit, no doubt inspired by the familiarity of her relationship with him when he was alive.]*

**355. J:** To put things right, you will have to compensate for it.

**356. P(F):** Yes, I don't have debts up to the present. Now, Honorable One, I have already made compensation . . .

**357. P(M):** I came here [thinking that] there were not any debts remaining . . . But speak well to us. If there is a lack somewhere . . .

**358. J:** That's why you are asked to redeem it.

**359. P(F):** Yes, I'm prepared to redeem it; your wife is here.

**360. J:** Now redeem it.

**361. P(F):** Yes.

**362. J:** Is it difficult to make a Guru Paduka offering? If it is, then don't worry about it.

*[Guru Paduka is a propitiatory offering to Siwa; each component – cakes, fruit, rice, side dishes, cloth – is replicated in four colors: red, white, black, and yellow.]*

**363. P(F):** Why would it be difficult for me to make that much? It's not.

**364. P(M):** No, you speak well. Tell us. What is there?

**365. J:** That's why I ask you to get rid of the wrongs now. So that the wrongs don't accumulate.

**366. P(F):** That's right.

**367. J:** Well?

**368. P(F):** Speak clearly to us, Honorable One.

**369. J:** Now about the postcremation ceremony, there were none, the offerings to Betara Sakti Sang Hyang Semara Tantra, there were none. Now, the cleansing in the houseyard, so you'll know. There were no "filling-up" offerings, and there were no *panambyag* offerings. Now I ask you to redeem those wrongs. Do you want to?

*[Offerings are made to Betara Sakti Sang Hyang Semara Tantra as part of post-cremation ceremonies because this deity presides over spirits in the afterworld that are to be released to be reincarnated in human form. Each spirit must pay its "debts" in offerings to this deity, or face the possibility of a rebirth stricken with misfortune. Panambyag offerings are clothes for the spirit at the cremation and postcremation ceremonies, which are hung up at the main offering stand, with the other offerings.]*

**370. P(M):** Yes, I comply. The reason it's been a long time is that when you left me [died] I was still very small. I ask your forgiveness.

**371. J:** So that you will not be pursued.

*[Mention of pursuit is probably a return to the earlier theme of pursuit (in a dream) as an omen of malevolent forces bearing down upon the household (cf. speeches 178, 234).]*

**372. P(M):**   Yes, I will follow your wishes, with your spouse.

**373. J:**   Now redeem it all.

**374. P(M):**   Yes.

**375. J:**   Mother will speak with me now? Make just one Guru Paduka offering to redeem the wrongs, twenty wrongs are those. Will it be difficult to redeem them with the Guru Paduka offering?

**376. P(M):**   Yes.

**377. J:**   That's all for now.

**378. P(F):**   Where do I make the redemptive offerings?

**379. J:**   At the main shrine, in the cottage temple. Give notice to Betara Sakti Duuring Akasa, Betara Siwa, Betara Guru, Betara Sakti Sapu Jagat, ask them [to redeem] the wrongs.

*[Here the spirit is referring to the central shrine in house temples, where offerings to major deities (such as those that follow) are presented.]*

**380. P(F):**   Yes.

**381. J:**   So you are freed from the consequences of your wrongs. If you can't perform the ritual now, make a promise to do it in the future with all the others.

**382. P(F):**   Yes.

**383. J:**   Well?

**384. P(F):**   Yes.

**385. J:**   That's all for now. Do you understand it?

**386. P(M):**   Now, just to make sure of things, because I'm an ignorant person. I don't know, well, should I make the redemptive offerings in the main house temple or in the cottage temple?

*[This query again shows the chief petitioner's preoccupation with sorting out the problem of his priorities vis-à-vis the king group's temple in the village and his own house temple at the cottage.]*

**387. J:**   In the cottage temple or wherever you please, you can summon [the deities], it's all the same! They become one.

**388. P(M):**   That's so.

**389. J:**   If you want to promise, make it there. If not, it's up to you.

**390. P(M):**   I promise, why should I not promise? . . . Your descendants ask to know your will so that there will be no more mistakes in the future. We ask you about it.

**391. J:**   But I've told my petitioners about all that. About the way to do it.

**392. P(M):**   Yes.

**393. J:**   Well, it's the same, isn't it?

**394. P(M):**   Yes.

**395. J:**   Now, that's all. The child will speak.

**396. P(M):**   Yes.

**397. J:**  A son, isn't it?

**398. P(M)**  Yes.

**399. J:**  Well, now I'm going to leave. I have a small request.

**400. P(M):**  What is it?

**401. J:**  Can I have a little whisky?

**402. P(F)**  There's no whisky. Where would we get whisky?

**403. P(M):**  I ask forgiveness.

**404. P(F):**  Forgive me, but there is no vendor. Where would we buy it?

**405. J:**  I ask for eleven [Chinese ceremonial] coins. With the money, I am going . . .

## H. Fourth discussion

**406. P(M):**  Where is the *kewangen* offering?

[*Kewangen is a small conelike arrangement of flowers with a Chinese coin fastened in a coconut leaf. It is specially made to hold between the raised hands when praying.*]

**407. P(M):**  Here's the money. We don't have eleven coins. [Hands the balian rupiah notes.]

**408. J:**  [Put it] there. [Points to their offerings.]

**409. J:**  Is it true you left the place empty?

**410. P(M):**  May I ask you, Jero . . .

**411. P(F):**  It was explained that the place was left empty.

**412. J:**  In a minute it will emerge. In a minute, there is still some more . . .

**413. P(F):**  I accept that, moreover . . .

## I. Fifth possession (boy's spirit)

**414. J:**  [Prayer repeated.]
Is Daddy here?

**415. P(M):**  Yes.

**416. J:**  I've come here.

**417. P(F):**  Yes.

**418. J:**  Grandma?

**419. P(M):**  I – your grandmother is here.

**420. J:**  Mummy?

**421. P(F):**  Your mother isn't here.

**422. J:**  What is she doing?

**423. P(M):**  She's unclean. Forgive us, Honorable One, and speak to us.

*["Unclean" here refers to the mother's ritual pollution during menstruation.]*

**424. J:**   Now what do you want to know? Do you want to ask about why I died, or do you want to ask about my purification?

**425. P(F):**   Yes.

**426. P(M):**   I want to ask about your death, that is . . .

**427. J:**   Don't make me talk like that. I'm lower down, [and] I don't want to make mistakes.

*[The child's spirit is referring to his status in the afterworld as "lower down." In the realm of death, recently dead spirits are thought to work as the servants of higher deities.]*

**428. P(M):**   No, what I mean is that I need to ask you about your death, Nengah. How did you die? Tell us now!

*["Nengah" was the boy's birth-order name. Although it is inappropriate to use "Nengah" in addressing a spirit, the father forgets himself when he is carried away by emotion.]*

**429. J:**   I was pierced through the lungs! [Cries.]

**430. P(F):**   Oh, no.

**431. P(M):**   Tell us now, Honorable One, so I'll know.

**432. P(F):**   Yes, speak well to us, Honorable One.

**433. P(M):**   Who is it who stabbed you – causing you to "run away" while you were still so small?

**434. J:**   It's your relative, a female, uncle's relative. I'm not game to say who, I'm not allowed, so that I won't make a mistake. Daddy?

**435. P(M):**   Yes.

**436. J:**   Don't bother about me.

**437. P(M):**   Oh, how can you say that? How could I forget about you? Everything will be arranged for you. How can you say "Don't bother"?

**438. P(M):**   No, the reason you have been asked to speak is so that all your ceremonies can be properly arranged by your father. Speak well to us now, Honorable One. How . . .

**439. J:**   When is my ceremony?

**440. P(M):**   No, well, I mean it's like this, Honorable One. The group cremation is to take place eighteen days before Galungan. So it won't – I mean, your mother has been crying about it, she's sad. But tell us what you want so the ceremony goes off well.

*[Galungan is the major festival of the Balinese 210-day calendar and celebrates the triumph of the forces of good over the forces of evil in the world.]*

**441. J:**   I want first some offerings to the Sun deity, a set of *durmanggala* offerings.

*[Durmanggala is an offering of exorcism and propitiation.]*

**442. P(M):**   Now?

**443. J:**   Whenever you are able to do it. Give me offerings to Brahma, Wisnu, Iswara, the Trinity. Do you agree, Daddy? I will cause sickness.

**444. P(M):**   Yes, I agree [indistinct] so that you don't . . .

**445. J:**   If that's the case, carry redemptive offerings for me to the main crossroads: offerings to Brahma, Wisnu, Iswara, the Trinity, with three rice cones: a red, a white, and a black, in a "helping life" offering. Give these to me.

**446. P(M):**   At the main crossroads? Yes . . .

**447. J:**   Well?

**448. P(M):**   Yes.

**449. J:**   That's all for now. If you're going north, Daddy, just go to the north. If you're going to the south, just go to the south.

*[Just keep to yourself.]*

Don't become confused. Later [you] will be pursued, the needles will be brought out, [pierced in] the back. What's right is said to be wrong, what's wrong is said to be right.

*[In this speech the son's spirit is warning his father that the sorceress is still a threat and that if members of the family are not careful they too could become the victims of the sorceress's (magic) needles (hence the reference to being "pierced in the back").]*

**450. P(M):**   What has caused this to be so? Please try and speak of it a little to your father, as you already know about the "great world."

*[In this passage the father is acknowledging that his small son's spirit now has greater knowledge of worldly events than the father does himself.]*

**451. J:**   I'm now allowed to say. How will it be arranged — If you agree, Daddy, I will organize it. I will cause the sickness, if you agree, I'll cause the sickness.

*[See discussion of sorcery in sections 5E, 6C.]*

**452. P(M):**   Yes.

**453. J:**   If not, then I won't.

**454. P(M):**   Yes. What do you want to make ill? Tell me about it.

**455. J:**   The one who cursed me!

**456. P(M):**   Yes. That redemptive *durmanggala* offering — it is to be . . . ?

**457. J:**   No! The redemptive offering to the Trinity, Brahma, Wisnu, Iswara.

**458. P(M):**   Yes. Speak well.

**459. J:**   So! I ask for a cleansing ceremony with a redemptive *durmanggala* offering. I should have had a *babayuhan badé* offering.

*[Babayuhan badé is an offering to placate demons at the burial ceremony.]*
But I never got a *babayuhan badé* offering. Daddy, you're confused, Mummy is confused. Don't be unhappy. Well?

**460. P(M):**   Yes.

**461. J:**   That's all, Daddy. Organize the offerings for me. I don't know anything.

## J. Fifth discussion

**462. P(M):**   [Still addressing the spirit.] Should the *durmanggala* offering be made on the day of the collective cremation?

**463. J:**   How did it go?

**464. P(M):**   My child was crying.

**465. J:**   He was pierced in the chest . . . Fix that up! It'll fall down!

**466. P(M):**   It fits – he was pierced in the chest – with . . .

**467. P(M):**   Where are you from? Bakas?

**468. P(M):**   He was sick, his stomach was distended. He died in the hospital.

**469. J:**   He was stabbed in the chest. The illness was in the chest, the lungs.

**470. P(M):**   . . . the doctor couldn't fix [him].

**471. J:**   That's all, is it? [It's been] five times . . .

# PART III

## The Medium Is the Masseuse: A Balinese Massage

# FILM SYNOPSIS

Filming of massage treatment: Jero Tapakan, Ida Bagus, Linda Connor, and Timothy Asch.

EVERY third day Jero Tapakan treats patients with massage and a variety of traditional medicines. In this film she begins by arranging her offerings and medicines while joking with the patients who are waiting their turn. Since all healing involves supernatural forces, Jero's preparations culminate in prayer.

Jero's treatment of Ida Bagus, a man who suffers from sterility and seizures, is shown in detail. Like all her patients, he receives a thorough massage, eye drops, and a medicinal tonic. The dialogue, which is subtitled, includes discussion between Jero Tapakan, Linda Connor, and Ida Bagus about the nature of his illness, as well as informal banter among people in Jero's houseyard. Jero treats her patients on her porch, beside the chairs provided for people who are waiting. Thus treatment is also a social occasion, and patients are frequently accompanied by other members of their family.

The film ends with an interview held four days later, in which Ida Bagus

175

and his wife talk about the history of his illness, their ten-year search for a cure, and their analysis of why they have had no children.

Through her treatment and her words, Jero reveals her conceptions of the human body, the nature of illness, the contrast between Western and traditional Balinese medicine, and the relationships between human beings and the cosmos. The massage is shown in sufficient detail to illustrate how and in what order the parts of the body are treated.

A 31-minute, 16mm, color film by Timothy Asch, Linda Connor, and Patsy Asch
Available on videocassette from Cambridge University Press
Available on 16mm film from Documentary Educational Resources
5 Bridge Street, Watertown, Mass. 02172, USA

# EIGHT

## *Ethnographic notes on*
# The Medium Is the Masseuse
## LINDA CONNOR

### A. Principles of massage treatment

THERE are hundreds of masseurs *(balian apun, balian uat)* practicing in rural areas of Bali. Massage is a popular therapy for a wide range of complaints, from aches and pains in the joints, lethargy, and fatigue to impotence, dysentery, headaches, influenza, sprains and strains, and the sorts of problems we see treated in the film *The Medium Is the Masseuse* – seizures and childlessness. Men and women, children and adults, all may have reason to consult a masseur. Balinese masseurs, like other balians, are guided by a unified philosophy of healing that takes account of indigenous conceptions of anatomy and physiology as well as of a spiritual order of meanings and the conviction that both ritual and somatic ministrations are necessary in the treatment of illness. Non-Balinese masseurs (mostly Javanese) are also popular, especially in the towns, where they compete with Balinese practitioners. The former in some cases have a more secular approach to therapy, but they are guided by similar folk theories of human physiology, particularly with regard to the *urat, or uat*, the "connecting channels" of the body (see section 8c).

Whatever techniques are utilized, the fundamental principles of healing as understood by Balinese practitioners constitute an integrated domain of ideas. Masseurs ascribe the same range of causes to the complaints they treat as do other sorts of healers, for example, fatigue, strain and overwork, congenital factors, sorcery by human enemies, and curses from ancestors or deities. Balians like Jero use their privileged knowledge of the realm of mystical power to explain and treat patients' problems.[1] Such explanations may be integrated with a more mundane order of causation. For instance, in Ida Bagus's case (recorded on film) Jero discusses the causes of his sterility in terms of his bodily weakness, brought about by illness that was itself caused by sorcery; a problem with the functioning of his wife's reproductive organs; and, for unknown reasons, the failure of a reincarnating ancestor to animate the union of sperm and egg.

---

[1] Balinese cosmology as it relates to healing is discussed in broader terms in section 3B.

Jero ministers to both the causes and the symptoms of her clients' problems, using ritualistic as well as somatic interventions. Thus, in the case of Ida Bagus, treatment has included massage, countersorcery offerings, spiritually potent medicines administered during attacks, and plans for a ceremony to facilitate the arrival of the reincarnating ancestor. In the case of clients who come to "ask for speech" at a séance, ritualistic interventions — offerings, prayers, and ceremonies — usually predominate, whereas massage patients seek Jero's skills in somatic treatment as their first priority. Many older patients come to obtain relief from chronic complaints, such as rheumatism. Such patients usually expect relief of symptoms rather than a cure. The opportunity to spend a few hours in the convivial atmosphere of Jero's houseyard and to discuss their complaints with a sympathetic healer and with other patients doubtless also contributes to a general feeling of well-being. Acute complaints also come under Jero's care. There is in fact no condition that may not be treated by massage if patient and healer see fit. However, Jero recognizes the symptoms of cholera and refuses to handle such cases, advising relatives to take the sick person to the district hospital. She acts similarly in other situations where she judges the patient's symptoms to be life-threatening.

Patients and healers are aware of the treatment that modern medical facilities offer. It is not uncommon for both patients and healers to compare and assess the practices of clinicians and balians and their relation to each other.[2] Patients see parallels between modern medicine and the balians' treatments, such as indicated by the following exchange between Jero and one of her patients.[3]

**J:**   Illnesses are named differently by the government and by Balinese. They have different names, but the illnesses are the same.

**P:**   Yes, the illnesses are the same. If you're ill, you complain about it.

This statement refers primarily to the symptoms of illnesses. When it comes to the causes and treatment of symptoms, patients and healers more often perceive a conflict between the two systems, as the following passage — a transcript of a recorded conversation among Jero, myself, and a patient — indicates:

**L:**   How many times has she been here, Jero?

**J:**   Over a long time. A year. She gets better and stays away. And then, if she gets ill again, she comes back. She always comes straight here. She's a seller of roast pig.

**L:**   Has she visited the clinic?

---

[2]  They also compare different balians and doctors, nurses, clinics, etc.; section 8D.
[3]  P = Patient (in this chapter).

**J:** Often. They told her she has — what's it called? — "Koplek" illness (*laughs*).

**L:** Lack of B complex?

**J:** Yes, lack of B complex. Even though she's a seller of meat! She never lacks meat. If she eats meat, she gets sick.

**L:** What's the Balinese interpretation of her illness?

**J:** The Balinese interpretation is an illness of the connecting channels. The ones from the abdomen are bruised. And those from the bowel are bruised. The channels are damaged, blocked.

**L:** Was there any improvement [at the clinic]?

**P:** I felt the same. Just after the injection I couldn't eat, I couldn't get up. I had no energy.

In this passage we learn of conflicting explanations for the symptoms and of different treatment regimens. The patient obviously considers Jero's treatment superior to that of the clinic. Jero's comments in the passage also reveal that she understands some of the illness-related concepts that clinic staff attempt to communicate to patients (i.e., about the possibility of correcting a vitamin B deficiency with higher meat consumption). On the basis of her knowledge of the client's symptoms and background, however, she is obviously skeptical about the validity of such ideas. We see the same skepticism of clinic explanations and treatments on the part of both patients and healer in the filmed case of Ida Bagus and again in the case of the *legong* dancer discussed below. During any particular illness or series of illnesses, assessment of the diagnoses and treatment options available is an ongoing process, and judgments are constantly being revised.

Jero's treatment includes not only massage and chiropractic-like manipulations but administration of a large array of potions with both spiritual and material efficacy. In every healing session there is some communication with the supernatural realm, by virture of the balian's status as a consecrated specialist. Thus even a person suffering from a minor accident, strain, or sprain who asks Jero for a massage will be instructed to make small "energy-enhancing" offerings (e.g., *pangenteg bayu* or *tulung urip*) to aid recovery and prevent recurrence.

The ritualized context in which massage occurs is seen in the film, where we observe Jero setting up a small shrine and then intoning several prayers. To the side of the offerings Jero places the bottles, boxes, and bags that contain her medicines — oils, plants, spices, roots, shells, rocks, holy water — which at other times are kept in her shrine house. After the table of offerings and medicines is prepared, each client in turn places on top of the tall offering tray his or her own small offering, *canang sesari*, which usually includes a small sum of money. Clients place any payment in kind (rice, sugar, coffee, etc.), which they may make in addition to or instead of a cash donation, on the offering table. There is no set fee; clients pay according to their means and inclination. Many people who have been successfully treated by Jero also repay her by offering their assistance (providing raw materials, making offerings, preparing ceremonial food, cleaning her house-yard) when she is holding an important ceremony. Others provide labor or raw materials when she undertakes some home improvements.

Before Jero can begin to treat her massage patients, she must ask for a blessing from the deities and ancestors who bestow healing skills upon her, and she must ritually purify the area where the treatment is to take place. This she does (as shown at the beginning of the film) by uttering a sequence of prayers while facing the small table of offerings. As in the prayers prior to a séance, the deities of the Balinese pantheon are beseeched for their blessings. Jero also throws a small offering to the ground during her prayers, a propitiatory offering to any demonic forces that may be present. Through her prayers she also purifies and strengthens the oils and other medicines she uses in her treatments. The film shows only the first of her prayers.

A conspicuous element of the prayers that precede the massage treatment is the mention of the Javanese ancestors (Betara Mas Majapahit) of the man from whom Jero inherited the practice. These ancestors are believed to be members of a lineage that can be traced back to the ancient Javanese king-dom of Majapahit, even though Jero's mentor, Pak Udeng, is a Muslim. This sort of syncretism can be found in many areas of healing practice and belief on Bali. It is reflected also in the style of offerings on the table, most of which are for the Javanese ancestors and are made, according to Jero, in the Javanese fashion taught to her by Pak Udeng. The most obvious Javanese-style components are the two cups of black coffee (one sweetened and one unsweetened), with side dishes of eggs and shop-bought wheat cakes. These foods are for the male and female manifestations of the Javanese ancestors, for whom Balinese-style offerings are unacceptable.

While Jero is reciting the prayers and preparing the oil she uses for massage (a mixture of coconut oil, sacred oil,[4] ginger, and garlic), the patients, often accompanied by friends or relatives, sit talking quietly at the other end of the small verandah or in other pavilions of the houseyard. By 7:00 a.m. on the day of *pasah* there may be several patients awaiting their turn, and more continue to arrive during the course of the morning. Jero has many days when she treats from 10 to 15 patients, working from early morning to sunset and taking only a short break to eat lunch. Patients are generally treated in the order in which they arrive, although exceptions are sometimes made for high-status clients or those who have to travel a long distance to their homes. Some people wait hours for their turn, so Jero has established a custom of serving each person coffee and a small snack while they are

---

[4]  See section 8C for an account of this sacred oil.

waiting. The time does not pass too slowly, as patients, some of whom may be acquainted, talk among themselves or joke with Jero as she carries out her treatments.

## B. Biographical background to Jero's initiation as a masseuse

Jero became a masseuse after ten years of practicing as a spirit medium. This new development in her career is not discussed in either *Stories from the Life of a Balinese Healer* or *The Medium Is the Masseuse.* I include an account here because Jero's initiation as a masseuse is an important step in her spiritual, professional, and personal development and because it illustrates a slightly different way in which a balian may arrive at his or her calling.

The early to mid 1960s was a time of widespread misery and turmoil in Bali (see Chapter 10), and these conditions were exacerbated for Jero, who had to cope with personal losses (the death of her husband and son; see Chapter 10) as well as with the misfortunes that affected many people on the island. There were men in her village who wanted to marry her but she rejected them, deeming remarriage inappropriate to the nature of her calling. By this time Jero's practice as a spirit medium was earning her a reasonable livelihood, so there were few economic pressures to find another spouse. But, she recalls, she could not escape the effects of the love magic that unknown suitors practiced upon her. A particularly severe case of bewitchment immediately preceded initiation to her new vocation, that of masseuse:

At that time I was already a widow, like I am now. I was bewitched with some (love-sorcery) oil [*lengis babajangan*], that's how it all started. Somebody wanted to make trouble for me, wanted to make me sick. I was like a lovesick young virgin, bewitched – I was the victim of a spell [*guna*], a man's spell, a spell to make me want to marry him. I was so confused, all I wanted to do was look for the one who did it. I just had to find him. But at the same time I was thinking that I couldn't marry, I was ashamed at the thought of marrying.[5]

Jero went to several balians seeking countermagic and medicines to alleviate her condition, but none of those she consulted could help her. Then a voice that came to her in a dream told her that an Islamic spell had been used upon her and that she would have to find an Islamic healer to obtain relief.

---

[5]  The phrase *lengis babajangan* refers to oil that has had a love-sorcery spell whispered over it. The would-be lover is thought to stand near the object of his desire (e.g., in a crowd watching a drama performance at a festival) and to brush her skin covertly with the oil.

So I set out to find an Islamic healer. Finally I found one. He was a policeman, stationed at Selokan, to the west of here. He was originally from the city of Bandung, in Java. He divined what was wrong with me [*tenungina tiang ditu*].[6] He said it was true that I had been bewitched with an Islamic oil [*kena lengis Islam*]. I had a spell [*sihir*] cast on me. So he gave me some medicine. It consisted of papaya seeds, *kelor* bark [*Moringa oleifera* Lamk], nutmeg, cinnamon, rice whisky, garlic, all mixed into a poultice. I was cured, but I still felt a bit confused. He gave me some oil [*lengis*].

> "Jero, put this oil in your shrine house. It's a mixture of bark, oil, and honey. Ask for a blessing for it in your shrine house."

He said he found it in the mountains, the holy mountains of Java.

> "Use this oil as an antidote for all sorts of poisons [*sebatek upas*]. For all sorts of itches, for snake bites, dog bites, all sorts of bites."

He kept saying:

> "Use it as an antidote for sorcerers' poisons, for all sorts of poisons [*upas papasangan, saluwiring upas*]. Ask for a blessing from the ancestors of Pak Udeng in the holy mountains of Java. Ask for their permission first."

In this way, a relationship was established between the Islamic healer and Jero, in which he treated her more as a colleague than as a patient. The next development, as Jero recalls, was that Pak Udeng's ancestors (who presided over his healing practice) informed Jero in a series of dreams that they wanted to transfer some of their powers to her. They wished to teach her how to massage and thereby expand her practice. Such a connection between Islamic ancestors and a Balinese healer is unorthodox but not unheard of. Balinese look to the ancient Javanese kingdom of Majapahit as the homeland of their ancestors. Thus they perceive a link with the Javanese that transcends differences of religion. Moreover, Pak Udeng was married to a Balinese woman. Probably the Javanese policeman wished to cease practicing as a healer, and Jero's arrival presented an ideal opportunity. A healer who merely ceased practicing would risk incurring ancestral or divine wrath.

Pak Udeng's ancestors instructed Jero through dreams. Then, after massaging her first patient, she decided that she did not want to continue with such work.

J:    Twenty days after that I had a dream. Pak Udeng came to me in the dream.

> "My ancestors are here, my forebears have come here."

L:    How did he know they'd come here?

J:    Because he'd prayed to them and there had been no reply.

---

[6]    Balinese use many divining techniques. Jero does not specify here what technique Pak Udeng used.

"My forebears have come here. They're not with me any more."

I asked him to take them back — I didn't know anything about it. Supposedly they'd moved to my place twenty days ago. It was twenty days since the last dream. But I didn't want to have anything to do with his ancestors. "You can be a masseuse as well," he said. But I didn't want to. I told him to take them home with him. I said I can't fulfill two functions at once, as a spirit medium and a masseuse. Then I told him that I would make some offerings so that their return to his place would be a smooth one. But these ancestors didn't want to go, they were happy here, they said, with a simple Balinese woman.

It was a shame. The ancestors were of a reigning family of Majapahit, they were venerated by Pak Udeng, but they wanted to stay here in Bali. Yes, they were of a ruling dynasty of Majapahit. But even if they resided here and bestowed their blessing on the sick, how was I to do the massage successfully? Pak Udeng said:

"It's easy. You just have to try it and at the same time ask for divine benevolence. That's all a person ignorant in these matters can do."

Then I was shown how to make the offerings, and I was given that book over there (*pointing to a book of Islamic prayers and teachings on divan*). That book was brought from Sanur! He brought me his medicines. I made a shrine for them here. Then I went to a lot of trouble to make the right offerings so that the ancestors would want to abide here. I dedicated welcoming offerings to them because they were reluctant to return to their place of origin.

So I started massaging. Then, for the next couple of years I was very busy. People came all the time seeking cures. I had a lot of energy then; I would walk a long way. There were no public vehicles.

Jero cannot read the pamphlet Pak Udeng gave her, but the document she refers to is considered powerful as a repository of the written word and warrants a place with other mystically potent substances and objects in her shrine house.

Jero began to practice as a masseuse on every third day, the day *pasah* of the Balinese calendar, which she considers inappropriate for invoking deities and spirits.[7] The massage clientele developed gradually over several years, as the other clientele had done. The two practices operate independently, with séance clients generally arriving on the first two days (*bateng* and *kajeng*) of the three-day week. Consultation through mediumship does not necessarily entail consultation for a massage and associated treatments, although some patients participate in both (as is the case with the patients on film).

---

[7]   Jero occasionally practices massage on other days as well, in emergency cases or for clients she considers too important to refuse (e.g., local officials).

## C. Techniques of massage treatment

Each massage with its associated treatment occupies between 30 and 40 minutes, depending on the nature of the patient's complaint. Jero does not shorten her treatments or quicken her pace if there are a lot of patients waiting — she merely finishes later in the day, and the patients wait longer, without complaint. The person about to be treated moves over to the divan, removing the top half of his or her clothing and loosening the lower half (usually a sarong or trousers). Jero is not embarrassed about treating males, although she points out that some women are reluctant to consult male masseurs. Women form, by a small margin, the majority of her clients. Her openness to treating male patients caused her some problems early in her career, as she recounts in her own words:

J: I had been doing massage for about a month. An impotent man arrived. Do you know what *wandu* [impotent] means?

L: Yes.

J: Everybody here laughed when he walked in. Laughed at me for treating somebody with that sort of complaint. They came from the north and the south [of the hamlet] and laughed at me for treating a case like that. But I was just silent.

L: Did you massage him?

J: Yes, I massaged him; treated him by massage. Everyone laughed at me, made fun of me. But I didn't take any notice of them. He was cured by me. Then another one came, an important person, a policeman. He said he was impotent. He wanted a massage although it was already nightfall. Just after I began, he said:

> "Jero, I feel very weak here (*she indicates that the man was pointing to his penis*). I need a massage."

Then he tried to seduce me. As soon as I got the chance, I hurried off to Pak Udeng's place. I didn't want to continue being a masseuse. I wanted to relinquish all ties with his ancestors. I didn't want to be a masseuse any more, not when it caused so much trouble. You can imagine how unhappy I felt. I went to Pak Udeng's place. I told him I wasn't going to be a masseuse any more.

> "It causes too much strife. I'm fed up. Please recall your ancestors. I can't continue with it."

He said:

> "Look, it's this way: you have to be able to discern whether they're feigning the condition or not."

He pretended he was impotent.

> "Now check me over first. First, if I'm suffering from impotence, you should check the channels [*uat*] [of the arm] first. Check to see if there are any hard lumps in the channels like beans. If there are, then it's a true case of impotence and you should treat it."

**L:** If not?

**J:** He said:

> "First check the channels [in the arm]. Don't start the treatment before the preliminary checkup. Then, after the checkup, there is a mantra. It goes like this: 'Now, Sir, you should feel some improvement. Be recovered.' Check the channels. If there are no hard lumps, and his channels are normal, then you must say the following: 'Sir, if you are truly impotent, go home and be recovered. But if you are not truly impotent and you come here and feign it, go home and be impotent.' That's what you say. Then loosen the clothes, take the channels and twist them around, so that he is indeed impotent. He asked for it. Don't worry about it, just do what I say."

After that, I felt I could continue with it again. One day a man came along feigning illness. I knew as soon as I took his arm, like this [illustrating with her hands], that he was not ill. So I said:

> "If you come here in good health, then go home impotent; if you come here impotent, then go home cured."

Then I loosened his clothes. He said:

> "Forget it! Forget it! I'm only suffering from fatigue. I've been playing too much volleyball."

**L:** Is that so?

**J:** "It's stopped me up!" [he said].

**L:** There have been people like that here?

**J:** Yes. But since that time, nobody has come with a false complaint. It was only at that time that there were a few people who said they were sick but in fact were not.

**L:** So what were they doing, just trying you out?

**J:** Yes, trying me out. So that man got up and fled. He didn't want to be made impotent.
That's what you do, twist the channels around so they make the man impotent. But after I first felt his channels to see if he really was impotent he said he was only exhausted from playing volleyball. Since that time, nobody else has come like that.

This anecdote of Jero's establishes two points about her practice. It makes clear that women who practice massage may be suspected of prostitution and that a new practitioner may have to work quite hard to build a reputation as an honest healer, not without personal suffering and embarrassment along the way. In Jero's case the trials she endured were almost enough to make her give up her practice. I have never come across any evidence that masseuses in rural areas do in fact operate as prostitutes, although both men and women who perform this treatment may be suspected of illicitly performing abortions (and some indeed do).

The anecdote also underlines the importance of the spiritual powers that balians are thought to possess. Jero's confidence about handling any future cases of fraudulent complaints probably stemmed more from learning Pak Udeng's powerful mantra then from acquiring the manual skills supposed to render her troublesome clients indeed impotent. And in the event, for the man feigning impotence, it was enough to hear Jero intone the mantra: He immediately retracted his story and fabricated another one that allowed him to leave unharmed.

### The massage

The massage, for both men and women, is the same. Jero begins with the person lying on his or her back. Kneeling or sitting beside the patient, she first massages the abdominal region with firm circular stroking and pressing movements. Jero says she starts at the abdomen and navel because this area, along with the small of the back, is the center of the body. She explains that the abdominal region of the body is analogous to the motor of a car. In this region are found the "great channels" (*uat gede*, discussed later in this section), from the small of the back to the abdomen, and from the abdomen to the shoulders and chest. Other *uat gede* run from the buttocks to the legs and feet and to the back. The massage of the abdominal region includes the groin, where channels connecting to the legs are found. Then she moves to the chest and shoulder area with a series of stroking movements, using the whole palm of her hand (effleurage). At this stage she also works on the side of the rib cage. Next, she sits at the patient's side and takes hold of first one arm and then the other. She massages the arm distally, that is, with strokes moving away from the heart, contrary to most Western massage practice. In these and other movements, it is apparent that Jero's technique is oriented to improving the condition of the connecting channels. Jero uses an interesting sideways rubbing movement on the forearm and hand. She also rolls the tendons of the forearm between her fingers, a movement she refers to as *ningtingang uat* ("lifting up the channels"). This is done to check which channels need attention, and to straighten any crooked channels so that the blood to the hand circulates well. At the end of the arm massage, Jero bends and presses the finger joints so they make a snapping sound. This adjustment is called *makepotin*, a word that Balinese use to refer to all sorts of "bonecracking." People like to work on their own finger and neck joints to achieve the same snapping sound, which Balinese hear as a "pot" sound. Hence the word is onomatopoeic.

After the arm and hand massage is finished, the patient is asked to turn over. Jero begins massaging from the buttocks and the small of the back, then proceeds up the spine and rib cage to the shoulders. She kneels or sits beside the patient and, for much of the back massage, she uses a strong pressing and rubbing movement with the heel of her hand. When she is through with the back and neck, she stands and massages the patient's legs and feet with her feet, using the heel of her foot in a circular, digging motion to exert pressure, after which she performs a chiropractic-like adjustment to the vertebrae of the lower back. She massages the muscles of the buttocks with the heel of her foot while the patient is lying on his stomach and then asks the patient to turn to one side as she continues to massage the upper buttock. She grasps the patient's lower arm and, exerting pressure on the buttock with her foot, lifts the arm raising the torso off the divan. As a result the vertebrae in the lower spine make a cracking sound, which can be heard in the filmed massage; this is also referred to as *makepotin*.

After the spinal adjustment has been made, the patient is asked to sit up so that Jero can work on the upper neck, the scalp, the forehead, the jaw, and the face. For the scalp and forehead, she rolls the palm and heel of her hand over the skin, pressing on the opposite side of the head with the other hand. For the face and jaw, she rubs and presses with her thumbs.

Essential parts of each treatment are the administration of elixir at the end and the application of spiritually potent medicinal oil (*tutuh*) to the subject's eyes, which causes some irritation, watering, and loss of clear vision for several minutes. In addition to these ministrations, patients may receive special medicines and instructions for offerings, according to the nature of their complaints. All the elements of this procedure, which is repeated with each patient, can be seen on the film. Although there are many similarities in the way different masseurs think about body functioning and work on the body, each practitioner has a different technique and sequence of movements.

When performing a massage, Jero gains insights about her patient's condition not only by touch but also by a mystical resonance between herself and the patient. She says that she can feel in her own body the corresponding problem areas in the patient's body. This resonance is attributed to the powers of her spiritual siblings (see section 3B), who communicate with the spiritual siblings of the patient. Jero also gains spiritual strength for the massage from the Javanese ancestors who preside over her practice. She says that while she is treating patients she does not feel tired, even if she has to work for many hours, but as soon as she performs the closing prayers for the ancestors, she begins to feel fatigue. She reports that sometimes, if she is very busy and her hands begin to feel "thick" or swollen, she massages her own forearms so that the feeling disappears. Most important for Jero, however, is the ancestors' blessing that enables her to focus her thoughts (*acepang kenehe*) exclusively on healing.

## Uat: "connecting channels"

The physical treatment of the body is focused on the *uat* (or *urat*), which may be loosely translated as "connecting channels." *Uat* are a primary element not only of Balinese thought about the physiological functioning of the body but of many other Indonesian regional cultures as well. *Uat* refer to any canal-like or sinew-like feature of human anatomy — tendons, veins, blood vessels, nerves, or muscles — but they are not conceived as identical to the structures identified in Western anatomy. *Uat* are critical in the physiological functioning of the body, although there does not appear to be a correspondence with any Western scientific concept.

*Uat* carry spiritual essences and life-giving fluids throughout the body; they are also vehicles for the elimination of toxic waste, which if retained may cause all manner of complaints. According to Jero, three types of fluids (*getah*) are conveyed by the *uat*: yellow fluid (*yeh kuning*), clear fluid (*yeh bersih*), and blood (*getih*). Yellow fluid is not the same as urine, which, according to Jero, is produced directly from ingested fluids. In the system of macrocosmic/microcosmic correspondences (see section 3B), *yeh kuning* is associated with the deity Wisnu, whose color is yellow; *yeh bersih* is associated with Iswara, whose color is white; and blood is associated with Brahma, whose color is red. Jero explains that all the fluids in the body have to flow smoothly, but the *uat* may become damaged by a fall, overwork, mental stress, or sorcery.

Massage technique is oriented to smoothing out damaged *uat* that are "bunched up" or "knotted" (*mapesel*), or "stiff" (*kaku*) and "frozen" (*beku*), thus facilitating the free flow of fluids and energies throughout the body. Often during her manipulations the masseuse locates small, lumpy, hard deposits in the *uat*, to which she attributes a particular complaint. These may be referred to as *berasan*, from the word for "raw rice" (*beras*), because of their resemblance to the feel of this grain. *Berasan* are believed to be constituted of hardened deposits of yellow fluid that have to be eliminated through massage and medicines. Other substances, such as sorcerers' poisons and even sorcerers' demons *(babai)* are also believed to lodge themselves in the *uat*, necessitating removal by mystical as well as manual means.

Theories of the way in which *uat* connect different parts of the body vary from one balian to another. Some balians derive their knowledge on this subject from traditional *lontar* palm-leaf manuscripts on physiology, but the information in these tracts also varies.[8] The parts of the body are thought to be connected through the "great channels" (*uat gede*) and by a series of secondary channels. Damaged *uat* may be located in a part of the body other than where the problem manifests itself. For example, Jero explained about one woman she was treating.

**L:**  Is she inflamed inside, or what?

**J:**  It's her nerves [*urat syaraf*]. The nerves are damaged — the nerves of the abdomen, the liver. They affect the head. They affect the ears. If it's the nerves, they affect all the body. It can make her dizzy.

---

[8]  See Weck 1976.

Jero, in treating a case such as Ida Bagus's infertility (seen on the film), considers that all the body's *uat* have to be treated through massage. She also acknowledges that the patient's other complaints (Ida Bagus's seizures) must be successfully treated before the problem will right itself. In cases where the patient complains of an ache or pain located at the specific body site, extra attention may be given to that area during massage, but *uat* in other parts of the body are treated too.

Malfunctioning *uat* are also thought to affect the flow of blood throughout the body. Jero suggested that in Ida Bagus's case "frozen" *uat* caused his blood to rise, which in turn contributed to his illnesses. "Frozen" or "knotted" *uat* may also inhibit blood flow at specific sites, causing sluggishness or aches and pains that are "cold" in character and have to be treated by "heating-up" medicines as well as massage. Different balians hold a variety of theories about the relationship between "hot" and "cold" complaints, *uat* damage and blood flow, as well as about the appropriate medicines to be used in each case.

*Bayu:* life force, or vital energy

Just as important as the physical repair of the *uat* is their spiritual rejuvenation. Through the *uat* travels *bayu:* life force, a mystical windlike power that animates the human microcosm. *Bayu* is personified and represented as a facet of one of the spiritual siblings *(kanda mpat)* that protect the welfare of their human host. *Bayu* is also deified and thereby represented as a supernatural force, with symbolic correspondences in nature. It is a male force as contrasted to the female force, *rasa* ("feeling"). Both are considered essential qualities of the human psyche. *Bayu* is also part of the trinity *bayu* ("action"), *sabda* ("speech"), *idep* ("ideas"), all nonmaterial aspects of human beings. In healing, *bayu* is emphasized over the other elements.

The *lontar* manuscripts include many tracts about the different types of *bayu* in the body. One manuscript, for example, lists *bayu prana* as the energy for breathing; *bayu byana* as the energy for digestion; *bayu kurmara* as the energy for laughter and enjoyment; *bayu kerekara* as the energy for anger and tears; and so on. It is most common for the texts to enumerate the ten different sorts of *bayu* in the body *(dasa bayu)*, although there are shorter and longer lists.[9] Ordinary people, and even balians who are not literate in the *lontars*, think about *bayu* as undifferentiated energy that is an essential element of bodily well-being. Those who are feeling ill and listless may explain it by statements like *wus bayun tiangé* ("my vital energy has

---

[9] A concept related to *bayu*, that of *vayu*, is known in Ayurvedic medicine of South Asia. In Ayurvedic texts *vayu* is also described as a windlike force, one of the bodily humors. For further discussion, see Charles Leslie, ed., *Asian Medical Systems: A Comparative Study* (Berkeley: University of California Press, 1977), pp. 4, 201. For a discussion of *bayu* in Balinese thought, see Mershon 1970, 1971; Hooykaas 1974; Weck 1976.

escaped'') and will point to the top fontanel as the place where *bayu* can escape from the body. Mothers often apply a thick herbal paste to the fontanels of their young babies to prevent escape of *bayu*. Of lively, strong babies, especially boys, people will admiringly say *gede bayuné* (''his life-force is strong,'' or ''great'').

The state of a person's vital energy is connected to the condition of his or her *uat*. Damaged *uat* may impede or weaken the quality and flow of *bayu* in the body, leading to a weakening of the person's hold on life; for example, in the film Jero refers to the presence of *bayu* in the *uat*.[10]

**L:**  Why do you massage his channels?

**J:**  So he can absorb energy [*bayu*], and everything is smoothly connected. So the blood circulates smoothly.

*Bayu* is amenable to manipulation not only by massage but also through offerings, which can be made on behalf of the sick person to the deified manifestation of *bayu*. In achieving an appropriate treatment regimen, adjustments of the person's spiritual condition through ritual are considered just as important as somatic interventions. There are many ways in which the functioning of the human microcosm may be adjusted by ritual means. In the case filmed, although we do not see Jero giving instructions for offerings, we learn that she considers prayers an important part of the healing process.

Another case, transcribed from a tape recording during a treatment, indicates the interplay between somatic and ritual ministrations and (in this case) the conflicting diagnoses and treatments of clinic staff and balian. The patient (P) is having a massage while discussing her treatment history and the cause of her illness with Jero and me.

**L:**  Have you been to the clinic?

**P:**  Yes. I paid five hundred rupiah. But I'm still sick.

**L:**  What did the doctor say?

**P:**  Dysentery. Excreting blood and pus.

**J:**  She's been four times to no avail. . . . She came here yesterday for treatment. She hasn't had a bowel movement since then. . . . She's "asked for speech" here yesterday [contacted deities, through a medium].

**L:**  What did the deity say?

**J:**  Swollen – because of a deity's curse [*kapongoran*]. Once she was a *legong* dancer. She never made the right offerings before ceasing to dance. She never asked permission to stop. When she was single she was a *legong* dancer. And

---

[10]  Vertical lines down the lefthand margin indicate dialogue included in the film, although the subtitles were often an abbreviated translation.

then he married her *(pointing to husband)*. She never got permission to leave. She never gave notice.

**L:**   To whom?

**J:**   To the deity of the Death Temple [Betara di Dalem].

**L:**   Why that deity?

**J:**   It is that deity which takes girls to be *legong* dancers.

**L:**   Is that usual?

**J:**   *Legong* dancers are taken into the service of God [*selangang Widi*]. . . . Now the deity still remembers. She was told to perform a *pangalap* ceremony. With Balinese concerns, if there is a wrong committed against God, then injections won't help. For God, one has to make offerings. Then things will improve. If the doctor can't help, then follow the Balinese way. If the Balinese way won't work, then go to the doctor.

**L:**   Did she go to the doctor first?

**J:**   Yes, four times to the doctor. She was diagnosed to have dysentery. She was given injections, but the illness did not go away. Then she "asked for speech" from God and was told of her error. Now she must redeem her sins and she will recover.

Medicines

On film we see Jero giving "tonic" and eye drops to Ida Bagus. Many masseurs administer such treatments to their patients after the massage. The coffee tonic is a rich mixture consisting of strongly brewed coffee, sugar, pepper, ginger, and the yolk of an egg. As Jero explains, the tonic activates and accelerates the flow of life-giving fluids and forces through the *uat*:

**J:**   It's like a car, Linda. You have to warm up the engine. The connecting channels are knotted and frozen. The medicine is a starter, like turning on a car engine. There's vibration and then perspiration.

Most patients seem to feel the mixture is doing them good to the degree to which they find it repulsive (as evidenced by the expression on Ida Bagus's face). The eye drops, another standard medicine, contain spiritually powerful oil, found by Jero under auspicious circumstances "in a white snail shell," "at the spring of the nymphs." As Jero points out, the medicinal potency of the oil lies in its capacity to allow the *uat* to function freely. The profuse watering of the eyes that it causes is also thought to have a beneficial cleansing effect through the excretion of bodily fluids, worth the discomfort such an intervention obviously causes.

The bottles, jars, and bags on the table beside the divan contain the ingredients for many other medicines, which Jero makes up according to the needs of particular patients. Some of the ingredients (such as the small white sea shells, *bule sutra*, which are ground up to form part of a variety

of cooling tonics) Jero collects periodically; others are bestowed by unpredictable and sometimes awe-inspiring acts of divine favor. In the following
anecdote, for example, Jero recounts in some detail how she came to find
a potent oil that she uses as an ingredient in her massage balm and in other
medicines as well:

One day, at night, about nine o'clock, a person walked into my yard. "Jero, Jero
Tapakan," he called at the door of my shrine house. At that time it was made of
bamboo, it was small, not like it is now. I opened the door.

>"Who is that?"
>"It is I."

When I opened the door, a temple priest was standing there. Tall, with white
teeth, alone . . .

>"Forgive me for asking, but may I know where you're from, Honorable
>One?"
>"I'm from the hill of the teak trees, Bukit Jati Kepalatan."
>"Who has accompanied you?"
>"I'm alone."
>"Please come in."

I opened up the shrine, and we sat down together. After we were seated, I asked:

>"How must I address you, Honorable One?"
>"I'm the priest of Teak Tree Hill."

He didn't give his name.

>"Why have you come here to visit me?"
>"I came because I heard that you are a spirit medium. That was the word
>I received at Teak Tree Hill. So I came here this night to give you some
>medicine. This is a special sort of fish oil that I bought for two hundred
>rupiah. The oil is to be blessed by the deity here [*sesuunan deriki*]" [at
>Jero's house].
>"Why should I do that, Honorable One?"

(It was hard for me to know if it was a man or a woman I was addressing.)

>"You are a masseuse. You can use this as massage oil."
>"But I'm not a masseuse."

I was very reluctant to admit to him that I was a masseuse. He said:

>"But I thought you could do massage?"
>"No, I can't massage, [I don't know] which are the channels [*uat*] or
>where is the stomach. No, I don't do that sort of thing." . . .

I was reluctant to give anything away. I was so confused when he arrived. I didn't
want him to know anything. I didn't want to be given the massage oil.

>"I don't know anything about those sorts of things. I can't even tell the
>difference between the parts of the body."

That's what I told him, so he wouldn't give me the oil.

>"Jero, don't be afraid. Just use this oil for massaging. You don't have to
>diagnose the illness in any detail. As long as you rub the person with this

oil the illness will disappear. You don't have to find the exact location of the disease."

But I didn't want to, and I didn't have the money. He was asking two hundred rupiah for the *kepyu pasih* oil.

"Oh, Honorable Priest, I don't even have a fraction of that amount."

I had used all my money to pay my debts.

"I don't even have a cent. Except that there are some Chinese coins here. Will you accept Chinese coins? I have a thousand in Chinese coins; in paper money I haven't got a cent. If I get money today, it's gone tomorrow. That's the way it is with me."

That's what I told him.

"Don't worry about the money now. You can try the oil out first on patients. If they get better, you can repay me later. I'll come here another time. I won't ask for the money in advance. The two hundred rupiah is only for my expenses. Here is the oil. I'll come again sometime to ask for the money. I wouldn't want to take it from you now.
"Try the oil first, so you can see how effective it is. Use it for cases of dysentery, vomiting, and the like. Mix it with water and honey."

Many of Jero's medicinal ingredients are anomalous natural objects found under unusual circumstances: a piece of petrified wood, which she refers to as "tooth of the lightning" and which appeared at the top of a palm tree following a bolt of lightning; or a strikingly gnarled, knotted piece of twig that she saw flying through the air out of a coconut tree where there had just been a flashing ball of fire. The correct use for these objects often comes to Jero as an inspiration during a healing session or in a dream. Many of her medicines contain elements of five or six such ingredients, crushed or ground in specified quantities. She often supervises the relatives of her patients, who make the medicines while she is carrying out the massage. These people may contribute the more expensive or difficult to obtain ingredients such as eggs, whiskey, limes, or spices. Jero frequently gives patients prescriptions for medicines and offerings to prepare at home.

Examples of some of Jero's commonly prescribed compound medicines follow:

*Simbuh:* a paste, mixed in the mouth with saliva, then blown onto the prescribed area of the body in a fine spray. This medicine was prescribed for a woman with protracted menstrual bleeding, in order to counteract the "coolness" within that was causing her to lose too much blood. Ingredients: roasted leaves of the orange tree, roasted nodules of turmeric, and salt mixed with soot from the kitchen fire.

*Boreh:* a liniment for weakness in the legs (e.g., during recovery from a prolonged illness). Ingredients (ground together): black rice, betel nut, young areca nut, cinnamon, nutmeg, garlic, and potato skin. This treatment is administered in conjunction with an elixir (*loloh*) containing chicken eggs, honey, orange juice, and ground *piduh* [*Impomcea pes-caprae* Roth] leaves. These two medicines are combined with a "mudpack," referred to as *lap*, that is applied to the legs. Ingredients (ground and roasted together): bark of the *pule* [*Astonia scholaris* R.Br.] tree, coconut milk, coconut, water, and onions.

*Loloh:* an elixir for sterility, given to both men and women and believed to help the growth of sperm and egg. Ingredients: mango, leaves and young tubers of the *temu* [*Curcuma*] plant, *bangle* [*Zingiber cassumunar*] leaves, laos, honey, gambier, rice whisky, and young palm leaves. The dry ingredients are ground and mixed with the liquid ones. A second elixir for sterility, taken with the first and given to both men and women, is believed to facilitate conception by enhancing bodily strength. Ingredients: meat of a young coconut, laos, orange juice, coconut oil, honey, *kap-kap* [*Piper betle*] vine, betel nut, and *piduh* leaves.

*Ubad lelengedan:* medicines for dysentery. The following ingredients are simmered together to make an elixir: young shoots of the betel plant, mature *paku* greens, *isep nanah* grass, *isep getih* grass, *jangitan* grass, sandalwood, onion, ground red rice, and extract of boiled coconut. This elixir is administered in conjunction with two "heat" and smoking treatments. In the first, the following ingredients are gently smoked in a coconut husk: onion, salt, and oil sprinkled on coals. The patient stands over or sits in front of the smoke for about two hours. In the second treatment the patient is exposed to the heat of gently roasting onion, salt, oil made from young coconuts, and *miana* [*Coleus atropurpucus* Benth].

## D. Background to the case of the clients seen on film

In 1978 Timothy Asch and I had filmed several segments of Jero's treatment of three patients. On our return trip to Bali in 1980, with Patsy Asch, we three decided a better film could be made with more intensive filming of one patient and a follow-up interview in that person's home. Although any one of the cases Jero treats is intrinsically interesting, some show better than others the complex relationship between a variety of treatments utilized by patients and their theories about the causes of illness. These considerations plus their wish to be in the film and their readiness to talk in some detail about their problems, led us to focus on Ida Bagus and his wife Dayu Putu.

Jero had been treating Ida Bagus and his wife for about six months prior to the filming, and they had consulted her dozens of times during that period. Like many of Jero's massage patients, they sought treatment fairly regularly over a long period. But, unlike most massage patients, their initial contact with Jero had been through consultation with her as a spirit medium, when they had sought the causes of Ida Bagus's seizures and of their childlessness. Ida Bagus, a clerk, had been transferred to a subdistrict office not far from Jero's home, and it was here that he learned of Jero's reputation as a spirit medium. The consultation with deities at the séance had revealed that Ida Bagus's seizures were caused by sorcery, not by a divine curse. They also suggested that the childlessness was caused by the reluctance of a reincarnating ancestor to animate the soul of a child and that a ceremony of purification was required. During the filmed massage Jero also explicates what she sees as other contributing factors in the couple's childlessness.

### Ida Bagus and Dayu Putu: biographical data

At the time of filming Ida Bagus and Dayu Putu were in their early to mid thirties and had been married for about 10 years. They both have Brahmana titles (the group from which high priests are drawn) and are distantly related. Their marriage was arranged and approved by both their families and had, it seemed, always been a source of happiness to both of them. They had lived since marriage in the *geria* (a generic term for Brahmana houseyards) of Ida Bagus's father, together with Ida Bagus's brother and sister-in-law, who were also childless. This *geria* is located in a town about seven kilometers from Jero's village.

In addition to Ida Bagus's salary and the income from a small amount of land, Dayu Putu earns extra cash by selling Balinese handicrafts that she makes or buys wholesale at the local market. She awaits customers at a scenic halt on the main road north of the town where tourist buses and limousines sometimes pause for a few minutes. Before his marriage, Ida Bagus worked as a clerk in the Malaria Control Office. In the first few years after his marriage he augmented his junior high school qualifications by undertaking extra study. These efforts landed him a better job in the Department of Education and Culture, first in the town and then in Jero's subdistrict office. He had been in the latter position for about nine months at the end of 1980. (I first became acquainted with the couple in September 1980.)

The couple not only frequently consulted Jero for treatment, but also spent many relaxed hours in her houseyard assisting with any offerings that had to be made or chatting with the people who passed through Jero's houseyard in a steady stream.

### Ida Bagus and Dayu Putu: case history

Although the main focus of the film is Ida Bagus, his case should not be discussed in isolation from Dayu Putu's. She is implicated in their childlessness and had sought concurrent treatment from Jero (prior to filming).

Ida Bagus recalls that he first started having seizures about a year after his marriage. He had never before experienced similar symptoms. Describing the attacks, Ida Bagus said:

**IB:**   The first time it happened to me I was in the bank. At first I didn't lose control, I was conscious of it happening. It was like a current, like coming into contact with an electric current. I felt myself going on and off, so that I had to get help.

**J:** Since you have been coming here for treatment, has it happened to you about once a month?

**IB:** Yes.

**J:** So, once a month. Before you came here, how was it?

**IB:** Well, it happened often. Sometimes twice a week I had an attack, in the beginning. I feel it starting here, in my left hand. It's like I've taken hold of a light bulb and got an electric shock. That's how my hand feels, and I have to get help.

**L:** Are you aware of what's happening?

**IB:** Yes, that's how I feel before I pass out.

**L:** And when you pass out?

**IB:** Well, when I pass out, I don't remember anything. According to friends who have helped me out at that time, I'm like a chicken with its head chopped off. I don't feel anything. I groan, groan, groan.

In my interview with Dayu Putu and Ida Bagus four days after the filmed massage, Dayu Putu described his attacks:

**L:** What's it like when you see one of his attacks, Dayu Putu?

**DP:** Well, I get apprehensive. I don't feel too well. When I see the illness coming on, I try to help a little. He starts to feel cold.

**IB:** That's how it is.

**DP:** When he feels cold, I loosen his clothes. After that I rub him down with mentholated oil.

**IB:** And she quickly fetches the "pill" [Jero's medicine].

**DP:** I give him the "pill" straight away.

**IB:** And also the rice-whisky mixture that we got over to the east [at Jero's place].

**DP:** And then I go and get my brother-in-law to help.

**L:** How often do you get these recurrences?

**IB:** Well, now . . .

**DP:** Seldom now.

**IB:** Only on certain days. As the Balinese say, on special days.

**DP:** It's most common on Friday, on *kliwon* Friday [a conjunction of the fifth day of the Balinese seven-day calendar and the fifth day of the Balinese five-day calendar].

**IB:** And on *kajeng-kliwon* [a conjunction of the first day of the Balinese three-day calendar and the fifth day of the Balinese five-day calendar].

**DP:** Yes, it used to happen on *kajeng-kliwon*.

**IB:** It happened on that special day.

**DP:** And it was in the evening.

The attack that stands out in Dayu Putu's memory, and that she recounts in some detail, is one that occurred while she and Ida Bagus were staying overnight at Jero Tapakan's home, during a period of treatment. By this stage Jero had identified sorcerers' demons *(babai)* present in his body as the cause of Ida Bagus's attacks; that is, he was the victim of sorcery. Ida Bagus attributed the motivation for the sorcery to jealousy of his educational qualifications and job promotions. The episode that took place in Jero's houseyard is noteworthy in Dayu Putu's estimation because it occurred in Jero's presence. Many Balinese believe that very few balians have enough spiritual power *(sakti)* to cause these demons to manifest themselves in the presence of a healer. The *babai* are thought to be afraid of such confrontations, in which the healer's superior powers might vanquish their own. Thus they are believed to remain dormant during treatment by all but the most superior balians. Dayu Putu is affirming the strength of Jero's spiritual powers as a healer when she describes how the *babai* manifested themselves while she and her husband were at Jero's home.

**DP:** Amongst all those balians [that they had consulted previous to Jero], never did Ida Bagus have an attack at their places. Only at Jero's place did he have an attack.

**L:** At the time of the attack, what did Jero do?

**DP:** It was the middle of the night. We were all asleep, including me. The first thing that happened – well, Ida Bagus has to relieve himself often. He came back from relieving himself, that's when it started. He said: "I feel pretty bad. What's happening? I think my illness is coming on." So then I called out: "Jero, Jero, come and help Ida Bagus, he has an attack coming on." Well, Jero came out, she was half-naked.

**IB:** She called her son as well.

**DP:** "Wayan," she called. "Wayan, Wayan, come and help Ida Bagus, he has an attack coming on."

**IB:** And then, I was like this: Bang! Bang! Bang!

**DP:** "Help, Ida Bagus is having an attack. I can't [restrain him]." He was resisting. He was resisting Jero's son, Wayan.

**IB:** I was grabbed by him.

**DP:** Yes, like that, held around the body. Ida Bagus struggled with Wayan. He hurt him. His relatives helped too.

**IB:** The ones in the northern houseyard.

**DP:** Yes, the ones to the north. And then the one called Rindu helped too.

**L:** What did Jero do?

**IB:** At that time?

**DP:** She got that oil.

**L:** She administered it?

**DP:** The oil.

**IB:** I wasn't aware of it . . .

**DP:** He doesn't remember. It's I who remembers. [She gave him] the oil. And then made some *simbuh* with onion in it. She told me to spray it on. [*Babai* are believed to find onion noxious.] And then . . .

**IB:** Somehow I came out of it.

**DP:** So I did it.

**IB:** And I came to myself.

**DP:** And then after that Jero gave him some potent oil [*tutuh*, usually administered through the mouth and nose, or eyes and nose]. All this at the same time, by Jero. She did everything.

**IB:** And then she asked [the *babai*] to go home [i.e., to leave Ida Bagus's body and return to the sorcerer who was their master].

**DP:** They were asked to go. But then: "I don't want to. I don't want to. I don't want to." That's what was said [by the *babai*]. "I don't want to . . . I'll go home. I'll go home. Don't do that to me. Don't do that to me." [This is the typical response of the *babai* when the healer's medicines start to vanquish them. It turns into a bargaining session where the healer usually promises to stop administering the potent medicines if the *babai* will depart their victim's body. So it is the *babai* who are conceived to be speaking at this stage, not Ida Bagus.]

**L:** Is that so?

**DP:** Yes, it was like that. Ida Bagus resisted every time he was held. He created a real scuffle. "Don't do that to me." That's how it went. But if he wasn't held up, he would just fall to the ground. He wasn't capable . . .

**IB:** Yes, that's what it was like.

**DP:** He'd fall down like this: Plop! He was so limp. That's what it was like. If he hadn't obtained treatment at Jero's place, well, nothing else . . .

**IB:** . . . would work.

**DP:** Nothing would work.

In 1980 Dayu Putu and Ida Bagus seemed to be more satisfied with the results of Jero's treatments than they had been with any of the treatment regimens they had experienced prior to consulting her. Like many people with chronic or long-term complaints, they had consulted many general practitioners, nurses, midwives, and even medical specialists, as well as many different types of balian.

**IB:** Well, I went to the one at – what's its name? – at Kepisah. That one's [balian's] opinion was that I needed calming down. What was used? Cold water.

**DP:** An elixir [*loloh*].

**IB:** It was a tranquilizing "pill," according to that one. Another one had been to Jakarta.

**DP:** And we went to Blahbatuh.

**IB:** To Blahbatuh. That one was a diviner.

**DP:** He gave an elixir. And took blood pressure, like a doctor. It was scientific, but like a balian as well.

**L:** Couldn't those other balians help you?

**IB:** No, they couldn't help.

**DP:** No.

**IB:** Not as yet.

**DP:** That is, every time we got treatment, for about six months he'd be better.

**IB:** Recovered.

**DP:** That is, if you take the time from the recovery to the recurrence. For six months, or for three months, after finishing at the balian's place – we've gone to so many balians!

**IB:** More than forty, maybe fifty.

**DP:** Fifty – even – fifty – even . . .

**L:** Did you go outside this district?

**DP:** Yes.

**IB:** We went to Kintamani, to Bukit Celeng, to the east.

**DP:** We've been all around. Wherever there are balians we've been there.

**IB:** Even the one here.

**DP:** And to one in North Bali.

**L:** Did you accompany him, Dayu Putu?

**DP:** No, not to the one in North Bali. But I accompanied him to the ones around here.

**IB:** To Peliatan.

**DP:** To – what's its name? – Labuhan Garam.

**IB:** Yes, we've been to Labuhan Garam.

**DP:** And we've been to doctors – to every general practitioner – for treatment.

**IB:** And the new ones.

**DP:** Yes, all the new doctors.

**L:** What were the opinions of those doctors?

**DP:** Epilepsy.

**IB:** Epilepsy – epilepsy grammica [Ida Bagus's pronunciation of "grand mal"].

**DP:** Grammica.

**IB:** Don't ask me what it means, it's a medical phrase.

**L:** Yes.

**IB:** But according to Jero it's called – what's its name? – *babai*.

**DP:** Yes, like . . .

**IB:** What sort of *babai* did she say? It's *babai* from sorcery.

**DP:** Yes.

**IB:** That's it. But it's also called – *babai.*

**DP:** The *babai* – well, according to the balian at Bukit Celeng, they're called *babai bikulisah.*

**IB:** They're all different . . .

**L:** What sorts of medicine did the doctors give you?

**IB:** Vitamins.

**DP:** Vitamins. What are they called? Those pills? Alinamine pills [an Indonesian brand name for vitamin B$^1$ pills].

**IB:** Tranquilizers.

**DP:** What was the name of the tranquilizers? Luminal [phenobarbitol], the most frequently prescribed was Luminal.

**IB:** Yes, that was it. Luminal.

**L:** How did you feel when you were taking the doctor's pills?

**IB:** Well, the doctor's medicine, it was only tranquilizers and tonics, that is, the vitamin pills. I didn't feel anything, it was just as usual. The reason for that is that the illness, according to the opinion of – well, the message through the spirit medium – this illness is outside the field of medicine.

**L:** What happens with Balinese treatments? Does your illness recur?

**IB:** No, not since this . . .

**DP:** Not since we've gone to Jero, there haven't been recurrences.

**IB:** No, there has been none.

**L:** And what happened when you were taking the doctors' medicines?

**DP:** There'd be recurrences.

**IB:** Yes, there'd be. . . .

**DP:** Before, there'd be recurrences, every week, or every month.

**IB:** Every two weeks sometimes.

**DP:** Yes, every two weeks.

**IB:** Sometimes three times a week.

**L:** Were you conscientious about taking those medicines at that time?

**DP:** Yes, he was conscientious.

**IB:** Yes, I was.

**DP:** Pills, injections, all the time.

**IB:** The reason is that – well, we who are officials are treated whenever necessary. [Treatment is free for government officials at the clinics.]

**DP:** Yes, that's how it is.

**IB:** But they weren't successful. Those doctors, according to their science, it's epilepsy.

**DP:** That's what the doctors call it.

**IB:** They always told me to be conscientious about taking the medicine.

It is obvious from their remarks that Ida Bagus and Dayu Putu evaluate Jero's treatments much more positively than they do those of the doctors and other balians they had previously consulted.

**L:** How do you feel, Ida Bagus, since you had the massage?

**IB:** For the last four days, there have been no symptoms, and I've felt that I have more energy. I just don't feel as if I have any symptoms – I feel calm, these last four days . . .

**L:** And before the massage?

**IB:** There were some [symptoms], for a day. That's why I went to see Jero again, because I felt bad. So I went to Jero and asked her about it. She made a "pill" for me again.

**L:** I see.

**IB:** It is a pill according to Balinese science. What's in it I don't know. Chemicals – but in the way of traditional healers. According to the doctors, they're not chemicals.

**DP:** She has an inspiration (*wahyu*).

**IB:** Yes, it's like that. She made about thirty-five. Thirty-six.

**L:** Jero Tapakan made them?

**IB:** Yes.

**L:** What are the ingredients?

**IB:** Of the pill?

**DP:** People aren't allowed to say.

**IB:** It's not allowed.

**L:** Oh, I see.

**IB:** Jero knows. She only says to me: "Eat one of these each day. If you feel a recurrence of the symptoms, the next day eat two. If you still feel a recurrence, then two days later take three at once, and so on. If it comes on for a fourth time, take four the next day." I have to keep taking them, for thirty-five days. If the thirty-five days have passed, and Jero is very busy, she may not have got around to making me some more pills.

**L:** The ingredients are Balinese medicines?

**IB:** Yes, according to Jero. She says, "My pills are different."

**DP:** But it's not allowed to name the ingredients.

**L:** Where are they made? Here or at her place?

**IB:** At her place.

**DP:** At her place.

**IB:** But she has said that they . . . contain serpent's dung (*tai naga*). But it's not allowed to speak of it. It's from a spiritual message, based on a dream, divine speech in a dream.

**DP:** I think it's a divine message.

**IB:** Yes, a divine message. Jero is told to make a cure for me. That's what's said.

**DP:** That's how the message is.

**IB:** That's why ever since I've been taking that [medicine] I have felt myself getting stronger.

**DP:** He hasn't had a recurrence since then.


During the massage, Jero talks about Ida Bagus's illness in more detail. She attributes his attacks to a form of sorcery called *babainan* in which live demons (*babai*, of which there are many named varieties, depending on the way they are bred) are introduced into the victim's body by magical means, to cause many different complaints; attacks such as those Ida Bagus is experiencing are among the most common. She rejects the medical diagnosis (epilepsy) of his symptoms.

**L:**   What's the Balinese diagnosis for Ida Bagus, Jero?

**J:**   In my opinion — well, I don't know anything, but according to my guardian deity, the Balinese diagnosis of Ida Bagus is called *babai*. "Baby" *babai (babai raré)*, "horse" *babai (babai jaran)*, that's what I think. But I don't know, it's not visible.
    Since you have been coming here for treatment, have you had an attack, Ida Bagus?

**IB:** Yes.

**J:**   Are you aware of it at the time?

**IB:** Just before the attack I'm aware of a quivering starting here in my left hand.

**J:**   When you start to run, how do you feel? Are you aware of it or not?

**IB:** I'm not aware. You, Jero, tell me that when I start to run, if I'm restrained, I get violent. But I don't remember.

**Waiting patient:** How would he know?

**IB:** That's right.

**J:**   I think that if he had epilepsy he couldn't run and speak normally. His bodily forces are strong. In his case, he just doesn't remember. The connecting channels *(uat)* are frozen, and his thoughts get agitated, the blood rises. But his blood isn't frozen. That's why he can run with such strength and not remember.

**L:**   How often are you having attacks now, Ida Bagus?

**J:**   Since you've been having treatment here? Oh, before you came here, how often were your attacks?

**IB:** Well, once a month, twice a week, I had attacks, but now?

**J:**   Since you've been coming here?

**IB:** There haven't really been any. If I feel an attack coming on, I dash over here and you help me. If it were epilepsy, that wouldn't work.

Further into the treatment, Jero again comments on the condition of Ida Bagus's *uat* while she is massaging his upper back.

> Here it's sore and tense, and here it's swollen. So I rub this way and massage toward the other side. Like smoothing a rumpled sarong. If there's damage here, it feels sore down there.

Apart from stressing the importance of the physical manipulation of the *uat* in order to realign them and to restore bodily energies, Jero also attaches great significance to the spiritual elements of her treatment and of all healing. A key concept in this regard is that of *maguruguruan*: the existence of a compatibility between healer and patient. This is thought to be not only compatibility of temperament but spiritual compatibility as well:

J: Healers and their patients must be compatible [*maguruguruan*].

IB: Yes, that's so.

J: If the spiritual energy[*bayu*] of the healer is greater than that of the patient, then the treatment will soon be effective. It's the same with all traditional healers. If the person who is ill has greater life force [*bayu*] than the balian, then they're not compatible. When the balian's life force [*bayu*] is great, and the sick person's is small, then they can quickly ask for a blessing. What's important is God's blessing, even if you're a doctor. God decides who'll get sick and who'll die. Doctors too have to be inspired by God. It's the same with traditional healers, it's still decided who will be sick and who will die. Traditional healers are inspired by God, too.

> When I think about it, the treatments of doctors and balians are the same, only it's like one is cooked and one is raw.

IB: Yes, medicine is scientific, everything is manufactured.

J: Balinese treatments are the most complex. Well, some are simple, some are complex.

IB: Yes, at the doctor's, they give you all sorts of things. Here [at the balian's] it's according to the illness.

J: When I'm ill, feeling run down, I go to the doctor, because I can't fix it myself. I get myself off to the doctor.

IB: Yes.

J: I look for the midwife,[11] or I look for the doctor.

Jero also emphasizes that the process of healing requires the spiritual co-operation of both the balian and the patient:

J: We pray together. We meditate together, because alone I am ignorant, am I not, Ida Bagus?

---

[11] Government-trained midwives often augment their incomes by establishing general practices in the afternoons and evenings.

**IB:** Yes, I join in with you.

**J:** Ida Bagus meditates strongly, and I join in because I don't know anything.

**IB:** It is you now who ask for blessing, Jero.

**J:** Yes, if you are strong enough to meditate, then I do not. When I am strong, then you do not. It works out the same.

**IB:** Yes.

Ida Bagus's and Dayu Putu's childlessness is a problem that over the past ten years has troubled them just as much as his seizures. Neither blames the other, and both have sought a variety of treatments from balians and medical personnel. In my interview with them they discussed their response to the problem.

**L:** I have another question, about your problem in not being able to have children. Jero Tapakan is treating that also?

**DP:** Yes.

**L:** What is her opinion?

**IB:** According to Jero Tapakan, Dayu Putu is fertile.

**DP:** . . . There are five of them.

**IB:** There are five — what's it called?

**DP:** Seed (*manik*).

**IB:** In Bali we call it the seed.

**DP:** I have five seeds. Before, they were small. As fine as hair that has fallen on the cement, those seeds . . . After I had some massages from Jero, the seeds started getting bigger. Only the length remains a problem.

**L:** Have you seen a doctor?

**DP:** Only a midwife.

**LC:** What did she say?

**DP:** I had high blood pressure, she said, and must visit the clinic regularly. After I went there, they said I was well. After that, I went to Balinese healers.

**L:** How many years had you been married then?

**IB:** . . . Nineteen sixty-nine.

**DP:** Nineteen sixty-nine.

**L:** How long until you started getting treatment after you were married?

**DP:** Started getting treatment? It was a year when Ida Bagus started treatment . . .

**IB:** We honeymooned [*bulan madu*] for a year . . . [Newly married couples without children are said still to be honeymooning.]

**DP:** Yes, for a year he was in good health. And after a year he started having attacks.

**L:** After you'd finished with the midwife, where did you go for balians' treatment?

**DP:** We went to Denpasar. He was called "Grandfather." He treated me regularly, every three days — for one month. Then everything was fine, there was nothing wrong, it all depended on whether there were seeds, he said.

**L:** What about the blood pressure?

**DP:** It was already normal. Then he said I was fine. He said I should look for a midwife to massage me. But I didn't. I went to another balian. A lot of my friends had been to midwives, and to doctors, to doctors who specialized in gynecology – but there was never any improvement. What's more they had a curette. It's better to consult Balinese healers.

**IB:** Although it might be better [at the doctor's], Dayu is frightened; she is frightened to have a curette.

**DP:** I am afraid of a curette.

**IB:** And they said she had high blood pressure, but she isn't thin – still, it's probably better if the doctor gives her a checkup but she is frightened of that.

**DP:** I've been everywhere . . .

**IB:** When I think about it – well, both of us – none of our ancestors were infertile. My mother had eleven children, and on her side Dayu's family had many children. So I ask myself, why don't we have any yet? I consulted my ancestors [at a séance]. I went to a spirit medium at – what's it called?

**DP:** Tegal.

**IB:** We "asked for speech" there.

**L:** What was said?

**IB:** Well, Balinese say – ah – there's an obstacle.

**L:** Was this at the medium's place?

**IB:** Yes. Ancestors wish to come back [reincarnate].

**DP:** It's his father who wants to reincarnate.

**IB:** Yes, my father wants to come back. But there's an obstacle that I don't understand. I don't know the reason.

**DP:** I keep having massages . . .

**DP:** I don't know how many balians have massaged me. There were two male balians who massaged me, no, three . . . The truth of it is, wherever I hear of one, I go.

**L:** What do you think is the connection between your illness and your childlessness, Ida Bagus?

**DP:** According to Jero Tapakan, "one is weak and one is healthy."

**IB:** That's right.

**DP:** That means one of his sperm is dead and one is alive [*spermane mati satu, bergerak satu*].

**IB:** Which means that it's weak.

**DP:** If it's dead, I can't conceive.

**L:** Did you go to the district doctor?

**IB:** Yes.

**L:** Did you have a checkup?

**IB:** Yes. It was said I needed rejuvenating. I was told to eat nourishing food.

**DP:** And so he took Hormoviton [a multivitamin tonic]. And there was a pill. What was its name? We bought it at Leba Pharmacy. . . . That was the medical treatment. I've forgotten all those pills, there were so many.

During Ida Bagus's massage, Jero also discussed the couple's infertility:

**J:** It's true you haven't been able to have children, Ida Bagus.

**L:** What's the treatment for that?

**J:** It's not important to treat that. What's important is to treat the illnesses, not the childlessness. Treat the other illnesses first . . .

**IB:** Beforehand?

**J:** . . . and then deal with the semen [*air mani*]. His semen isn't strong enough yet.

**IB:** It's still . . .

**J:** It's sluggish. In Bali we think of it like lightning. The lightning's flash isn't strong enough. It strikes, but it's weak. It strikes, but it's weak. It has to be strong to be effective.

**L:** Can you treat that by massage?

**J:** Yes, you massage to repair the connecting channels so they are taut. I can't say whether he'll recover or not. If it's his connecting channels, they can be repaired. If they're in the wrong place, if they're bunched up, they can be repaired.

**L:** In connection with their childlessness, has Ida Bagus's wife come here too, Jero?

**J:** Yes, she has. Her eggs are healthy, quite healthy, that's already fixed.

**L:** What was the result of the checkup?

**J:** Covered by fat, her eggs. I have fixed that by massage. Now she's fine, but this one is not well yet. [Many of the ideas about the physiology of reproduction probably come from observations of the anatomy of chickens, e.g., the finite number of seeds, their length, and the fact that they are covered by fat.][12] And there's one more thing, Linda. His reincarnating ancestor doesn't wish to be born yet. There are three obstacles: from his illness, from his ancestor, from his wife. Now his wife is fine. The ceremony for the ancestor has yet to be held. It's not known when the ancestor will appear, as the Balinese say. He has to ask for the ancestor's blessing.

Ida Bagus and Dayu Putu told me of their intention to perform a ceremony for the reincarnating ancestor. It was to be held at the home of a high priest in the town, a relative of theirs, and was to be an elaborate ceremony of exorcism and propitiation to purify the couple as the receptacles for an ancestral spirit and to redeem any wrongs they may have committed that

[12]  Balinese ideas about anatomy and physiology are discussed in Weck 1976.

continue to hinder the ancestor's appearance. They both expressed their hope that the ceremony would facilitate the conception of a child. The couple also reiterated their faith in Jero's treatment and their intention to keep consulting her.

Follow-up with Ida Bagus and Dayu Putu, 1982–4

In 1982 Timothy and Patsy Asch returned to Bali with a videotape of the massage footage, which they showed to Ida Bagus, Dayu Putu, and Jero Tapakan. All were delighted with the footage and expressed no objections to its content. At that time Dayu Putu still had not conceived.

In 1983 and 1984 I met Ida Bagus and Dayu Putu again. By November 1984 they still had not conceived a child. In the intervening years, they had both continued the pattern of consulting all sorts of clinicians and balians, especially those who tried a new technique or medicine. Ida Bagus was occasionally experiencing seizures. He still consulted Jero from time to time, particularly when he felt an attack coming on, but neither he nor Dayu Putu visited Jero as frequently as they had in 1980. At our last meeting in 1984 he said he was beginning treatment by a medical doctor who used acupuncture techniques. In undertaking all these treatments, his main concern was to remedy the childlessness rather than the seizures, but he also underwent treatment for the latter because he viewed the problems as linked.

Dayu Putu, too, had continued to consult both balians and clinicians in an effort to increase her fertility. Just prior to my visit in 1984 she had summoned up the courage to undergo dilation and curettage, which she had been afraid to do in 1980. She viewed this operation as a curative treatment rather than a diagnostic procedure, and she hoped that it would enable her to conceive within a few months. Dayu Putu said that the specialist told her that he could find nothing wrong with her on the basis of the D&C procedure.

When I questioned Jero about the case in 1984, she said that her advice, which she had conveyed to Ida Bagus, was that he should be consecrated as a Brahmana high priest. It was Jero's opinion that this was the ceremony that the reincarnating ancestor required before it would descend. Jero said that her diagnosis of both Ida Bagus and Dayu Putu had essentially been confirmed by the medical specialists both had consulted: She said that one specialist had told Ida Bagus that the ejaculation of his sperm was too weak; in Dayu Putu's case, the D&C had confirmed that there was no fertility problem. Ida Bagus, when asked about his intention to have a very elaborate high priest's consecration ceremony, said that he did not think that recourse would solve their problems. Although it is evident that Ida Bagus and Dayu Putu still discuss their health with Jero, there is no longer the same consensus about the causes of their afflictions as there was in 1980, when they were fully engaged in treatment with her.

## E. The language used in the massage film

Unlike the stylized, formal speech of the séance film, with its heavy use of metaphorical language, the language of the massage film is informal and colloquial, corresponding to the atmosphere of relaxed anticipation and pleasant conversation in Jero's houseyard on massage days. This is echoed in Jero's conversations with the person she is treating, who often, as in Ida Bagus's case, is well known to her. Conversation under these circumstances is not constrained by the necessity of cultivating acquaintance. Moreover, unlike clients at a séance who withhold information about themselves so as not to jeopardize the verity of the possession speech, massage clients come with health problems they are willing to discuss with anyone prepared to listen. They, like Jero, respond to everyday events going on in the house-yard around them, which can be a source of great entertainment. During the film we see an example of this when Jero engages in an animated exchange about the local priest, to the amusement of everyone around.

The most formalized speech patterns in the massage film occur at the beginning, when Jero is setting up her offering table beside the divan and asking for the blessing of the ancestors. She conducts the prayers for several minutes in a mixture of high Balinese and Kawi (see section 5I). They are similar in content to the prayers uttered before a séance, except for the invocation to the Javanese ancestors to descend and inspire her practice as a masseuse. She also greets with formality clients whom she does not know, asking in polite language where they come from and their titles. Clients known to her are likely to receive more casual greeting.

The main factor determining the form of language used by Jero and the patient during the massage is the status of the patient, as indicated by title and occupation. Jero communicates, with language and gesture, consid-erable deference toward those of gentry title or prestigious occupation such as policemen or officials, especially if they are not well known to her. Status factors affecting language become particularly salient in the case of the subject we see on film, Ida Bagus, because he has both an elevated gentry title and a job as a government official. The formality of the language with which Jero addresses him is mitigated, however, by the fact that they regard themselves as friends. He does not (as is customary toward people of lower title/rank) speak completely informally to Jero, because she is a consecrated practitioner who is treating him. I suspect, though, that they both speak a little more formally than usual because they are both conscious of being filmed. For the same reason, I too addressed Jero in more polite language than I would use in a more private interaction.

Jero sometimes has difficulty in speaking appropriately refined Balinese with clients such as Ida Bagus, as she does not know some of the elevated vocabulary used in polite address. Some Balinese words having to do with personal functions – eating, drinking, bathing, sleeping – and bodily parts are highly discriminated according to status; there may be as many as five or six gradations depending on status of speaker, status of subject, status of addressee, and context. Early in the massage film there is an example of Jero's difficulty. Jero wants to say that she has examined Ida Bagus's body, but either she does not know the correct polite word for "body" or she is nervous about an inappropriate word being recorded on the film. She uses instead a more neutral Indonesian word, *badan*, but still gropes for the right Balinese word.

**J:** I've examined his "body" [*badan*] – what's the right way to say it, Ida Bagus? May I use *badan*? I don't know the right way to address you.

**IB:** Yes, "body" [*raga*, a fairly polite word] "body" [*badan*], yes. The Indonesian is *badan*.

Thus Ida Bagus indicates that he does not mind the use of the Indonesian word, but he also provides Jero with an appropriate Balinese word.

Because relative status is also expressed in relative head height and because Jero must often have her head above Ida Bagus's to massage effectively, she is careful, especially when standing, to apologize for this breach of convention with the words: "Excuse me, Highness" (*Sugra, ratu*). This phrase is often used when she first touches the body of a titled person, another breach under normal circumstances. However, she dispenses with the latter formality when treating Ida Bagus, as she has massaged him so often.

During most of Ida Bagus's massage the participants use a mixture of familiar and polite Balinese, along with a few Indonesian words; both find this acceptable. It is usually difficult for most people to keep up a flow of very polite Balinese in what is essentially an informal situation.

# NINE

## Editorial notes on
## The Medium Is the Masseuse
PATSY ASCH

### A. Background

In 1978 Tim Asch and Linda Connor filmed Jero as she treated several patients with massage and traditional medicines. In 1980 I edited a massage film, using the most complete treatment filmed: that of a woman suffering from general aches and pains. Although the footage was beautiful, when we showed it to people we were dissatisfied for two reasons: The particular ailment of the patient was a kind that might lead a Westerner to seek a masseuse rather than one that indicated distinctive Balinese interpretations of the illness, such as sorcery or divine curse; and the film revealed little of the history of the patient or why she had sought treatment from Jero. We transferred this film to videocassette and added subtitles as an archival record but did not produce a final film. (There is a copy in the Anthropology Department at the Australian National University.)

When we returned to Bali in 1980 we decided to film another massage treatment. Tim and I met Linda at Jero's early in October but could stay only two weeks. Jero's practices as a spirit medium and as a masseuse were interrupted because she was participating in a final mortuary ceremony that involved her extended family. We were able to take Jero to a neighboring town to show her cassettes of our 1978 footage and to film *Jero on Jero* and we held several public showings of our footage of a collective cremation in Jero's hamlet, but we could not film anything else.

During those two weeks we met Ida Bagus and his wife Dayu Putu. They spent many relaxed hours in Jero's houseyard, chatting with us and helping to make the elaborate offerings necessary for the mortuary ceremony, and they accompanied Jero's extended family on a pilgrimage to many shrines on the island as did we. We learned a great deal about Ida Bagus and Dayu Putu but did not consider filming them because we felt that Ida Bagus's medical history was too complex.

Tim and I were not able to return to Jero's village until mid November, only two weeks before Linda had to return to Australia. Our first priority was to finish filming stories from Jero's life and to show people the cremation footage and record their reactions, as part of an attempt to make films that incorporated feedback. It was only in our last week that we were sure we had enough footage to film an additional massage. We discussed it with Jero while Ida Bagus was there. When he volunteered to be in the film, we decided he would be our best choice after all, because his enthusiasm and openness would be assets as we tried to show the history of a persistent illness.

Ida Bagus and Dayu are not personal names but inherited titles used as polite forms of address. "Putu" is a birth-order name such as most Balinese posses. The couple live in a town several miles from Jero's hamlet. When Ida Bagus began working in a subdistrict office of the Department of Education and Culture near Jero's house, he heard about her renown as a spirit medium. He and his wife decided to visit Jero to consult their ancestors about the source of his illness. They were told his illness was caused by sorcery, not by a divine curse. Unlike most clients who consult a medium, they decided to seek additional treatment from Jero. When we first met Ida Bagus and Dayu Putu, Jero had been treating them both for about six months.

Our earlier massage footage included a number of features that we wanted to duplicate, particularly Linda's participation. Linda was not visible in our séance footage because séances are formal events during which it would have been inappropriate for Linda to ask questions, although there had been times when Jero had asked Linda to write down the ingredients of offerings or medicines for clients who could not write. Anyone may listen to a séance, but only the petitioners and medium speak. In contrast, massages are informal social events, usually characterized by light banter in which anyone may participate. We decided it would be best to have Linda record sound and to include her in the footage in order to illustrate the way she had done fieldwork and to elicit Ida Bagus's medical history. One less foreigner would be involved, but it did mean sacrificing sound quality because Linda could not concentrate on recording while participating in the conversation.

We expect the *The Medium Is the Masseuse* to raise two kinds of questions: those about Balinese concepts and practices and those about the viewer's own concepts and practices. We hope the material provided in the film and book will stimulate people to compare Jero's ideas with their own ideas about the causes of illness, the nature of human energy, and the relationship between individual well-being and the cosmos. Interpretations of the nature of illness and health usually reveal a person's fundamental concept of the universe and of the place of human beings within it.

The paragraphs that follow go through the film chronologically. I have commented only on dialogue or images that I think might be ambiguous. The headings link the comments to specific shots in the film.

## B. Opening still shots

The opening title shot is of Jero massaging Ida Bagus's jaw. We wanted a simple image of their faces as Jero treated Ida Bagus. I photographed the second still, of Linda recording sound and Tim filming while Jero is treating Ida Bagus, during the actual filming. I included it both to show the spatial relationships between Tim, Linda, Jero, and Ida Bagus and to introduce Linda, through the credits, so that when she first appears in the film the audience will know who she is. The third still, Jero with her grandson, is taken from the end of *Jero Tapakan: Stories from the Life of a Balinese Healer* and serves to introduce Jero. The final still, from a slide of the central volcano, Gunung Agung, and the rice fields, was taken across and up the street from Jero's houseyard. It was included to give a sense of the beauty of Jero's hamlet.

## C. Preparations for a day of massage

We began filming at 9:00 a.m. on 17 November 1980. By that time seven patients had arrived, each carrying a basket of offerings. On massage days, held every third day, Jero sets up a table next to the divan on her porch where she arranges bottles of medicines and a tray of offerings (see Diagrams 1 and 2). The film opens as she brings the last of her medicines from her shrine house and arranges her offerings. The patients have set their baskets of offerings on the ledge in front of Jero so that they will be blessed when she blesses her own offerings. One of Jero's nephews, who lives in the adjoining houseyard, brings two cups of coffee from the kitchen. As he walks across the houseyard, Jero's daughter-in-law, two of her children, and a relative are visible sitting on a bench in front of the kitchen. They later joke with some of the patients. The shots of the preparations, which I cut fairly short, are included to show the informality of the situation and the way that Jero establishes rapport with her patients, epecially those who are strangers. Whenever two Balinese strangers meet, they must discover their relative social status in order to know how to speak to one another properly. This is what Jero is doing when she asks the woman from Tabanan her "seat," or title. Jero's teasing exchange about the woman's being "love-sick – hopefully" is typical of the banter that goes on at Jero's on massage day, and it is one of the reasons people enjoy coming to her for treatment.

Jero must dedicate her offerings, and those of her patients, before she can begin treatment. These prayers are similar to those at the beginning of a séance, except that Jero also asks the blessing of ancestors from the Javanese kingdom of Majapahit. Jero acquired the massage practice of a Javanese policeman (see section 8B), thereby inheriting his Javanese ancestors, who inspire her practice as a masseuse. After Jero finished dedicating the offerings, Tim asked her if the baskets could be moved from the counters so that they would not obstruct his view. Each patient took his own basket. The deities consume only the essence; the remainder of the offerings is taken home, and the edible parts are eaten.

Jero usually treats people in the order in which they come to her house-yard, and when she had finished her preparations and prayers she treated the two patients who had arrived first. Thus we had to wait about an hour until she was ready to treat Ida Bagus. The film resumes as Jero comes out of the kitchen with something to add to the medicine she then makes for Ida Bagus.

### D. Medicine for Ida Bagus

Jero spent considerable time mixing medicine, talking with Linda, and chewing areca and betel nut. I have cut this section fairly short because we wanted time to show all the major steps of massage treatment. Although the dialogue is interesting, we did not have film to cover many of the statements we wanted to include. Therefore several of the shots – those looking the whole length of the porch and the close-ups of Jero grinding – are not synchronized with the sound track but have been used as cutaways to try to create the illusion of continuous interaction. The two shots of faces – the woman in red and the priest – were included to allow time for Ida Bagus to come and sit down. I have cut a long segment in which the second patient comes out of Jero's room to receive eye drops. It is then that Ida Bagus actually sits down.

Like the tonic she prepares for Ida Bagus, most of Jero's medicines are made from commonly available ingredients using traditional recipes – brewed coffee, sugar, pepper, ginger, egg yolk – but she usually adds something special, something found in an unusual location or in connection with a dream or vision. These added ingredients are thought to lend spiritual potency to her medicines (see section 8C).

When Jero asks Ida Bagus what word to use for "body" it is probable that she is reacting to the filming. Because Ida Bagus inherited a Brahmana title, he should be addressed in the most refined Balinese vocabulary possible, but over the months they have known one another he and Jero have slipped into less formal exchanges. Terms for the human body are the most sensitive and have the most options; Jero may have forgotten which is considered the most refined and therefore the one she would like to use in the film. It is increasingly common for Balinese to slip into Indonesian when status ambiguity or uncertainty makes it difficult to speak Balinese (see section 8E).

When Ida Bagus talks about paying for past sins, he means spiritual sins such as neglect of ritual; "paid in past lives" refers to previous lives in the chain of reincarnation. This diagnosis of his illness came from consulting deities and ancestors through Jero and through other spirit mediums who were possessed during séances.

**L:** When did you "ask for speech" here [from deities and spirits]?

**IB:** It would be – about six months ago.

**L:** What did the deity say?

**IB:** My illness is caused by a sorcerer.
A divine curse is not involved.
The deity is satisfied. I've paid for my sins in the past.

**J:** He has paid in past lives.
Now he has no sins.
He's lucky that he's living. He's unlucky that he's sick.

In this segment of the film Jero asks one of the waiting women for some betel nut, laughing as she does so. Quids of "betel nut" (*base*), consisting of betel leaves, areca nut, gambier, and lime, sometimes with the addition of tobacco, are commonly chewed throughout Indonesia. The mildly narcotic mixture is used primarily by older people who have not replaced the habit with cigarettes. Balinese include betel nut in some offerings. Jero probably laughs because of the filming; she knows Westerners do not chew betel nut.

## E. The massage

Jero massages all patients in the same sequence: (1) the chest and stomach; (2) the arms and hands; (3) the back; (4) the feet and legs, followed by adjustment of the spine; and (5) the neck, temple and jaw (see Linda's detailed account of the massage in section 8C). She may adjust the amount of time spent on each area, depending on the patient's illness and the feel of each set of muscles and tendons. During treatment of Ida Bagus, Jero is occasionally distracted by conversation with Linda, but her sequence is not altered.

As Jero begins to massage Ida Bagus's stomach, using oil to lubricate her hands, she jokes about his taking off his clothes. Both the joking and the reference to doctors are undoubtedly in reaction to being filmed. This is one of the reasons I included another still shot of Tim and Linda filming; I wanted the audience to be aware of their influence on the social interaction and to see how they were working.

Further joking and a period of silence were cut. There is a disjuncture in the film dialogue at this point because Tim was changing film rolls. The new roll begins as Jero is explaining to Linda that the spiritual energy, the life force (*bayu*), of a balian must be stronger than that of the patient, in order to overcome his illness (see section 8C). During the close-up of Jero's hands as she massages Ida Bagus's stomach, image and dialogue are approximately synchronized.

The words that we have translated as "cooked" (*lebeng*) and "raw" (*matah*) are the same words used in reference to the preparation of food, but they also can be used to refer to maturity or immaturity. ("When I think about it, the treatments of doctors and balians are the same, only it's like one is cooked and one is raw.") We chose "cooked" and "raw" because they seemed closest to Jero's meaning and because we found the parallel with Lévi-Strauss amusing.

Jero's frequent assertion, in all the films, of her own ignorance is both an expression of the general view that the deities and spirits direct human existence (the healer is simply a vehicle) and a way of absolving herself of all responsibility for her treatment or for what is said when she is possessed. Her guardian deity guides her practice as a masseuse and as a spirit medium.

Elsewhere Jero says the deities and spirits revealed that *babai* had entered Ida Bagus's connecting channels. *Babai* are sorcerers' demons, little creatures who enter the body and obstruct the *uat*, the connecting channels — including blood vessels, tendons, sinew, and nerves, as well as intangible connections related to the flow of energy. In footage we have cut from *Jero Tapakan: Stories from the Life of a Balinese Healer*, Jero attributes her husband's death to *babai*; thus his illness, too, was caused by sorcery.

The physical strength with which Jero massages can be seen most clearly while she is massaging Ida Bagus's arms and hands. It is common for patients to groan with pain as she manipulates certain muscles, and yet I can attest that one does feel relaxed and limber once she has finished; perhaps it is the relief of knowing the treatment is over.

When Jero refers to epilepsy, it is not because she thinks Ida Bagus's illness is similar to epilepsy but because he had reported that several doctors had diagnosed his illness as epilepsy. His symptoms do not seem to her to be those of an epileptic. She argues that if he had epilepsy her treatment would not prevent his attacks; they had occurred several times a week, but after he began treatment they all but ceased.

Jero's discussion of Ida Bagus's semen reflects her concept of *bayu* (life force, vital energy). She tries to strengthen her patients' *bayu* by physical and spiritual treatment.

Linda has suggested that Jero's notions about female eggs may derive from her knowledge of the anatomy of chickens: a series of eggs of increasing size, lying next to one another.

There is another break in the filming between Jero's statement that Ida Bagus has to ask for the ancestors' blessing and her description of the massage. The title, "If there's damage here, it feels sore down there" reflects the view, common among practitioners of massage in the West as well as

Asia, that the location of pain does not necessarily indicate the point of injury or the point where treatment should be applied.

Placing one's feet on another person's body, particularly a person of high social rank, is normally an extreme breach of etiquette. Jero usually apologizes, except to patients she has treated many times, such as Ida Bagus.

## F. Jokes about the priest

The priest had been sitting at the foot of the divan throughout the massage. It was our impression that he had come in order to be in the film. Jero asked him to move so that she could massage Ida Bagus's feet. It is Jero's daughter-in-law who begins teasing Jero about not treating the priest. She is the woman sitting across the houseyard, seen in several shots during this exchange. Jero is not always tactful, particularly toward people like her daughter-in-law. Here she gets irritated, perhaps at the implied criticism, but then shifts the joke onto the priest. When Jero says, "He came and didn't bring anything," she probably means he didn't bring any offerings: Patients seeking treatment always bring offerings, because the deities and spirits are thought to be responsible for healing. I suspect Jero was annoyed because the priest kept hanging around while we were staying with her; hence the accusation that he was not minding his own business: "If he weren't a priest he'd be accused of just wandering about." This type of banter is typical and seems to be enjoyed by almost everyone. We showed it because we were afraid that by including Linda and focusing much of the conversation on the history of Ida Bagus's illness the film would not provide a sense of the typical atmosphere of Jero's houseyard on a massage day.

While the joking continues, Jero massages Ida Bagus's hips and then arranges his body carefully so that when she pulls on his arm, with her foot holding his hip down, a cracking sound comes from the joints in his spinal vertebrae. Western chiropractors make similar adjustments to the lower spine.

## G. End of treatment

Little of the massaging of Ida Bagus's neck and head was filmed. Instead, Tim filmed the people sitting across the courtyard so we would be able to see those previously heard joking about the priest. Jero's conversation with the woman lapsed. Her comments about the channels to the eyes and those around the jaw having hard lumps were in response to Linda, who had asked why she was massaging the face. Silence followed.

When Jero finished massaging Ida Bagus, she began to mix his medicine. Here we show a close-up of the bottles of medicine that actually was recorded at the beginning of the day. Tim resumed filming just as Jero broke an egg and threw away the white, placing the yolk in the medicine she had begun to mix earlier in the film. Most patients find the taste of the medicine unpleasant and, like Ida Bagus, grimace as they swallow it. The eye drops are an oil that causes eyes to tear for about five minutes. This treatment is consistent with Jero's aim to eliminate any obstructions in the patient's connecting channels (*uat*). Ida Bagus's treatment consisted of a thorough massage, a tonic, eye drops, and a liniment.

The scene ends as Linda asks Jero about the origin of the liniment. Jero's apparent reluctance to answer probably shows that she is getting bored with Linda's questions. Linda has asked the question for the film record and Jero knew that Linda already knew the answer. The source of medicines, even mystically powerful ones such as the oil from a white snail shell, is not considered confidential information in Bali.

### H. Interview with Ida Bagus and Dayu Putu

We wanted to include footage of Ida Bagus and his wife at their home, but we were unable to visit them until the day before Linda left Indonesia. As we arrived it began to drizzle. The sky got darker and darker, and we did not have any lights. We waited more than four hours and finally, an hour before sunset, it suddenly cleared enough for Tim to get an acceptable exposure on the hillside above the trees surrounding their house. Ida Bagus and Dayu Putu suggested we film in a small, open pavilion, and we all rushed up there and began immediately, fearing we would not have time before the light faded. The only place that was light enough was right at the edge of the platform, so Tim and I could not sit inside with them, which meant Tim was not filming from an advantageous angle. Our purpose in filming this interview was to allow audiences to compare Ida Bagus's and Dayu Putu's interpretation of their condition with Jero's and to allow the couple to relate the history of their problems in more detail. We included most of their discussion of their childlessness because that had not been discussed in detail during the massasge. We were tempted to include Dayu Putu's description of Ida Bagus's illness, but it was very long (see section 8D for Linda's translation of this account).

The interview was difficult to edit because what interested me most was the interaction between Ida Bagus and his wife, the way their speech over-lapped and the way they finished each other's sentences or repeated each other's phrases. To capture these features one needed to see uninterrupted interaction. We filmed about 16 minutes but felt that about five minutes of their conversation was all that we could include and still keep the right balance between films of the massage and of the interview. We decided to limit our films to 30 minutes so they could be incorporated into lectures or used to stimulate discussion.

In a number of places I was forced to use cutaways of Dayu Putu and Ida Bagus in order to bridge a gap when I cut dialogue. These cutaways are fairly obvious. At other times, I simply used a jump cut, and that too is obvious.

The final shot in the film, under the credits, is a continuation of the last shot taken during the massage. We included it to show that Jero began treating her next patient in the same way that she had begun her treatment of Ida Bagus, even though the woman was suffering from quite different symptoms. Linda is continuing to ask Jero about where she found the white snail shell and the curative oil used in Ida Bagus's liniment.

# FILM SYNOPSIS

Linda Connor and Jero Tapakan.

JERO Tapakan tells Linda Connor about her life before she became a healer, over 25 years ago. She begins with an account of her family's extreme poverty that culminates in her decision to leave her husband and children and to wander as a peddler rather than seek a "wrong" death by drowning herself. Jero then describes some of the mystical experiences she had in North Bali, experiences that finally led her to recognize her own "madness."

In the footage taken two years later, Jero describes her return home and the diagnosis of "blessed madness," which was repeated through the many spirit mediums she and her husband consulted. The deities and spirits proclaimed that she could be cured only if she held a consecration ceremony and became a healer. Although she eventually held the ceremony and reluctantly received clients, Jero says it took over ten years before she was able to repay her debts from the money she earned as a spirit medium.

Jero's son, Wayan Data, is brought into a brief discussion about signs which indicates that he might inherit Jero's practice as a masseuse. The film concludes with a ceremony for Wayan Data that will permit him to work in sacred places as a carpenter. This ceremony is an important step in Wayan

Data's purification but does not in itself ensure that the deities will choose him to become a healer.

Although Jero's account is unique and she is a person with a vibrant personality, the themes of poverty, mysticism, madness, and humility toward her calling are common elements in the autobiographical accounts of many Balinese healers. Jero's narrative style frequently resembles the style of traditional Balinese folktales and dramatic performances.

A 26-minute, 16mm, color film by Timothy Asch, Linda Connor, and Patsy Asch
Available on videocassette from Cambridge University Press
Available on 16mm film from Documentary Educational Resources
5 Bridge Street, Watertown, Mass. 02172, USA

# TEN

# *Ethnographic notes on* Jero Tapakan
## LINDA CONNOR

## A. Background to the stories

Life history material provides a way for anthropologists to understand the social reality of peoples they study from a personal perspective. When people recount incidents from their lives in a storytelling mode, they select information they regard as important rather than provide answers shaped by questions considered important by the investigator. Data from life histories provide us with insights into both the idiosyncratic aspects of a subject's personality and life situation and the social and cultural forces that set constraints on key life choices.

Biographical material was important in developing my understanding of the place of balians in Balinese society. I worked with about 60 balians, and early in these acquaintances I discussed with each one how he or she first took up the vocation. These biographies provide valuable insights into the personalities and aspirations of balians as well as into the social processes in which they were involved.

The story of Jero Tapakan stands apart from many others I recorded, not so much by any extraordinary qualities inherent in it as by the wealth of detail, a feature attributable to the long period of time over which I collected the information. The incidents were enlivened by Jero's obvious enjoyment in relating them and by her vibrant personality and talents as a raconteur. She was the balian with whom I established the strongest relationship during my fieldwork. Although there were several balians in the district whom I visited at least once each week for many months, I was Jero Tapakan's neighbor and associated almost daily with her and her family. My knowledge of her life is derived from many anecdotes told to me by Jero herself and by her friends and relatives, as well as from a series of discussions, each lasting one or two hours, that I tape-recorded on five occasions during my first field trip (October 1976–October 1978) and on one occasion during my second field trip in 1980. The three filmed sessions compose only a small proportion of the material I collected on Jero's life. These filmed sessions, and those recorded on tape, took place in Jero's houseyard, usually on the verandah of her sleeping pavilion (*gedong*; see Diagram 1). On most of these occasions members of Jero's family and neighbors sat nearby to listen to all or part of the story, as Jero is a compelling and amusing speaker.

It was Jero's wish that I should formally record her story, and she encouraged Tim Asch and me to film her as she recounted it. A grateful client had once offered to write down her biography but had so far not taken the opportunity. Most villagers resisted any attempts to formally elicit their life stories on the grounds that their lives were ordinary and not worthy of note, but Jero, like many balians, felt that she had had an extraordinary life. She expressed regret that so few people knew about the sufferings she and people like her had endured, both as a poor peasant woman and as a balian. For Jero, as for many balians, her experiences are a charter of her professional qualifications, which receive popular ratification in the retelling.

### B. Literature, oral traditions, and Jero's life story

In Balinese literary, narrative, and dramatic traditions the life story figures largely as the recounting of a series of epic incidents in the lives of legendary heroes. Jero's account shares the same basic concerns as these forms. Chronicles (*babad*) frequently include accounts of the mystical adventures of founding ancestors of descent groups, including periods of isolation, privation, and wandering preceding divine inspiration about the course of action.[1] Although Jero cannot read these manuscripts, she is familiar with the stories they relate, which are frequently enacted in a variety of dramatic genres, particularly *topeng* (mask drama), performed as part of many ritual events. Important temple ceremonies often include *mabasan* sessions in which classical texts read aloud by one participant are rendered into vernacular Balinese by another. Jero cites her own power to heal as a trait inherited from one of the earliest ancestors of her own descent group (Pasek Pulesari) who, a *babad* recounts, had many mystical experiences while wandering alone in a forest. Jero would have heard most of this story at *mabasan* sessions in her descent group's temples.

Jero's account of her past is suffused with a mythical time scale such as pervades the *babads*. She neither relates the events of her life in strictly chronological order nor presents them in an everyday time scale. The intervals between significant happenings collapse, with rarely any narrative indication of the length of time that has elapsed. During the telling of important events, time appears to stand still so that the listener has little knowledge of (and is presumed to have even less interest in) the actual duration. For example, when Jero first recounted her wanderings in the forest my impression was that her divine encounters had occurred over a period of months. Many weeks later I discovered, quite by accident, that the whole

[1]  See Worsley 1972.

journey had occupied just half a day! Chronological indicators, when offered by the subject, are personalized and often imprecise – for example, "before the Japanese came"; "when I was a young girl"; "after a long time." My attempts to elicit a more precise time scale were among the questions that Jero impatiently dismissed.

Structurally and thematically, Jero's story (and those of other balians) also lies within the oral tradition of Balinese folktales (*satua*). The *satua* is not a prerogative of either gentry or commoners, and it is transmitted by literate and illiterate alike. It is of secular and domestic significance rather than public entertainment, and it does reflect, perhaps more than any other genre of oral or written literature, the way of life of the peasantry.[2]

*Satua* generally relate a series of incidents concerning one or several individuals. The narrative may be arranged in a variety of sequences by linking passages, any of which may be simplified or elaborated by the teller. This structuring is particularly evident in the way in which Jero tells her life story. To refer to it in the singular as a "story" is misleading, for it consists of a series of significant incidents told on separate occasions, all having relevance to her major theme: her induction and practice as a balian.

The content of Jero's story also shows parallels with the *satua* genre. The simple characters of folktales, servants and clients of the powerful, are often to be found wandering in the forests where strange circumstances befall them. Nothing is ever what it seems in the forest, an eerie liminal zone between socialized human space and the supernatural realm. In her story, Jero elaborates at great length on the significance of her strange experiences when as an itinerant hawker she became lost in the forest. Her sojourn into this liminal zone represents a turning point in her life. She later resolves to return home and eventually becomes consecrated as a balian.

Because of their entertaining qualities and because they are usually told in the houseyard at night after a day's work, adults as well as children are drawn to listen to the storyteller. The language used is simple and everyday. Jero uses familiar forms of Balinese to relate her story, using polite Balinese only when she is putting words into the mouth of one of her characters for whom such language would be appropriate. She often speaks the parts of the characters as if she were an actress in a play. The adoption by the narrator of the first-person role is a common feature of *satua* style.

At frequent junctures in the narration, especially after an interruption or diversion, Jero returns to the main flow with formulaic phrases like "and after that" (*suba lantasanga sekéto*) or "after a long time" (*makelo makeloné*). This is a common feature of *satua* narration. Another characteristic of the style of *satua* narration is the conclusion of a significant passage with a

---

[2] More detailed information about *satua* can be obtained in Raechelle Rubinstein, "Satua Pan Balang Tamak: A Balinese Folktale" (B.A. thesis, Sydney University, 1977).

summary of its moral import. Jero frequently uses this technique. For example, when speaking of the period of poverty and suffering before she became a healer, Jero says:

J:    I repaid the debts only after I became a medium. I remember how badly I felt. Nobody helped us then. So now I feel I have an obligation. If anybody comes here to ask for a loan, I can't refuse them. I know how hard it is to have to borrow. It doesn't matter what they ask for, coffee or anything, I can't refuse them. I don't get angry at them, but other people do.

The narrative is also enhanced by Jero's own individual style of storytelling. She is a raconteur and uses rhetorical devices (repetition, questions, paraphrasing) extremely effectively. She is also creative in her use of metaphor, as some of the passages translated below indicate. But perhaps the most interesting parts of Jero's stories are attributable to the rich texture of moods she is able to construct through gesture, facial expression, and changes in her tone and voice and style of speaking. Many of these qualities are lost in the translation, but they can be appreciated when Jero is seen on camera. It is worth remarking in this context that almost all of the narrative that Jero has been exposed to in her lifetime has been presented as performance rather than read from manuscripts.

## C. The setting

Jero has lived all her life in a rural hamlet (*banjar*) in a district (*kabupaten*) of South-Central Bali. Jero's hamlet is one of seven in the administrative village (*desa dinas*), with a total population of approximately 4,000 in 1980. The *desa dinas* has an elected head (*prebekel*) who, with the hamlet heads (*kelian dinas*), is the local representative of the national government. In the everyday lives of the inhabitants of Jero's hamlet, the customary village (*desa adat*), a ritually cooperating group with responsibility for temples as well as for many local religious and civic affairs, is more important than the *desa dinas*.

The hamlets of Jero's village are distributed north to south along a ridge (elevation, approximately 1,000 meters) on the slope of the second-largest mountain on the island, spanning the border where the last wet-rice fields give way to the dry fields of the cooler, drier mountain climate (see Diagram 3). Seventy percent (353 hectares) of village land is dry field (*tegalan*), and 30 percent (161 hectares) is wet-rice land (*sawah*). The land here compares unfavorably with the lusher, more fertile expanses of the coastal plains and foothills of South Bali. Thirty percent of families own no land at all and rely on sharecropping arrangements as a major contribution to subsistence. Most of the small landholdings are not sufficient to support a family, so that sharecroppers and small landowners alike are forced to seek other employment.

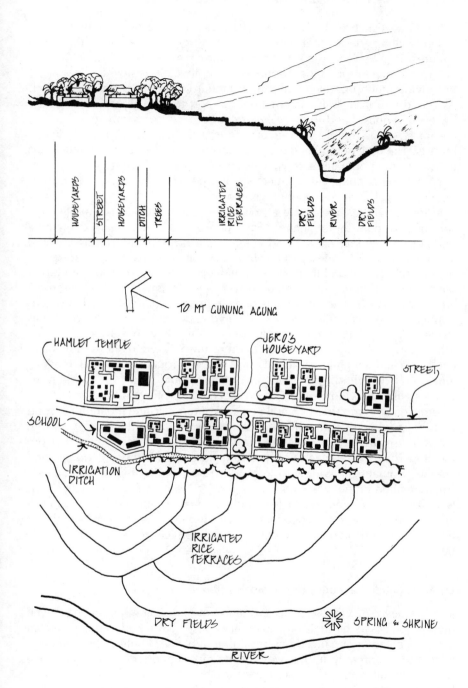

Diagram 3. Plan and section of Jero's neighborhood.

Census statistics for 1976 reveal that at least 10 percent of the inhabitants of Jero's village derive their primary income from sources other than agriculture – in government service, manufacturing, trade, transport, or tourism. The rate of expansion of these sources of employment is slow and not likely to provide much improvement in the standard of living of the population. As one drives from Bali's international airport to Kuta Beach, then to the town of Denpasar and to the elegant coastal resort of Sanur, one can see the taxis, shops, hotels, and entertainments associated with the influx of tourists. The flow of foreign dollars is uneven, however, and very little finds its way to the populations of villages far from the main centers of tourism. Jero's village is about 60 kilometers from the southern coast, and opportunities for gain are correspondingly remote.

In Jero's hamlet, houses are arranged on a north–south axis along each side of two main thoroughfares. Each houseyard (*pakarangan*) contains a number of sleeping, eating, and ceremonial pavilions as well as a house temple (common Balinese: *sanggah*; polite Balinese: *pamerajan*) for patrilineally related kin and their wives (usually parents, married sons and their wives and children, plus unmarried sons and daughters) (see Diagrams 2 and 3, pp. 84–5). The inhabitants of each houseyard are divided into economically separate units (*kuren*) for everyday purposes, each of which has its own kitchen. The *kuren*, or smallest economically viable group, is usually a husband, wife, and unmarried children. (In polygynous households it is each wife and her children. Ideally, the husband rotates between kitchens.) Jero now lives with her married son, his wife, and their four children, as well as with the widow of one of her deceased brothers-in-law.

Jero's daughter married several years ago (to a patrilineal parallel second cousin) and now lives in a house in the southern part of the hamlet. Within Jero's houseyard her son, his wife, and their children occupy the western pavilion (*bale dauh*), Jero occupies the northern pavilion (*gedong*), and another woman, the widow of Jero's deceased brother-in-law, occupies a small pavilion to the west of the *gedong* where she cooks as well as sleeps (see Diagram 2). Since 1979 Jero and her daughter-in-law have shared a kitchen because Jero's preoccupation with her practice does not allow her time to buy and prepare food, nor is it economical to do so for just one person.

## D. An expanded account of the stories filmed

Jero has been selective in the presentation of her biography. She has given most emphasis to the trials preceding her consecration and to incidents that have validated or enhanced her position as a balian. I believe her selection is governed primarily by her view of the most important events that have shaped her life and, to a lesser extent, by her knowledge of my interest in her vocation as a balian.

In this section, I have interspersed translations of segments of Jero's stories with discussion intended to clarify and enrich the account. The lengthy translations that follow supplement the brief excerpts that make up the film by providing a more complete and detailed picture of the development of Jero's vocation. The translated material is taken not only from filmed sessions but from other tape-recorded sessions as well. I begin with a brief summary of Jero's early life.

Jero was born in early 1930s in a South-Central Balinese village, the same one she resides in now. At the age of about 17 she married her patrilateral parallel cousin, who was about 19 at the time. Jero recalls that she was reluctant to marry the youth — indeed, she was reluctant to marry at all at that time — but was coerced by her parents. She said she had previously suffered a period of emotional confusion, which was attributed to the sorcery of a rejected suitor. Her family feared there might be a recurrence of such episodes (referred to as *babainan*) if their daughter did not marry as soon as possible. The boy's parents also pressured Jero, declaring that there were too many sons and not enough daughters in the family and that they needed a female to help look after their house. Jero, looking back on that period of her life, says that she was very gullible and easily influenced. However, she does not regret her marriage with her husband, which was mutually supportive throughout many years of privation.

The houseyard Jero now inhabits is immediately to the south of the one where she grew up. After some years of marriage she and her husband moved alone into the present houseyard and built the pavilions themselves. Jero's husband had inherited several small plots of not very fertile land from his father: two irrigated rice fields and two dry fields suitable only for co-conuts and sweet potato. The productivity of the latter fields has been improved in recent years by Jero's son, who planted clove trees. The land amounts to about two-thirds of a hectare in all, not enough to meet the family's yearly subsistence needs.

During her early marriage, Jero worked as a petty trader in the local village market and at the side of the road. She had had little experience outside the village. At the age of 9 or 10, she had been sent as a servant to work for several months in a gentry household, in a small center of Dutch administration about 25 kilometers from her hamlet. When the Dutch suddenly evacuated the island, under threat of Japanese invasion, Jero was sent home. During the Japanese occupation she lived with her family in the village, and she vividly recalls the harshness of the Japanese regime. All valuables, clothing, and surplus foods were seized, and those villagers who hoarded or were disrespectful to the Japanese were summarily executed or physically mutilated. Jero recalls this time as one of great fear and misery. By comparison, the arrival of the Allied forces was welcomed, and the soldiers' generosity and good humor were much admired.

Jero married in the early 1950s, not long after Indonesian independence was declared. Although she cannot recall a time when she and her husband were not poor, when her children were born (three in all, two sons and a daughter, born between about 1952 and 1958) the debts began to reach unmanageable proportions. Jero acknowledges that times were hard for everyone after the war and during the protracted struggle for Indonesian independence, but she is emphatic that she was worse off than most of the people in her hamlet. This she attributes to the series of illnesses she suffered, which often prevented her from working and were directly related to her becoming a balian.[3]

J:  My husband worked in the fields. We'd just get ahead and then we'd be in debt, again and again. We were always hungry. We worked hard. We had fifteen coconut trees. Every time they bore fruit, it would disappear. We had to borrow to get food to eat.

L:  Whom did you borrow from?

J:  We borrowed from anyone willing to lend. It didn't matter whether they were relatives or not, as long as they were willing. It was the only way for us to survive then, by borrowing.
Now I cry when I remember those times. The children never had enough to eat. We had sweet potatoes, we couldn't afford rice. Then my husband bought me one little packet of rice from the foodstall. As soon as I opened it, the children came and sat in front of me. They were still tiny. I divided it up so they could have some. My husband was angry that I did so. He went and bought me another one on credit. Even one packet of rice, we had to get it on credit! He made the children a toy motor car and sent them out in the road to play with it. Then, when the house was empty, he gave me the rice.

Jero's earnings, like those of most rural women, were crucial to the survival of the household. More affluent households may recover rapidly from slight misfortunes because of their greater flexibility in deploying their resources. But households that exist at a subsistence level may be crippled for many years by a poor harvest or sickness.

J:  I borrowed money at a high rate of interest, and I set up a stall selling coffee, near the bridge to the east of our village, where the road starts up the hill. But I got sick again. We used up all the money I borrowed when I couldn't work. The debts started piling up again. I went everywhere looking for the right medicine.

L:  What was wrong with you at that time?

J:  It was as though I were deaf and dumb, my eyes were sore. I was like that for

---

[3]  We have placed a vertical line down the left-hand margin to indicate dialogue included in the film. Of course, the translation is expanded in this version, because there are not the time constraints of subtitling.

a month and seven days. . . . I couldn't hear anything. . . . Then I recovered from
that illness. We had a lot of debts, from the time I was sick, paying for the
cures. We borrowed anywhere we could. Then I set up a stall at the cock fights,
wherever I thought there'd be some business. . . . I followed the crowds everywhere. Every time I started to make a profit, I'd get sick. . . . I'll pass over a few
incidents at that time, so we'll get up to the time when I went mad.
I'd get sick, I'd get into a lot of debt. I'd have to buy my trade goods on credit.
Then I'd get better again, when the debts were enormous.

Each time Jero fell ill she had to give up her trading activities, and the
family's debts grew. At the time, she recalls, the cycle of illness and in-
debtedness seemed like unwarranted misfortune. Now she interprets these
events as signs of her calling as a balian and of the inappropriateness of
trading as an occupation. She also recounts that these illnesses put her in
closer contact with the spiritual world, particularly through her dreams.
Many Balinese, especially healers, attempt to decode the messages in their
dreams, which are considered a means of communication with spiritual
forces. As Jero recounts in one passage, sometime the cure for illness can
be conveyed in a remembered dream. The most striking description of a
dream message prior to Jero's consecration comes in the following passage,
which we did not include in the film because of its length and complexity.
The dream takes place in a mystical landscape through which Jero moved.
In retrospect, Jero has no difficulty in interpreting the significance of the
dream.

Jero begins the story of the dream by recalling her illness and suffering at
that time.[4]

**J:**   Little by little I repaid the debts [which had accumulated from her previous
illness] until finally they were all paid off. Then I got sick again!

**L:**   What sort of sickness?

**J:**   I was constipated. I couldn't urinate. My stomach was huge. I tossed and turned.
I was delirious. I was swollen, inflamed inside.

**L:**   Could you walk?

**J:**   No, I couldn't walk. I traded at the side of the road here. Then we went to a
spirit medium to ask advice, the Balinese way. . . . The diagnosis was that somebody had asked me for a loan. They wanted to buy some rice. But they didn't
get it [from me]. It was that person who cursed me. It was true, there was
someone who asked to borrow money. I didn't have any. So they cursed me.
. . . My stomach was swollen.

We went to the spirit medium at Sema Agung. But he couldn't cure me. I was
still writhing with pain. We went to the healer at Tempidan, but that one couldn't
help. I was in pain. He gave me an enema. Then we went to Tulisan, but that

---

[4]   This is not the same version of the dream as appears in Connor 1982*a*, pp. 40–6. This is
a later version, which Jero retold especially for the filming.

one couldn't help either. They wanted to take me to the hospital, but I wouldn't go. I thought I was going to die. I said I didn't want to be taken everywhere in search of a cure. I didn't have any money, and I was in debt. I said:

"The best thing is when I die, borrow five silver coins to use for the mortuary offerings. If I go to the hospital, and I die there, a lot of money will be spent and there will be no way to redeem the debts."

The illness couldn't be cured, I was surely going to die. There were constant pains in my stomach . . .

I was tossing, turning, writhing. I would "forget," then "remember," "forget," then "remember," like that [i.e., lose consciousness and regain it repeatedly].

**L:** You looked as if you were pregnant?

**J:** Yes. I couldn't urinate, and I was constipated, for a month and seven days. Then I had a dream. I dreamt that I was summoned to court. The headman from my village came looking for me. He called my name:

"Men Jata, you are summoned to Peladan, to the law court, to be tried. This is a summons. If you are proved guilty, you will be imprisoned immediately. If you are not guilty, you will be freed. You can't postpone the trial, it must be today."[5]

So I had to go. I had no clothes, Linda! I didn't have time to fix my sarong. I was dizzy and swaying. So in the dream I set off. I set off; my hair was loose. I thought about how embarrassed I would be later at the court. But at home everybody was weeping for me. They regarded me as dead. But I was still dreaming! When we reached the crossroads to the south, there was a "relative" [*nyama*].[6]

"Where are you going?"
"I'm going to Peladan."
"What are you going to Peladan for?"
"I was summoned to court by the headman."
"What have you done wrong?"
"I haven't done anything wrong, as far as I know."
"Well, in that case come with me to the south."

We went southward, toward the cemetery. But it looked like a palace. A very grand palace . . .

Then we came to three lakes. One was of steaming water. One was muddy. And one was blue and clear. My "brother" left me. I didn't know who he was. He told me that he was my "brother," but I didn't know anything about it.

"Just stay here. Someone is looking for me over to the east" [he said].

Then a policeman came along in the dream. A military policeman. He approached me.

---

[5]   "Men Jata" ("mother of Jata") is a pseudonym for Jero's teknonymous name, by which she was addressed before becoming a consecrated practitioner.
[6]   See Jero's interpretation of the identity of this "relative" or "brother," later in this section.

"Where is your letter? Have you paid for the ticket? If you have a ticket, you may come here! If not, you may not!"

I didn't have a ticket. So I wasn't allowed to stay there.

"Who brought you here?" [he asked].
"I came with my brother."
"Who is this brother?"
"I don't know."

Then he brought out a book. He turned the pages while holding the book.

"Live people aren't allowed here! [he said]. Go home!"

I was told to go home.

"I don't want to. My brother will be looking for me."
"Are you game to try this water?"
"Yes, I'm game."
"If it's hot, will you bathe in it?"
"Yes."

I really wasn't game to bathe in the water. He stirred the water up, until it was bubbling and overflowing. "I'm not game, I'm not game," [I thought].

After he finished, it settled and became clear again. Then I was escorted to the palace [Dalem] into the place called *jero* in everyday life.[7] I went to watch the *legong* dancers, little girls the same size as that one (*points to child in her yard*) were dancing. Their bodies were swaying. I wanted to go in and have a look around. But I was asked for my ticket. I didn't have one. I would have paid anything to get in. Then I was chased out by some huge dogs. I ran away, looking for my "brother." I ran toward home. I was reunited with him. Then things went black again; everything spun around. At the crossroads near the marketplace he pushed me toward my house.

Then I woke up to hear the sounds of everybody crying.

**L:**   They thought you were dead?

**J:**   Yes, except that I was still not completely cold. Everyone was crying. I had seen them all at the pond [in the dream] and they had been laughing. They had only been laughing at the pond, but here they were, every one of them, with eyes swollen from crying.

**L:**   What is the meaning of that dream? Is it a dream or something else?

**J:**   I felt like I was dreaming, but to all external appearances I was dead. Everyone here said I was dead. To living people like you, Linda, I appeared dead, but I felt like I was dreaming. That's the reason why if somebody dies one shouldn't be sad. They're dreaming.

**L:**   Well, what does it mean?

**J:**   I wasn't guilty of any wrongs; I wasn't in the wrong. That's the reason I was sent home. It was a curse [*pemali*] over me, but I eventually returned to the

---

[7]  As well as being a term of address as described in section 6B, a second and related meaning of *jero* is "inside," especially in reference to the space inside the precincts of gentry palaces.

crossroads. The crossroads was where I returned to the everyday world. Whoosh! Like that. Later I was given instructions for a recipe. I was told to find some leaves – *krepetan* leaves. Old "Grandfather," a nearby balian, found the leaves and made the medicine that cured me. The ingredients were *krepetan* leaf, garlic, coconut milk, and coconut water, simmered together. Later a lot of pus came out of my anus, with the feces. It smelt terrible, like a rotten corpse.

**L:**   The smell?

**J:**   Just like a corpse! My husband had to carry me outside. A lot of pus came out with the feces, a bucketful. My husband would carry me back to bed each time. He was exhausted from caring for me. I was excreting pus for a month and seven days. He was exhausted.

I wanted to buy some thanksgiving offerings, *apejatian* offerings. I promised to dedicate them as soon as I was capable of walking to the temple. But I couldn't even make it from here to there. I only had to move and my stomach felt sick!

The dream landscape is full of images that also prevail in drama, folktales, and shadow puppet performances: a purgatory-like landscape (referred to as Tegal Penangsaran, "Field of Suffering," by Balinese) with the stern guardian and the ponds in which souls of the dead suffer for the wrongs they have committed in life. The glorious palace, abode of deities, is another colorful image from this mythical world.

In an earlier recounting of the dream[8] Jero explained to me that it was a mystical message (*sabda*) and constituted a test that she had to endure before becoming a healer. She interprets the "brother" in the dream as one of her protective spirit siblings (*kanda mpat;* see section 3B) who guided her through the realm of death and back into the world of the living. Once again the instructions for medicine that came to her during this dream proved efficacious where other cures had failed.

Jero eventually recovered from this illness and began working as a peddler again. She recalls that her family's financial situation continued to worsen no matter how hard they all worked:

**J:**   Everyone wanted money. They all gossiped about us. We survived the best we could. I worked as a peddler, every day, day and night. I'd carry the coffee around to people wherever they wanted it. I'd get credit for ten days but after fifteen still wasn't able to pay. . . .

No matter how we arranged our finances, no matter how we counted the money, the debts and profits, we still had difficulties.

I cried about it; my husband cried. There was nothing we could do; we'd pawned everything we owned. Our clothes were tattered and torn. . . . No one trusted us to pay our debts; they wouldn't give credit. Even credit for sweet

---

[8]   See Connor 1982a, p. 46.

potato and red rice, we couldn't get.[9] We even stole . . . The coconut harvest was all pawned.

L: You even pawned the coconuts?

J: Yes, the coconuts, everything. We had nothing to eat. One day my husband came home with Nyoman.

L: Oh, Nyoman was born at this time?

J: Yes, we had Nyoman by this time. She was born after I recovered from my illness. That made three children. Three children then, with Nyoman. We had nothing. We were hungry. We couldn't work out how to feed them. We looked for edible leaves and grasses. . . . We tried to get some sweet potato and rice. We got into more debt. We also used to go and glean at the sweet potato harvest. So, you know what *munuh* [to glean] means?

L: Yes.

J: We gleaned at the harvest of sweet potato and taro. My husband went, not me. He'd come home with the food. But we had no coconuts to spice the food. The *cacah* mixture had no rice in it. It wasn't tasty at all.

All the children were listless and apathetic. We tried to get credit and we couldn't. They said we had to pay our other debts before we could get more credit. . . .
And then [I said to my husband]: "Go and find a coconut."
We stole one of my [pawned] coconuts. We didn't steal anyone else's. If we were discovered, we would ask for it. We wouldn't steal anything else. It was too much. The children had no food, and they were still small. We'd only ask if we were caught. If we weren't discovered, we'd steal it. We didn't do it openly.

He climbed the tree. After he climbed up, the coconut thudded to the ground. Just one coconut, to flavor wild greens.

The owner of the crop arrived from the east. He swore at us . . .

They [the owner and Jero's husband] fought over the pieces of coconut. I didn't say anything. I just cried. I feel like crying now. It was just money in order to eat, coconuts in order to eat. We worked so hard, but everything was carried away.

"Pay for it!" [he said].

I had never picked a coconut like that. It was the first time we'd stole anything. Only one coconut.

I didn't say anything. I couldn't reply to him. It was after that, I started wandering.

L: How did you feel when you set out?

J: I'm going to cry. Turn the tape off. I can't speak.

Here there is a break of several minutes while Jero collects herself to go on with the story.

---

[9] This mixture (called *cacah*) is the cheapest, most inferior form of staple food.

**J:**   I started wandering. I wanted to kill myself so that I would be free of this suffering. I wanted to drown myself. I thought by drowning myself I should be free of my burdens. So I went to the big river over to the west. But I didn't throw myself in.

> "Why should I kill myself when the world is so vast? The best thing to do is to leave here and wander. If somebody kills me then that death is a blameless one. But if I commit the wrong here of killing myself, then it's I who will be guilty."

That's what was going on in my head at the time. So it didn't come off. I went home. I decided to get some offering dishes on credit, in the town. Five . . .

I set out for the forest in Buleleng. Nyoman was just five months old.

**L:**   Nyoman was just . . . ?

**J:**   Just five months old. I got the offering dishes; they were given to me on credit in the town. The arrangement was as follows:

> "Just pay your debts first. You can have the offering dishes on credit. However many you sell, that's all the debt will be. Just pay your debts [to other creditors] first."

So she gave me five aluminum offering platters on credit. I took them with me to the forest.

Jero fled her creditors by leaving her hamlet and going to the northern harbor town of Buleleng to work as an itinerant hawker. Buleleng had been an important port since the 17th century, but Dutch mercantile penetration in the 19th century changed the nature of trade and made mountain areas like Jero's district economically important for the coffee and cattle they produced. Jero was following in the path of many impoverished villagers before her.

She set out on foot for the distant harbor town, with just the few trade goods she had obtained on credit. These goods, she stresses, were carried less with the hope of making a profit than to indicate to strangers that she was an honest peddler and thus to avoid being molested.

On the road, Jero "asked for rice" in return for small chores about the houses of strangers. In Buleleng she sought out some matrilateral relatives and stayed with acquaintances she met on her travels. These people cared for her, and she began life as a small trader again. At one point in her absence of several months she made a return visit to her husband and children, carrying some food and money to repay some of their debts. Their situation was miserable, she recalls, and she set out again for Buleleng, feeling that the family was better off with one less mouth to feed. Besides working in the big central market in Buleleng, she peddled her wares in the sparsely inhabited foothills behind the harbor town, moving from one settlement to another as she heard word of a coming village festival that might attract customers.

It was during this time that Jero experienced many strange visions. The culmination of these vivid and often frightening visions occurred one day when she was walking in forested country in the foothills around Buleleng, accompanied only by a young child, the daughter of the people she was staying with. In Jero's story, as in many myths and drama performances, the forest appears as a place where all the usual conventions about space, time, and social intercourse lapse. She and the child were heading for a remote village to sell offering platters to people holding a ceremony there. They got lost and never reached their destination. In the early part of the day their only encounters were with a lone man who seemed to misdirect them and with a huge and terrifying wild pig, which they succeeded in passing safely, though not without some fear. Their next encounter was with an eccentric woman living alone in a stone house guarded by seven savage dogs.

J: After that [getting past the pig] we kept walking. We came to a house as big as that one (*indicates pavilion in her yard*). That's how big the house was, but the walls were made of mud [*abing*].

L: What is *abing*?

J: You know, at the river, the bank of the river.

L: Yes.

J: That's called *abing*.

Then, at the highest point of the forest, there were lots of *ambenan* trees. Down below was the mud-walled house. Out came seven dogs. "Dog."[10]

L: Were you still with that girl?

J: There were just the dogs; just the dogs came out.

L: No, I mean were you still with that young child?

J: Oh, yes. I said: "Let's turn back. There's a house there. We'll be assaulted, our money will be taken."

I was scared I was going to die then. If we were assaulted at that place who would help us? What's more, I was worried because I had the child with me. If I had been by myself it wouldn't have mattered.

"Let's go home now" [I said].

"I'm scared of the pig" [which they would have to pass again on their way back].

"I'm scared of that house" [I replied]. "Sit down here."

We sat down and set down our goods. We sat there. Then the seven dogs came. They were fawnish-colored, and huge. They were howling.

"Woooo . . . woo . . . wooo . . ."

We faced them sitting down.

"Woooo . . . woo."

---

[10] Jero uses the English word, which I had previously taught her.

I crouched down, with the child here (*indicates her lap*). I watched from behind the baskets. They moved closer.

"Woooo . . . wooo . . . "

Silently, I prayed:

"Oh, Holy Goddess, I am one of Thy humble servants from the Holy Springs of Tirta Empul. If I have sinned, end my life now. If I'm innocent, if my thoughts are pure, I beg Thy protection."

Do you know what *liput manuk* means? To be free from harm.

"I'm Thy humble servant from the Holy Springs" [I prayed].

I kept watching while I was crouching. The child was huddled in my lap. They kept howling: "Wooo . . . wooo . . . ," seven of them! I was trembling by this time. Now it looked as if they were going to kill us. The seven of them were making a racket as if they were about to kill us. We didn't move. Suddenly a woman emerged from the mud-walled house. She peered at us.

"Oh, it's Men Jata. Come here!"

**L:**   From the house?

**J:**   She came toward us. The house was a long way from us. I was still frightened.

"Men Jata, you've come at last."

"Ketut, get up. She knows my name! How does she know that? [I asked]. She must have heard about us. Get up! She knows my name."

I was relieved because she knew my name. We got up. I cried out:

"I'll be bitten by those creatures."

"No, they won't hurt you. Get home!" [she yelled at the dogs].

**L:**   Were they sacred dogs?

**J:**   I don't know. I wasn't game to say "dogs."[11] I was scared.

"They'll bite me. I daren't approach" [I said].

"No, it'll be all right. Get home!" [she yelled at the dogs].

They obeyed. The seven of them walked away. She called out to me:

"Come here!"

"Get up, Ketut. She knows us."

The little one got up. When we got there, I said:

"Ma'am?"

"Yes?"

The house had no kitchen. There was nothing. Just stools, a table and nine stools. The seats were made of stone [*paras*]. In the middle lay a rice mortar, a tall one made of wood.

As soon as I walked in, I felt confused.

---

[11]  To call the creatures by the ordinary word "dog" would have been inappropriate if they had indeed been sacred animals attached to a temple, or the property of a deity. Their exact status is never revealed. Balinese regard ordinary dogs as one of the lowest forms of life.

"What sort of a house is this? [I thought]. Is she a jinn? No, she looks the way I do. This part is normal (*indicates her lip*). She has a grooved lip. She looks quite attractive, like an ordinary person."[12]

That's what I was thinking. She was an ordinary person.

**L:**   An ordinary person?

**J:**   Yes, an ordinary person. Although jinns don't have a groove, I still *felt* as if she was a jinn.

"Sit down, Ketut" [I said. And then] "Ma'am?"
"Yes?"
"Where shall I sit?"
"Not here, or here, or here. You can sit on the rice mortar."[13]

It was made of wood.

"May I sit here?"
"You may."

I sat down. And then after I sat down, I asked:

"Do you wish to purchase something?"
"Yes, I'll buy something."
"Let's begin as I haven't much time."
"Men Jata, who told you to come here?"

I thought it was the person who had sent the message for me earlier in the morning.[14]

"I thought that you sent a message for me? Isn't this Kedu village?
"No, this isn't Kedu. This is Bukit. Bukit Puncak Landep. This is my home. [Then she said] Have some rice first here. When you've had some rice, I'll buy something."
"I don't want any rice, I'm not hungry."
"Why don't you want any rice? In that case I don't believe you're in a desperate condition, that you've come all the way from Bangli, abandoning your home, your children, and your husband. If you don't want to accept my rice, I don't want to buy anything from you."

**L:**   Was it night yet?

**J:**   No, it was only one o'clock. We had been out since about ten in the morning. I said:

"If that's the way it is, I'll have some rice so that you will buy something. In

---

[12] *Jinn*, from the Arabic word, is a generic term used by Balinese to refer to mischievous, often harmful spirits who inhabit wilderness areas and prey upon humans who pass by. It is said that one way to distinguish jinns from humans is by their smooth upper lip.

[13] The lower parts of the body should not come into contact with a vessel used to process food. Therefore, this is an extraordinary place to invite a guest to sit, another indication that perhaps the woman is not "an ordinary person."

[14] Earlier in her story Jero had recounted how, that morning, a woman whom she did not know had come to her house to tell her that she could sell some of her offering platters in Kedu village in the mountains, where a temple festival was soon to be held.

Bangli I would be ashamed to ask for rice like this, but around these parts I will accept it. I ask for rice all over the place."

"Eat first" [she said].

"Thank you for the food" [I replied].

She brought out a big round piece of food. "Eat this." It was sweet potato. It was ordinary sweet potato, it certainly tasted like it, but the size of it! As big as a *juet* fruit.


Here there is a short break in the story while I changed cassettes.


**J:**    So I took one and peeled it. The small one I offered to Ketut.

"Do you want some rice?"

I was afraid to say it wasn't rice.[15]

"I'm sorry that's all there is. I have no vegetables or salt, only dry rice. I live in the forest, I never get to the market" [she said].

"That's all right. If I'm hungry I can eat anything. Even raw sweet potato."

**L:**    Raw sweet potato?

**J:**    Yes. It can be made into a spicy salad. So that's what I said to the woman.

"If I'm hungry and there's no rice, I can even eat raw sweet potato."

I gave some to Ketut.

"Here, Ketut, eat the rice."

She shook her head.

"I don't want it."

"If she doesn't want it, Men Jata, don't give it to her" [said the woman].

Then she turned to Ketut and asked:

"What's this?"

"Sweet potato" [said Ketut].

It was true. I thought that she was mad [*buduh*].[16] Then I said:

"I've had enough, thank you. I'm satisfied. Would you like to take this?"

I still didn't know what sort of a woman she was.

"May I ask you, Ma'am, how you came to know my name? Where have you met me?"

"I know because I have heard stories, although I never met you. I just heard the news. Men Jata, they said, has left her small children and her husband and has gone to the forest where she sells offering platters. Then when I saw you carrying the platters just then, I thought that it must be Men Jata."

"Oh, so you guessed it."

---

[15]   This behavior is another indication of the woman's strangeness. Because sweet potato is an inferior food to rice, a host would usually apologize for serving it. This woman, however, treated the food as if it were rice.

[16]   Jero here seems to be doubtful of her own perception of the situation and welcomes the child's statement as confirmation of her doubts about the woman.

"Yes."

"May I ask you, so that I can speak of you in the correct way, whether you're a titled person or an ordinary person? I don't know."

"I'm just called Sister Suci, and my husband is Brother Gede Merta. My husband just went out before you came. He'll be back in a minute."

**L:** What was his name?

**J:** Gede Merta.

"I see [I said. Then], "Do you want to buy an offering platter now? It's getting late. It's two o'clock already."

"How much is this one?"

"Usually I sell it for seven *ringgit*, but you can have it for six."[17]

I called her Sister Suci.

"What about this sarong, the patterned one? I want to give it to my husband. How much is it?"

"I usually sell it for twenty-six rupiah, but you can have it for twenty-five."

She took it. Then she noticed the ragged cloth I used to cover up all my goods.

"Let me buy that covering cloth."

She wanted to buy that cloth!

"This one is dirty. Wait until I have a new one for you to buy."

"If you don't sell me this one, Men Jata, you'll never see me again, even if you come here four times. Sell this one to me."

"I bought it for twelve rupiah. Because it's already worn, you can have it for ten."

She took it and spread it out. I was apprehensive. She paid for it.

"I'll get you the money."

She fetched the money. I counted it. Three times I counted it. There were fifty *ringgit*, no, fifty rupiah.

"You've given me too much money."

"How much extra?"

"You bought forty rupiahs' worth of goods, but you've given me fifty."[18]

Then she shouted at me:

"Men Jata, it's right that you should have it. For the child and because you had to come a long way to get here. Anybody else who received extra money, even one rupiah, would not tell me about it. Even if I asked them they wouldn't tell me. You got nine rupiah extra. Don't be so stupid. Use it for the child. It's right you should have it."

"Well, it's like this. I'm a poor, unfortunate woman. I just accept what's

---

[17] A *ringgit* is a unit of price based on the old Dutch coin of the same name; it is worth two and a half rupiah.

[18] This overpayment, plus the woman's interest in the tattered cloth and her lack of any desire to bargain, are further signs of her eccentricity, which add to the strangeness of the whole experience. Jero does not comment directly on these aspects of the exchange – they would be obvious to a Balinese audience.

given to me, so I'll take the money. Profit from theft or deception I could never accept. But of this 10 rupiah, I will return you one in payment if you will show me the way home to Panji Abasan. Otherwise, I'll get lost."

"I'll look after you. Take the money; I don't want any payment. And keep the nine rupiah. I don't seek any payment. Where did you say you were going?"

"To Abasan."

We started climbing.

"See that *pulé* tree, the large one? Wherever you are, take your bearings from that whether you're to the east or the west. You can't get lost that way. Use it as a landmark."

"Thank you."

"Off you go."

"Goodbye."

Then I began climbing.

**L:**   With the child?

**J:**   Yes, with the child.

Soon after that, we came across monkeys raiding beehives. They were in a tree with a huge trunk, a *dap dap* tree. There was a beehive there. They got the honey out. One passed it to its mate up above. While they had their backs turned we could get some honey too.

"Let's get some, Ketut. They wouldn't know if we took some while their backs were turned."
"No, they're looking for food, they'll attack us."

So we ran away and kept climbing. A little farther up, we came across a *cempaka* tree. Do you know that tree?[19]

**L:**   Yes.

**J:**   It was such a huge tree. The trunk was as big across as my shrine house. The branches were as thick as coconut tree trunks. There were fourteen branches; I counted them so I'd remember:

"One . . . two . . . three . . . Oh [I thought], if I had one of these at home I'd be a wealthy woman."

It was true people around there never went to market!

"Gracious, look at all those blossoms. They're so dense they make it dark! [I said to myself]. Oh, Sacred Deity Who resides in this forest, Who possesses these flowers, I beg permission to take just enough to carry in one large leaf."

I found a broad leaf and formed it into a cone; then I picked some of the blossoms from the lower branches. I've never seen anything like it! The leaf

---

[19]   *Cempaka* [*Michelia longifolia* BL] is a medium-sized tree that bears fragrant blossoms resembling very small gardenias. It is a prized flower for offerings, and *cempaka* flowers fetch a good price when sold in the markets.

cone was full, with about a thousand flowers in it! Then, whoosh . . . the tree disappeared! It completely disappeared!

"Oh, I must be crazy! Otherwise, how could I ever see a *cempaka* tree as big as that!"

**L:** What about the child?

**J:** She didn't say anything. She was quiet. She just followed me. After the tree disappeared, I felt like I was going mad. I picked up one of the flowers.

"What's this, Ketut?"
"A flower."
"What sort of flower?"
"A *cempaka* flower."

I couldn't be mad then.

"Where's the tree now?"
"I don't know. I don't know."

The child just didn't know. Then, whoosh . . . there was a little house shrine! Do you know what *cukcuk* means? A small shrine made of saplings. It suddenly appeared!

"Oh, Holy Deity, I request Thy permission to pick the flowers. It was not my intention to steal them. I asked permission prior to taking them. I ask Thy leave to depart now."

I took the flowers with me. It was already four o'clock or perhaps three o'clock. We got to the head of the river, Bangka River it was called. Gracious, there were so many monkeys! There were black ones and brown ones, all fairly small, some carrying their young. They were clambering on the branches. There were lots of oranges around. They're called *klanyuagan* in that region. They were everywhere.

"If we take some, they'll attack us."

It was difficult to get any. And then:

"Just give us one" [I said to the monkeys].

But the monkeys prevented us from taking any. They screeched at us:

"Kreook . . . kreook . . . kreook . . . "

**L:** The monkeys?

**J:** Yes.

"Kreook . . . kreook . . . kreook . . . " [they went].
"Give us one."

They took one and threw it away. We picked it up again. The orange was tossed around as if we were playing ball.

"Give us one."

We grabbed it. They took it again.
Then we decided to go. They kept screeching:

"Kreook . . . kreook . . . "

I was frightened. They threw one orange away. We ate that and some sweet potato. The orange tasted sour, like a lemon. So we ate it, and then we went home. When we arrived at the house, they asked:

> "Why has it taken you so long, Men Jata?"
> "I couldn't find the village. I got these flowers, and we saw some sights and met a woman there."

I told them the story.

> "Who directed you to that place? It's a mystical place! I've never been there myself. Who directed you there? You were fortunate to come back from there. If you say it's going to rain there, it rains; if you say you are going to get hungry, you're hungry; if you say it's hot, you'll feel hot; if you say you're exhausted, you'll feel exhausted. Gracious, it's such a mystical place at Puncak Landep, at the top of the forest. Don't go there again."[20]

**L:**   Did you have the desire to go there?

**J:**   No, I only ended up there because I was lost. I was looking for Kedu village, but I ended up lost at Puncak Landep.

The series of incidents in the forest is typical of periods when Jero felt herself to be so disoriented and confused that she knew she was going mad; at other times she remembers feeling lucid and calm, although others treated her as if she were mad. While staying with relatives and acquaintances in Buleleng, she reported meetings with people from her own village and district who reprimanded her for not returning to her family. The people with whom she stayed denied the reality of those meetings, however. One of the figures who appeared to her was the high-ranking regent of her local administrative district, a most unlikely personage to be concerned with the welfare of an itinerant peddler:

**J:**   I came back from trading in mid morning and went to sleep at someone's house. Then the lord regent arrived.

**L:**   What do you mean?

**J:**   The lord regent. With his retinue . . .

**L:**   The raja?

**J:**   Yes, the raja. He was still alive then. So then His Lordship arrived. I was asleep.

> "Where's I Tami? I've been told she's staying here."[21]
> That's the voice I heard from my bed.

**L:**   Did you see anything?

**J:**   No, I just heard the voice. I woke up with a start. I reached for . . .

---

[20]   Although the exact meaning of this passage is unclear to me, it implies that in the forest people are subject to strange laws.

[21]   "I Tami," the name by which the regent addressed her, is a pseudonym for Jero's personal name (shortened to "Tami" in the film *Jero Tapakan*). A personal name is a coarse term of address, used only by those of high status to those of low status, or by familiars.

"That person must be from home, otherwise he would not know my name" [I thought to myself].

I never told anyone my name.

"Uncle, Uncle, where's my ceremonial sash? The lord regent is here."[22]

I came out of the house.

"Lord Regent who?" [asked the person who owned the house].

**L:** This all happened in the middle of the night?

**J:** No, in mid morning. It was daylight.

"Which lord regent?" [asked Jero's host].
"The regent from Bangli" [I kept on repeating].
"But there's nobody there."
"Quick, give me my ceremonial sash."

I went off to put it on. Then I went outside.

"My Lord Regent, where is your destination, my Lord?"
"Oh, she's mad! She's mad! Why is she paying her respects there? She's mad! There's nobody there!"

They said I was mad. They wanted to know where my home was.

"Where's her home? Go and look for her home."

I didn't answer them.

"Where are you going, Lord Regent?"
"I came here looking for you. I heard that you have abandoned your children, and your husband. Your children are still small, isn't that so?"
"That is so, my Lord."
"Why did you abandon your children? Go home."

He told me to return to my home.

"I left home, Lord Regent, to 'halve the cooking pots.' I don't just ask for food."
"Well, return home in three days with what you have. Don't make any more trouble; you will humiliate yourself. It's a shame, your children are fretting for you."
"As you wish, Lord Regent. It was never my intention to stay away permanently . . ."
"Don't forget my words, I'm leaving now."
"Forgive me for not accompanying you, Your Highness. May I ask where Your Highness is going from here?"
"I came here especially to find you. Here is a ring for you."

I was given a ring, to carry for good luck.

**L:** The regent gave you a ring?

**J:** Yes, he gave me a ring.

---

[22] Use of a kin term is a common way to address strangers, neighbors, or acquaintances, indicating respect and good will; it does not necessarily imply a kin relationship.

"Oh, dear, the trader has gone crazy."

Everybody gathered around.

"Where is Men Jata's home? She's gone mad here. Where is her home? She's really mad."

I didn't say anything.

"Don't forget to return home" [said the regent].
"Yes. I do not just ask for food. I left home to 'halve the cooking pots,' Your Highness. Excuse me for not accompanying you."

And then he left. So I asked:

"Uncle, Brother, why are you calling me mad?"
"What were you doing out there alone?"
"That was the lord regent, from Bangli."

They said there was no one. There was nobody there, but I was acting as if I were speaking to the regent of Bangli.

"Uncle, he has been looking for me. He's concerned about me."
"There's nobody there. You're mad. Oh, Lord. Come to your senses" [he said].

I was unhappy. It was the first time I felt at all crazy. It was like this:

"If I'm mad [I thought to myself], then it's not true that the regent came to the forest. If His Highness goes out, to my village or wherever, he goes by car."[23]

But the resemblance was so strong, I must have been mad. That's what I felt at the time.

I was unhappy. I slept. I was depressed and felt crazy. Everybody said I was crazy. I slept for three days. I didn't ask for rice anywhere. I got thin and wasted. My thoughts were racing. I was unhappy and felt crazy.

These visions and voices seemed real, so real that it was difficult for Jero to respond to and communicate with the people around her when they vehemently denied the validity of her experiences and tried to control and modify her behavior:

L:   Weren't the others frightened when you were mad?

J:   No, they were just sad. I didn't remember much about being mad. I was too unhappy. Before I started seeing things, I didn't feel crazy. Although they said I was mad, to me it seemed as if a real person were there.

"So that's what happens to mad people [I thought]. If it looks like they're real, then one is mad."

I began to feel as if I were mad. When I was talking to him [the regent] I didn't feel mad. It was just like me here talking to you.

[23] At this time, Jero was in fact residing in a village not far from the town of Buleleng, but that area is regarded as something of a hinterland and is therefore referred to as a "forest" by townspeople and by people from Jero's home district.

Soon after this, in response to further exhortations from the figures she was encountering in her visions, as well as from her hosts, Jero decided to return home. She suffered an outbreak of painful boils on her legs and made a pledge to the deities that she would go home in three days if her condition improved. That night a recipe for a healing poultice (*boreh*) came to her in a dream. She applied the poultice, and within three days the boils disappeared. She then set out for her hamlet. But after her return home, she recalls, she felt more deranged and disoriented than ever.

From her description, it appears that at this time Jero's subjective experiences and behavior began to be publicly interpreted as *buduh kadewandewan* ("blessed madness"; lit.: "madness from the deities").[24]

J: | After I got home, I was mad. I was raving. It was blessed madness.

L: While in the forest, you weren't in a state of blessed madness?

J: No.

L: Well, what sort of madness was that?

J: I had the vision of the regent, I met the balian, I met the woman at Puncak Landep, I picked the flowers, that was the sort of madness [*buduh*] I suffered.

L: That's not called blessed madness?

J: No. It was only after I arrived home that I was in a state of blessed madness. "My Lord" this, "My Lord" that, I kept saying. And offerings were made for me. Offerings of exorcism at the sea [*lukat di pasih*]. They made *sorohan* offerings. *Segehan* offerings were made on my behalf. I demanded lots of offerings then. I'd ask for some *segehan* offerings, 100 of them. If they weren't made, I'd cry. I'd ask for another 54 *segehan* offerings. If they didn't appear, I'd cry. I'd ask for some small rice-cake offerings. Everything I'd ask for, I'd want to be made for me immediately. [See section 5F for a discussion of offerings.]

Her husband was worried and decided to consult spirit mediums to discover the real cause of all these illnesses and strange events. The couple traveled all around the district, consulting one spirit medium after another. All pronounced that Jero herself had been chosen to become a spirit medium. These diagnoses provided public endorsement of her illness as "blessed madness" and not just deranged behavior, as it had been classified in Buleleng, far from close kin and neighbors.

We consulted mediums eight times. All said that I should consecrate myself as a medium; then the madness would go. . . .
Finally, it was resolved at the medium's place in Srikadu, the medium called Jero Beneh. It was said that I must hold the consecration ceremonies [*matelah*]. If I didn't, I would never be in good health again. I was told I should perform the ceremonies in order that I be purified, so that the deity would have the earthly

---

[24] The remaining quotations come not from the filmed text but from a previous recording. Vertical lines indicate passages that are similar.

vehicle it required. After the deity had come down to speak through a medium, I was told that I had to fast and meditate for a month and seven days. After that, I could either become a medium or not, as I chose.

I was prepared to have the ceremonies but not to become a medium. I thought I could satisfy the deity and absolve my obligations. I'd just have a six-monthly anniversary ceremony. Under those conditions I was prepared to go through with it. . . . So the deity would have an earthly vehicle, and I would have the anniversary ceremonies [*odalan*] every six months.[25] Then I could become a trader again, I thought. Under those conditions I was willing.

The sequence of suffering, wandering, and visions forms an oft-recurring pattern in the lives of spirit mediums and other consecrated people, although Jero's experiences are more intense than most or at least more vividly recalled.

Jero and her husband held the consecration ceremony,[26] with encouragement from the balians they had consulted and from some of the customary officials in her village. The elaborate preparations meant that the household became further indebted:

Three days later, the deity said [through Jero, possessed] that we must perform the big consecration ceremony on the full moon of the tenth month. But we didn't have any money, we didn't have any food. I talked to my husband about it. He didn't have an answer. I had to get everything on credit. My sister lent me the rice, we also got some eggs, beans, all the ingredients for the offerings. Before the ceremony I borrowed fifty silver coins and went to the big market at Bangli. I bought a pig, food for the official guests: the head of the village [*prebekel*], his deputy, and the local ritual expert.

I asked the medium from Selokan, whom I had consulted while still suffering from the madness. Also Priest Munjuk from Paludan hamlet, who had come out looking for me when I was wandering, mad, in the forest. Also Jero Nyarikan [a customary official and temple priest in Jero's own hamlet].

That evening I took a ritual meal to all the people who would be official witnesses. I couldn't invite other friends and relatives; we were too poor. I took the *sate* and rice — it's called *pakeling* — to the houses of the witnesses. I told them the date of the consecration ceremony and asked them to come.

Then I went to the Death Temple [Pura Dalem] to inform the deities there of my intentions, then to all the shrines and temples [in the village].

After the preliminary ceremonies, we performed the consecration. We dedicated offerings for a whole day.

Jero recalls that her first experiences of possession were during her consecration. At a difficult point in the ritual, when the order of the proceedings

[25] Reference is to six Balinese months, or 210 days.
[26] The subject of a consecration ceremony must undergo it with a partner of the opposite sex, usually a spouse. The partner often acts as an assistant after the ceremony and in some cases may take over all ritual functions after the subject's death.

was not clear, Jero was possessed by her guardian deity, who corrected the mistakes that had been made in the ritual. When the correct offerings were presented, the deity departed. This happened twice during the ceremony.

After the ceremony, Jero undertook to fast and meditate (*mayasa*) for 42 days, to ensure the blessing of the guardian deity who had presided over her consecration. During this period she bathed daily at a sacred spring near her home and ate only a few sweet potatoes and vegetables, with a little coffee. Every day her family made offerings on her behalf, and she herself took offerings to the local temples and asked the blessing of the deities associated with each temple, as is customary after a consecration.

During the period of fasting and meditating, Jero experienced many visions that confirmed the efficacy of the ceremonies. She also received several objects and potions that could be used for medicines and curative charms. These objects came to her in strange circumstances. (They are the objects and potions that are visible in the shrine house, behind Jero, in the film *A Balinese Trance Séance*.)

Sometimes the meaning of her experiences was unclear to her, but she followed the instructions of voices that came to her in dreams or that she heard during her waking hours, without comprehending what the outcome would be:

The next day I was told to go to a sacred bathing place at Cukik. On the night of the full moon I was to seek some medicines. I was exhausted, but I set out in the middle of the night. There was nothing there. Just as I was deciding to return home, when the moon was at its brightest, I saw a part of a plant, from a small shrub, on the bank of the river. I thought: "Perhaps it is this which is meant for me." So I went over to it. I found a fruit with a stone in the middle, although usually that sort of plant never bears fruit. It looked like sweet potato. I picked it. Then I went home. I showed the fruit to my husband. He cried:

"Why did you bring that home? Throw it away!"

As soon as it was thrown away, it disappeared. He said:

"Why did you bring that fruit home? There's nothing special about it!"

The next day I was reprimanded . . . by my ancestors. It was said to be a medicinal plant.

Jero successfully completed the period of fasting and meditation, although not without scorn and ridicule from some fellow hamlet members who found her elevation in status pretentious. Another local healer refused to recognize her new status, because she constituted a threat to his own practice. All refused to address her by the honorific title "Jero," which was rightfully hers after the completion of the ceremonies.

Jero stood firm in her resolution not to undertake the duties of a spirit medium. The first séance, as she recounts it, was a response to pressure by others, particularly Jero Nyarikan, a local customary official (*kelian adat*) and temple priest (*pamangku*) who played a major part in establishing Jero as a professional medium.

Her first clients arrived without any forewarning, presumably because they had heard by word of mouth of the consecration of a new medium in the district:

> Then some people came to "ask for speech" [*nunas raos*], but I didn't want to do it. I cried. I didn't want to serve the gods in that way. I said that I was ignorant and illiterate. Jero Nyarikan encouraged me to give it a try.
>
>> "Just sit cross-legged at the shrine, and sprinkle the offerings with holy water. They already know that you don't know much about it."
>
> I didn't want to "ask for speech." I cried and protested. But they wouldn't leave until I carried out their wishes.... I didn't want to become a medium. I just wanted to have the ... consecration ceremonies, so that I would be cured of my illnesses. I thought that I would just have the anniversary celebration every six months.
>
> But Jero Nyarikan persuaded me to go through with it. I said I didn't know how to go about it. Since I had had the consecration, I hadn't been possessed by the deity. I was very calm. Before the consecration I had messages and commands all the time.... Now, I said, I didn't know anything about arranging the offerings, or how to intone the prayers and chants.
>
>> "Just sit up there and sprinkle some holy water, you only have to use the simplest offerings" [said Jero Nyarikan].
>
> So I did as he said. I sprinkled the offerings with holy water and lit the incense brazier. Then I couldn't remember anything [*sing inget*]. It felt as if there was something coming from above me.... A voice from above, it felt like. Later, I came to myself again [*suba inget*] and asked the people how it went.
>
>> "We found out what we wanted to know" [they said].
>
> But I didn't know anything about it... I don't remember saying anything myself, just the last sprinkling with holy water. When I "stopped remembering" [*suba sing inget*], it felt like a night with a full moon, that other world...

The newly consecrated are deemed to have particularly strong powers, which prompts people to try them out. Most mediums slowly build up a practice by word of mouth. Jero was no exception. The original clients had come to her from her own village. Doubtless they had heard about her consecration ceremony, since village officials must be invited to a consecration.

The clients were satisfied with the "speech" they obtained through Jero. Word spread, and people began consulting her regularly.

> Then people started coming, once every three or four days, then every two days, then every day. After six months, there were two or three groups every day. Then it became fairly constant, never too many and never too few. Then I knew I had to pay my debts to the deity. Because everybody in the village was ridiculing me and not talking to me.

"If your Lordship wills it, inspire me in my task. Grant me success in healing. Don't allow me to fail. I only ask for the means to live simply and repay my debts. My debts are many. As for those who are angry with me, I will have a feast for them. I will sponsor a *wayang* [shadow puppet] performance."

So I promised to repay any debts and obligations to the deity.

It wasn't until she had been practicing as a spirit medium for nearly ten years that Jero was able to afford the shadow puppet performance (*wayang*) and the feast she had promised the deities. (The *wayang* was performed publicly as an offering to Jero's guardian deity but served also to create social harmony among the sponsor, Jero, and the villagers who always enjoy these performances.) By this time Jero had been accepted in the village as a practicing balian and had, in fact, helped many of her fellow villagers with their problems. Local villagers tend to consult her about minor matters, going to more distant mediums about major problems when they prefer anonymity. In turn, as her reputation spread, more distant clients began to come to Jero with serious problems.

During the years that Jero was building up her practice as a spirit medium, her life was dogged by other misfortunes. Her second son died in 1961 or 1962, after an illness that could not be cured by either Western or Balinese medicine. In 1963 Gunung Agung, the highest and most sacred mountain on Bali, erupted violently; lava destroyed many villages in eastern Bali, and most of the island suffered famine as a result of the rain of volcanic ash that fell for weeks afterward, destroying food crops. Times were so hard, recalls Jero, that the provincial government organized free public cremations for the many casualties of the eruption and famine. Her son was cremated at that time. Jero's husband died suddenly just after those cremations were completed, thus missing the chance of a rapid liberation. It was only in 1978 that Jero was able to muster enough resources to participate in a simple collective cremation for the release of her husband's soul, together with 28 other members of her hamlet.[27]

Jero's fortunes again took a steep downturn when national events impinged on the village and the whole island was embroiled in the violent reaction against the Indonesian Communist Party in 1965–6. Although Jero was not directly implicated, she and many others without political party affiliation were adversely affected by the general atmosphere of turbulence, fear, and fatal reprisals.

Since the mid 1960s Balinese villages have enjoyed a respite from serious political upheavals and islandwide natural disasters. In these years Jero's life has been relatively uneventful, and she has been able to enjoy a small measure of economic stability as her practice has grown. Her position further improved after she began practicing as a masseuse a year or two after her

[27] This cremation is the subject of a forthcoming film by Asch, Asch, and Connor.

husband's death (this part of her life is discussed in section 8B). Each practice draws a steady stream of clients, and she is now one of the most popular balians in her district.

In discussing her initiation as a masseuse, as with her call to become a spirit medium, Jero represents herself as bending to the force of divine will. Most healers, whether they come to the calling by divine inspiration or by scholarship, claim that they are mere instruments of divine powers. Jero denies that her ability to heal stems from her own skill and attributes the talent to supernatural agents who are beyond her control: her guardian deity, who has been speaking through her since her consecration, and Pak Udeng's ancestors (section 8B). She never acknowledges the breadth of her own knowledge of healing and ritual matters or her skill in communicating with clients when not possessed. The Balinese classification "knowledge" (*ka-wikanan, kawisesan*) is reserved for the realm of literate scholarship and mystical power, not for the range of skills Jero possesses.

The same rationale persists when Jero discusses the future of her practices. As discussed at the end of the film *Jero Tapakan*, in recent years there have been some indications that Jero's 30-year-old son, Wayan Data, should one day take over his mother's massage practice. As he says toward the end of the film, he has been told on four different occasions by his deceased grandfather's spirit (who possessed Jero) that he should begin the preparations to become a healer himself. The spirit discouraged him from seeking supplementary income as a laborer in the town and advised him to stay at home as much as possible to learn from his mother the arts of massage and making medicines. Several of his dreams and of Jero's, as well as a mystical omen in the form of three semiprecious stones found in the belly of a fish he was cleaning, have strengthened Wayan Data's conviction that he should follow his grandfather's advice. However, as Jero is still at the peak of her career, the transfer of the practice from mother to son may take many years.

In 1980, when we were filming the second part of the film, Wayan Data took an important step toward his eventual consecration as a balian when he (and his wife) underwent the less elaborate *makaladewa* ceremony, or "craftsman's consecration." This ceremony which purifies the craftsman (a carpenter, in Wayan Data's case) so that he can work in temples and other sanctified spaces without polluting those abodes of deities and spirits, sets Wayan Data apart as a consecrated person who may expand his spiritual concerns into other areas, in his case healing. However, both he and Jero are adamant that each step along the way to his eventual recognition as a balian must be prefigured by ancestral and divine decree. For this reason, the question of who might take over Jero's practice as a medium in the future is somewhat problematic, as there has been no supernatural guidance on this matter. If the careers of other spirit mediums are a guide, there may be no indications until after Jero's death. Mediumship, because it is not believed to require a learned skill, is not thought to be transferred by training. In some families the vocation dies out when a suitable successor does not emerge through revelatory means after the practitioner's death.

# ELEVEN

## *Editorial notes on* Jero Tapakan
PATSY ASCH

### A. Introduction

For *Jero Tapakan*, I have not reproduced the subtitles in full or described each shot, as I have done for *A Balinese Trance Séance*. In Chapter 10 Linda provides much longer excerpts from Jero's stories than we have included in the film, and in a translation far richer than subtitles permit. With the exception of a few cutaways used to bridge gaps in Jero's stories, what the audience sees is a series of shots of Jero sitting on her porch and telling Linda some stories from her life. Toward the end of the film she is joined by her son. The film concludes with a few shots of her son's consecration as a carpenter.

The main difficulty in editing this film was deciding how much of our 80 minutes of film to include. One-third of the footage was of Jero's account of her family's poverty, an account that made her feel depressed and was less lively than her recounting of subsequent adventures. Some of the most interesting material, such as her dreams and experiences of "madness," were not sufficiently covered on film to permit inclusion. We did not know how long audiences would want to watch a woman talk, and we got contradictory answers; but most people who saw the footage argued that shorter was better. Now that the film is finished and I have watched it with varied audiences, I think we have edited too short a film.

Several people suggested that we illustrate Jero's stories with pictures of Balinese life, particularly life in Jero's hamlet. We discarded this suggestion immediately because Jero's account reflects a set of private images and thoughts, not all of them grounded in the physical world as others see it. In a sense this film is about the nature of reality. The most powerful figures in Jero's stories were either figments of her imagination or supernatural beings, and the most dramatic episodes have qualities she identifies as mystical. Perhaps we could have illustrated her narrative by using Balinese art, but this would have created a very different film, one that interpreted Jero's stories as a culturally standardized account rather than one that raised the issue of the relationship between her autobiographical stories and Balinese culture.

When we first showed the footage to the ethnographic filmmakers David and Judith MacDougall, they suggested we needed an introduction, something that would convince the audience that Jero was worth listening to. We searched for comments by others about Jero that would validate her importance within her hamlet but could not find anything that was appropriate. Then we tried introducing Jero with a series of excerpts showing her in a wide variety of contexts − as spirit medium, masseuse, grandmother, participant in a temple ceremony, person possessed during a cremation ceremony − but these either were too superficial or created expectations that the film did not fulfill. Next we tape-recorded Linda explaining how she had met Jero and why she became interested in Jero's life. Although Linda's narration contained interesting information, it seemed to place the audience at a distance; it was another example in which filmmakers were saying, "These people are human because they are friends of this Westerner, who is someone you can understand." It became a film about Linda's Jero, not the viewer's Jero. We finally settled on a quotation from Jero, one recorded only on Linda's cassette recorder:

I didn't remember much about being mad. I was too unhappy. Before I started seeing things, I didn't feel crazy. Although they said I was mad, to me it seemed as if a real person were there. "So that's what happens to mad people," I thought. "If it looks like they're real, then one is mad." I began to feel as if I were mad.

We hoped this quotation would tell the audience that they were going to see a film about a woman's point of view of herself and of a period of madness that she experienced, and that Jero's words would be sufficient to create interest in her stories.

The length and structure of the footage posed problems. In order to shorten the film we felt we needed explanatory titles to bridge the gaps between stories and between film rolls. We tried not to interject our own interpretations but to make these titles factual (Linda's analysis can be found in Chapter 10). Editorial decisions were based on our wish to create a coherent film so the many cuts would not be too distracting and to emphasize certain features of Jero's story: her experience of severe poverty, her attitudes toward shame and suicide, the mystical quality of her wanderings, her feelings of insanity, and the consequences of her being diagnosed as suffering blessed madness. In the remainder of this chapter I discuss the editing of each segment of the film and give additional ethnographic information.

## B. Description of poverty

The film opens with a 360-degree pan around Jero's houseyard. Tim wanted to give the viewer a picture of the physical and social environment in which Jero was speaking (see Diagrams 1 and 2). The camera swings clockwise, beginning and ending with film of Jero seated on the divan she uses to treat people with massage. The long pan shows, in order, her shrine house (where *A Balinese Trance Séance* was filmed); the family temple (where Wayan Data's consecration as a craftsman was filmed); the guesthouse and ceremonial pavilion (replaced in 1980 with a more substantial building); Jero's grandchildren playing with coffee beans that had been set out to dry; Jero's son, Wayan Data, sitting on the steps of his house and talking with his cousin; a woman, the widow of Jero's deceased brother-in-law, standing in the doorway of a small house she has used for many years; a patient and her child waiting on the porch for massage treatment; and then to Linda and Jero again. The sound is continuous and synchronized with the picture. The directional microphone, which Linda used with a Nagra tape recorder for the film, is pointed at Jero. It is so sensitive that it picks up a whine from Linda's small cassette recorder, which she has placed on the table beside Jero, amid the paraphernalia set out for massage.

During the first 15 shots of the film Jero talks of the circumstances of her early life: deepening poverty, hunger, illnesses, rising debts, and decreasing resources. Jero attributed her early sicknesses to sorcery:

The diagnosis was that somebody had asked me for a loan. They wanted to buy some rice. But I didn't give it to them. I didn't have any. So they got angry and made me sick. My stomach was swollen.

We have cut most of Jero's account of her family's poverty. The cuts in dialogue occur whenever a cut appears in the picture and a new shot begins. Several cuts appear as jumps whenever there are two shots of Jero filmed from the same angle and focal length.

This phase of Jero's life concluded with an incident in which Jero and her husband stole a coconut from one of the trees they had been forced to pawn. Jero still finds the theft deeply disturbing, although it occurred more than 25 years ago. When she began to cry and asked Linda to stop tape-recording because she "couldn't speak," Tim did not understand immediately what she had said and continued to film, but he soon felt embarrassed and panned to the children, who were still playing with the coffee beans. I think the absolute silence on the sound track increases the tension. At any rate, we found it too painful to watch Jero crying and cut to the children sooner than Tim had.

After about three minutes Jero prepared to resume her story; she rearranged her hair in what seems to be a typically Balinese way of restoring one's composure. When the old woman comes out of an episode of possession at the end of Bateson and Mead's film *Trance and Dance in Bali* (1951) she uses the same gestures; in the footage we have of a woman possessed during a cremation, she, too, redoes her hair as she regains her composure; and in *Trance in Bali* (1960) Belo describes similar behavior.

### C. Contemplation of suicide

We included a shot of Linda striking the microphone to remind the viewer that synchronized-sound filming was resuming and that Linda and Tim were part of the interaction. The close-up of Jero that follows is from the same shot. We cut a zoom while Tim focused on Jero's face. Her manner and voice as she tells about contemplating suicide contrast with the previous footage and with the footage that follows: She is subdued, reflective, and sad or tired. Jero considers suicide a "bad" death because the spirit either suffers in limbo or returns through reincarnation as a lower form of life. Here "sin" is like the Christian notion of a moral transgression.

### D. Transition shot

We included a shot of the rice field to indicate passage of time and to show something of the environment in which Jero lives (see Diagram 3, p. 229). Like most Balinese, Jero likes to bathe twice a day. She goes either to the secluded spring halfway down the ravine seen in the film or to a large irrigation ditch in the middle of rice fields to the east of her house. This shot was actually recorded two years later when we were planning to make an introductory film about Jero's hamlet, a plan we abandoned as we did not have enough footage.

### E. Wandering in the forest

The shot of Wayan Data and his children feeding the chickens was also included to indicate passage of time and to permit an explanatory title to introduce the next story. This shot was actually recorded during the previous day of filming.

In the filmed version (although not in other versions Linda recorded) Jero described the regent's imaginary visit before recounting her adventures in the forest. We have reversed these two stories because a chronological account seemed to flow more smoothly. We wanted to end on her awareness that she might be crazy and on her decision to return home. Linda has translated both these stories in full (section 10D). It is Jero's account of her adventures in the forest that most closely resembles traditional Balinese folktales in both style and content. Elements in this account, such as her hand gestures when the wild dogs depart, reminded us of shadow puppet performances, in this case the puppets' motions as they leave the screen.

### F. Cutaway of Jero's grandson

Because Tim took no additional shots of the houseyard when Jero resumed her story, we used a shot of Jero's grandson taken the previous day of filming. It looks as though he has suddenly realized that Tim is filming him; he stops his antics and walks over to his father. Previously his sister had also been dancing around the yard. We wanted a break in order to move to a new episode, and we wanted to include a summary quotation about the mysterious and dangerous nature of the forest. Like the opening quotations, this sound comes from Linda's cassette machine.

## G. The regent's visit

During Jero's account of the regent's visit she uses "mad" or "crazy" much as laypersons might, to refer to someone who suffers from delusions. It is only after she returns home and begins to visit a series of spirit mediums that her condition is diagnosed as "blessed madness." It was after recounting the regent's visit that Jero told of her growing sense of madness, quoted at the beginning of the film.

At the time of the regent's visit, Jero was apparently living among strangers who did not wish to be responsible for a "crazy" woman. Kin terms used in this story, such as "uncle," do not necessarily denote genealogical ties; they are formal terms of address used to signify respect. Balinese rarely refer to an adult by a personal name, preferring inherited or achieved titles such as Ida Bagus or Jero, birth-order names such as Wayan, teknoyms such as mother of X or grandfather of Y, or simple kin terms.

Throughout the early part of Jero's life the regent (or raja) of Bangli, the person she thought had come looking for her, was the most powerful political figure in her district. An interesting aspect of this part of Jero's story, not obvious in the English translation, is Jero's use of language: When she is quoting the regent she uses coarse terms, as an aristocrat would when addressing a peasant, but when she is quoting herself speaking to the regent she uses the refined terms appropriate when addressing a superior. Exchanges between Jero and the "uncle" are at an intermediary level. Jero's capacity to switch levels of address in a narrative is an indication of her skills as a raconteur and as a socially adept healer. Proper language usage is highly prized in Bali; yet many peasants have few opportunities to hear and practice refined speech, and some adults still do not know Indonesian (see section 5I).

## H. Jero's daughter-in-law

It is typical for a Balinese woman to come and live with her husband's family and join in the economic and ritual activities of the new household. Jero's daughter-in-law does most of the family cooking, cares for her children, and makes most of the family offerings – both the small, daily offerings and the important offerings used at major rituals. She frequently serves coffee and cakes or bananas to Jero's massage patients and to visitors.

### I. End of filming in 1978

We planned to make a film from just the 1978 footage, but when we began to edit Jero's stories we were frustrated: The climax of the stories – her realization that she was suffering from "blessed madness" and could be cured only by holding a consecration ceremony – had not been filmed. The stories lacked Jero's interpretation of their meaning. We decided to wait and try to film more of her account when we returned to Bali in 1980.

Although we say here that this is the last roll of film Tim had in 1978, the last roll was actually used during Jero's account of her adventures in the forest (see section 11E). We felt justified in saying this was Tim's last roll because we had rearranged the story chronologically. These two stories were told on Tim's last two rolls of film, so he could not film her account of her return home or of her consecration as a spirit medium.

### J. Jero's return home: consecration and first clients

In 1980 we asked Wayan Data to participate in the filming because there were signs that he might inherit his mother's massage practice. Like Jero, many Balinese healers have visionary experiences and suffer periods of madness before their consecration, but it is also possible to inherit a practice from a close relative through an apprenticeship. In either case, divine blessing is required. We hoped the inclusion of Wayan Data in the footage would enliven and broaden the account. Instead, perhaps because he had heard the stories many times, his presence seemed to dampen Jero's style. It was probably our goals that had the most detrimental effect on Jero, however. We thought we had an interesting film, one already too long, and we wanted Jero to draw together the strands of her story in a succinct account of her return home and of her progression to consecration as a medium. Jero, on the other hand, had her own script, her oft-told stories, and our effort to shorten the account meant that Jero's natural talents as a storyteller were frustrated; shortening the film by drastic editing further attenuated her stories.

Each new shot indicates a point where I have cut footage. In her translations (section 10D) Linda has included excerpts from other recordings (more detailed than those made during filming), about Jero's search for an explanation for her madness and about her consecration ceremony. We have cut out most of the account of Jero's many visits to spirit mediums and her cyclical periods of madness as she kept changing her mind about whether or not to hold the consecration ceremony. It is common practice to visit many spirit mediums before being consecrated; people want to be sure they understand divine messages, which tend to be ambiguous and complex. And although no Balinese said as much to Linda, these experiences may provide role models and be a form of training.

A consecration ceremony requires elaborate offerings and gifts of food for the invited guests who must witness the event. It was only with the support of relatives and of the local priest and ritual expert that Jero and her husband were able to hold the ceremony. As in all consecration ceremonies (see Wayan Data's at the end of the film), Jero's husband was consecrated too.

A 42-day period (a Balinese month plus seven days) of fasting and meditating was an important part of Jero's consecration. She identifies this period of withdrawal as the time when she began to acquire spiritual power (*sakti*) and to form a close bond with her guardian deity, who presided over her consecration and now guides her practice. When the 42 days were over, she was still reluctant to practice because she felt she was too ignorant. After her consecration Jero was in an even less favorable position to undertake ordinary work. The behavior of consecrated people is restricted: Certain foods are taboo, and nothing can be carried on the head, a serious prohibition for peddlers, such as Jero had been, who usually carry their goods and often a table on their heads.

Newly consecrated spirit mediums are believed to be particularly powerful. As word of a consecration ceremony spreads, clients seek these new mediums. Initially those who came to Jero were from her own vicinity, but as her reputation grew people came from considerable distances, because Balinese prefer to go to a medium whom they don't know personally (see section 5C).

In describing her first séance, Jero quotes the priest: "Go and sit cross-legged." This is the position in which some mediums sit while holding a séance. "Sitting cross-legged," "holding the brazier," and "forgetting" are ways Jero talks about achieving a state of possession. "Forgetting" is in keeping with the belief expressed by many Balinese that one does not remember what occurs when one is possessed (see sections 5B; 6B, shot 1). Throughout the first 20 years of her practice, the priest and Jero were close friends and allies. It was he who gave Jero the opening prayers she uses to bless offerings and seek possession, and he taught her much about ritual performance. However, he is not the priest seen at the end of this film or in the massage film.

Between Jero's descriptions of her first clients and Linda's question about whether Wayan Data would inherit Jero's massage practice there is a long gap where the following dialogue was cut:

J:    After the debts were half-paid, my child got sick. For fifty days. We tried all sorts of treatments. We asked for an injection, but it wasn't given. We tried to force medicine into him. He was big and he resisted, biting us. He died after fifty days.
L:    What caused his death?
J:    He was taken because of somebody's wrongdoing. We had an enemy. [She is referring to sorcery.]

J:    Three years after my child died, my husband got sick with chills. I didn't know how to treat him. I tried everything. Nothing worked. The best I could do was bless offerings. He was sick for two years. This way didn't work; that way didn't work. We consulted a medium, but there was no speech [the deities and spirits declined to descend and speak]. His fate was sealed. A healer from Badung said a sorcerer's demon [*babai*] had entered his body, and treated him for that. He vomited blood. He sang and then he died. Again I was griefstricken. The sickness and debts were endless. In those days it was hard. We didn't cook [i.e., there was no food to eat], there was sickness, and many people derided us. Now times are good. The deity grants what is asked.

We also cut a long passage about Wayan Data's childhood that seemed stiff and uninformative. We had hoped he would talk about his memories of Jero's madness and consecration, but he didn't.

### K. Wayan Data's consecration ceremony

Like those of most Balinese, Wayan Data's economic activities vary: He farms the dry fields inherited from his father, where he has recently added clove trees to the coconuts, mangoes, papayas, bananas, and root crops already growing; he works as a casual day laborer on community projects such as road construction; and he works as a carpenter, a trade he is trying to expand. When he is around the houseyard he occasionally assists his mother.

If Wayan Data wants to work as a carpenter in temples without being cursed (as might happen to an impure person who climbed on a shrine), he must be ritually consecrated. This ceremony is only one step in his purification, however; it is not directly related to inheriting Jero's practice.

In all four films Balinese ritual is mentioned frequently. We included Wayan Data's consecration to give the viewer the sense of a small, family ritual. As in all Balinese rituals, offerings are made, prayers are recited, and people are sprinkled with holy water. The purpose is to inform the spirits and deities of the activities of men and women and to ask their blessing. The ceremony was held in the early evening, four days after we filmed Jero talking about it. It was held amid the family shrines in the most sacred corner of their houseyard. Jero's brother, nephew, sister-in-law, grandchildren, and a female relative attended, as well as a local priest. We had only one battery for lights, and so we filmed the event in short, impressionistic snatches. Most of our footage of the 25-minute ceremony has been included. The informality of all Balinese ritual is evident in the way Jero talked even during the prayers. She does appear a little self-conscious about the filming.

Jero calls the priest "Jero Mangku." "Jero" is an honorific title shared by sanctified people such as balians and local priests. "Mangku," short of *pamangku* is a person chosen by a community to be the caretaker priest of a local temple, as opposed to a *pedanda*, a learned, Brahmana priest who has studied classical Hindu-Balinese religious texts. *Pamangkus* perform many private ceremonies in family temples.

After being blessed with holy water, Wayan Data and his wife don white clothes, symbols of purity, usually worn by sanctified people when they are working in temples. The final credits are shown over images of everyone praying and of Jero teaching her youngest grandson to pray. This was the conclusion of the ceremony.

# Glossaries

**Balinese terms**
**(Linda Connor)**

This glossary defines Balinese words that occur frequently in the text, as well as those of particular relevance to the subject matter of the book. The glossary reflects common usage in the district of Bali where most of the information for this book was obtained.

*atma:* the human soul; the manifestation of God in each human being

*babad:* chronicle originally written on *lontar* palm, structured around a dynastic genealogy

*babai:* sorcerers' demons introduced into the victim's body by magical means; *babainan:* an attack by these demons, during which there are marked behavioral disturbances

*balian:* indigenous healer of Bali

*balian apun, balian uat:* masseur

*balian kebal:* practitioner who administers spells, charms, and rituals to enhance the client's spiritual strength

*balian manak:* midwife

*balian taksu, balian tapakan:* spirit medium

*balian tenung:* diviner

*balian usada:* practitioner who uses traditional manuscripts on healing

*banjar:* hamlet or ward, a residentially clustered group of households that cooperate in economic, social, and ritual concerns

*banten:* generic term for offerings of all types

*bayu:* life force, or vital energy in the body

*berasan:* small, lumpy, hard deposits in the body's channels (*uat* ), located and treated during massage

*betara:* generic term for a lofty deity of the Balinese pantheon; also used as part of a deity's title, e.g., Betara Siwa

267

*boreh:* ointment, liniment, or poultice made from natural ingredients

*buana agung:* the "great world" or macrocosmos; the whole of existence

*buana alit:* the "small world" or microcosmos; the human body in its physical and spiritual aspects

*buduh:* mad, madness; *buduh kadewandewan:* "madness from the deities," blessed madness

*buta:* demonic spirit

*canang:* one of the commonest small offerings, consisting of a small tray of woven coconut leaves on which are placed perfumed flowers, betel nuts, rice, and sometimes other ingredients as well; balians' clients often place a cash donation on the tray

*dewa:* deity; can also refer to purified spirit of the dead, as in *hyang dewa*

*durmanggala:* offering of exorcism and propitiation

*Eka Dasa Rudra:* centennial festival of exorcism, propitiation, and purification

*engsap:* to forget; used by Jero to refer to some possession experiences

*gedong:* pavilion closed in on all sides; in household architecture, the brick pavilion in the more sacred, mountainward direction [*kaja*] of the houseyard where the most senior person or couple often sleeps

*hyang:* purified spirit of the dead, as in *Hyang Kompiang*; also used to refer to a deity, especially as part of a title, e.g., *Ida Sang Hyang Widi Hasa*

*inget:* to remember; used by Jero to refer to the experience of returning to ordinary awareness from possession

*jaba:* commoner or "outsider"; person without gentry title

*jero:* (1) term of address, applied to all those to whom the speaker wishes to show respect but who are not of gentry status; commonly used to address commoner wives of gentry men or consecrated commoners such as temple priests and healers; part of the title of these persons; a polite way to address a stranger; (2) "inside," especially in reference to the space inside a gentry palace, inhabited by *wong jero*, "inside people"; by extension, *jero* or *jeroan* may refer to any sanctified space, such as the inner court of a temple complex; a polite way to refer to somebody's house

*kajeng-kliwon:* conjunction of the first day of the Balinese three-day calendar and the fifth day of the Balinese five-day calendar; a day on which *babai* often attack their victims

*kala:* demonic spirit

*kanda mpat:* four spiritual siblings associated with each human being

*karauhan:* from *rauh*, "to arrive"; sometimes used by Jero to refer to her experience of possession by a purified spirit or deity *kelian adat:* hamlet or village official with responsibilities in the sphere of ritual practice and customary law

*kemasukan kekuatan:* Indonesian, lit., "the introduction of strength"; administration of spells, charms, and rituals to enhance the client's spiritual strength

*kepeng:* Chinese coin, once a unit of currency; now used for ritual purposes

*leak:* sorcerer; also refers to the appearances sorcerers assume when practicing their skills

*loloh:* infusion, decoction, or elixir made from natural ingredients

*lontar:* traditional texts inscribed on palm leaves that have been dried, treated, and bound; includes tracts on healing; after the tree of the same name (*Borassus flabelliformis*) from which leaves are obtained

*maguruguruan:* compatibility between healer and patient

*makaladewa:* purification ceremony for a craftsman so that he can work in temples and other sanctified spaces without polluting these abodes of deities and spirits

*makepotin:* onomatopoeic word from the root *pot*, the snapping sound made when joints of the body are bent and pressed; e.g., finger joints or vertebrae of the neck; also used by Jero to describe her adjustment of the vertebrae in the lower spine, which produces a snapping or cracking sound

*matelah:* colloquial Balinese term for a consecration ceremony for a balian or local temple priest

*ngaben, pangabenan:* cremation ceremony

*ngisep:* lit., "to inhale"; used by Jero to refer to her experience of possession when she holds the incense brazier under her face during a séance

*nunas raos:* "to ask for speech," from deities or spirits, who speak through a medium at a séance

*nuntun:* final purification ceremony for spirits of the dead, when they are called to reside as deified spirits in the temple of their descent group

*nyama:* sibling, relative; colloquial way of referring to the four spiritual siblings (*kanda mpat*)

*nyekah:* from the root *sekah*, the name of the central effigy of the 12-day postcremation ceremony (*roras*), in which it is the most important ritual (colloquially, *nyekah* and *roras* are used synonymously); also used in séance idiom to refer to a particular type of cremation ceremony, where effigies of the deceased are burned in the village, with symbolic earth dug up from the graveyard

*palebon:* polite word for cremation ceremony

*pamangku:* local temple priest

*panengen:* from the root *tengen*, "right"; magic of the right (as opposed to left) path, "white magic"

*pangarep:* chief petitioner at a séance, who has primary responsibility for resolution of the problem

*pangiwa:* from the root *kiwa*, "left"; magic of the left path, "black magic"

*pasah:* third day of the Balinese three-day calendar, considered inauspicious for conducting séances but used by Jero for her massage practice

*pedanda:* high priest, literate in the *lontar* manuscripts and having a Brahmana title

*pejati, banten apejatian:* offering used in many different types of rituals, containing roasted poultry and a coconut in addition to the basic elements of rice, other foodstuffs, flowers, and woven coconut leaves

*perentah:* illness caused by sorcery

*pirata:* uncremated, and therefore unpurified, spirit of the dead

*pitra:* spirit of the dead that has been purified by cremation

*pura:* temple

*Pura Dalem:* temple to deities of the realm of death, often referred to as "Death Temple"; situated in a seaward direction (*kelod*), from the village, next to graveyard and cremation ground

*purnama:* day of the full moon, an auspicious day for conducting séances and many other ceremonies

*Puskesmas:* acronym from Pusat Kesehatan Masyarakat (Community Health Center); a clinic situated in each subdistrict of Indonesia

*rantasan:* offering consisting of a pile of clothes decoratively folded on a tray; may be for a deity or, as at séances, for the spirit of the dead person whom relatives wish to contact

*roras, ngroras:* purification ceremony performed 12 days after cremation

*sabda:* message from a divine or ancestral source, often through dreams

*sakti, kasaktian, kasakten:* spiritual power

*sang mati:* uncremated, and therefore unpurified, spirits of the dead

*satua:* folktale

*segehan:* small ground offering made to demons, consisting of cooked rice and spices

*simbuh:* medicinal paste, in which ingredients are mixed in the mouth with saliva and then sprayed onto the prescribed area of the body

*sudra:* Sanskrit word used to refer to a commoner or "outsider"; person without gentry title

*tapakan:* from the root *tapak*, "palm of the hand" or "sole of the foot"; (1)

commonly used to refer to spirit mediums, often forming part of their title; (2) base, foundation, or as in reference to support, any person who becomes possessed as the *tapakan* of the possessing agent; also statues and other objects that represent deities; *katapak* is sometimes used to describe someone who is possessed

*tapakan palinggih:* offering commonly made at séances, consisting of a round bamboo tray on which is placed a bed of rice, a length of cloth, and a string of *kepeng* with a *canang* atop

*triwangsa:* Sanskrit word used to refer to persons with a gentry title (including the Brahmana groups from which high priests are drawn)

*tutuh:* spiritually potent medicinal drops, usually containing oil, administered by balians to the patient's eyes, nose, ears, or mouth

*uat:* Indonesian, *urat*; connecting channels of the body

*usada:* traditional *lontar* manuscripts on healing

*wahyu:* Indonesian; revelation from a divine source, often through dreams, which may help in the resolution of everyday problems; e.g., in the case of balians, instructions for treatment of a difficult case

*wandu:* sexually impotent

*wuku:* seven-day week in the Javanese-Balinese calendar of 30 weeks (or 210 days); used to determine many ceremonial cycles in Bali

## Film terms
### (Patsy Asch)

An *image* is a two-dimensional representation or likeness recorded through the film process: exposure, development, and printing.

A *frame* is a single image, separated from other film images by a black line. It is the smallest meaningful visual unit in a film, analogous to a single word in a sentence.

A *shot* is a series of film frames recorded consecutively and continuously. A new shot begins whenever the camera is turned on and ends when it is turned off.

To *frame a shot* is to compose an image.

*Exposure* is the amount of light that reaches each frame. Exposure is determined by the time and intensity of illumination. An *over-exposed* frame has received too much light; an *underexposed* frame, too little.

The *focal plane* is the plane on which parallel rays of light, refracted through a lens, focus to form a sharp image. Each film frame is exposed while it lies in the focal plane.

*Focal length* is the distance between the optical center of a lens (set on infinity) and the focal plane. Usually focal lengths are measured in millimeters (mm). A short focal length collects light from a wide scene, whereas long focal length has a narrow field so that images filmed at a distance appear magnified.

A *wide-angle lens* has a short focal length that covers a wide view. Wide-angle lenses are usually used in confined spaces, such as Jero's shrine house, to film objects close to the camera; however, the perspective is exaggerated because width is compressed.

A *telephoto lens* has a long focal length. The longer the length, the narrower the width of the area filmed. Telephoto lenses are used to bring objects closer to the viewer, but they produce images that appear flattened because the distance from the camera has been compressed.

A *zoom lens* is capable of altering focal lengths, usually through a range from wide-angle to telephoto. Our films of Jero were filmed with a zoom lens with a range of 10mm (wide-angle)–150mm (telephoto). A zoom lens permits filmmakers to alter magnification within a single shot.

A *zoom* is a continuous series of frames recorded as the focal length of the lens is changed. Zooming from a wide-angle to a telephoto setting is called *zooming in*; the reverse, *zooming out*.

*To pan* is to move the camera horizontally while filming. (The verb *pan* is sometimes extended to include vertical camera movement.)

A *pan* (from *panoramic*) is the series of film frames recorded while the camera is being moved; for example, a pan of rice fields from terraces on the east, past those to the south, to the ravine on the west. Such a scene is too broad to encompass in a single frame, even at an extreme wide-angle setting.

A *close-up* isolates a detail, such as a face, a hand, or an offering. A close-up is usually a telephoto shot.

A *cut* is the point between two frames where the footage has *literally* been cut, the point where two shots are spliced together.

A *cutaway* is a shot that is not part of the chronological sequence but has been added to bridge a time lapse or to separate two shots that do not look well juxtaposed or to allow dialogue to continue when a shot ends.

*Synchronized (sync) sound* is sound recorded at the same time as film. Thus the sounds heard correspond to the images seen.

*To synchronize* is to align sync sound with the film frames that were photographed as the sound was recorded.

A *fade-in* begins with a black frame; each consecutive frame is lighter until optimum exposure is reached. A *fade-out* gradually goes to black. Scenes often begin with a fade-in and end with a fade-out.

A *dissolve* is the optical effect of overlapping the end of one shot, as it fades out, with the beginning of the next shot, as it fades in, thus super-imposing one image over another. As the intensity of one shot diminishes, the intensity of the next increases. Fades and dissolves usually last from one to four seconds.

# Bibliography

*Note*: This bibliography includes only readily available sources, in English, on Bali.

PRINTED WORKS

Bateson, G.
    1970 [1937]  An Old Temple and a New Myth. In J. Belo, ed., *Traditional Balinese Culture*, pp. 111–136.
    1973 [1949]  Bali: The Value System of a Steady State. In G. Bateson, *Steps to an Ecology of Mind*, pp. 80–100. St. Albans: Paladin. Also in J. Belo, ed. (1970), *Traditional Balinese Culture*, pp. 384–402.
    1975  Some Components of Socialization for Trance. *Ethos* 3(2):143–155.
Bateson, G., and M. Mead
    1942  *Balinese Character: A Photographic Analysis*. New York: Special Publications of the New York Adademy of Sciences, vol. 2.
Baum, V.
    1973 [1937]  *Tale of Bali*. Jakarta: Oxford University Press/P. T. Indira.
Belo, J.
    1949  *Bali: Rangda and Barong*. Monographs of the American Ethnological Society, no.16. Seattle: University of Washington Press.
    1953  *Bali: Temple Festival*. Monographs of the American Ethnological Society, no. 22. Seattle: University of Washington Press.
    1960  *Trance in Bali*. New York: Columbia University Press.
    1970a [1935]  A Study of Customs Pertaining to Twins in Bali. In J. Belo, ed., *Traditional Balinese Culture*, pp. 3–56.
    1970b [1936]  A Study of a Balinese Family. In J. Belo, ed., *Traditional Balinese Culture*, pp. 350–70.
    1970c [1935]  The Balinese Temper. In J. Belo, ed., *Traditional Balinese Culture*, pp. 85–110.
Belo, J., ed.
    1970  *Traditional Balinese Culture*. New York: Columbia University Press.
Bendesa, K. G., and M. Sukarsa
    1980  An Economic Survey of Bali. *Bulletin of Indonesian Economic Studies* 16(2):31–53.
Boon, J. A.
    1974  The Progress of the Ancestors in a Balinese Temple Group. *Journal of Asian Studies* 34:7–25.

1977 *The Anthropological Romance of Bali, 1597–1972.* Cambridge: Cambridge University Press.

1979 Balinese Temple Politics and the Religious Revitalization of Caste Ideals. In A. Becker, ed., *The Imagination of Reality: Essays in Southeast Asian Coherence Systems*, pp. 271–91. Norwood, N.J.: Ablex.

Connor, L. H.

1979 Corpse Abuse and Trance in Bali: The Cultural Mediation of Aggression. *Mankind* 12:104–18.

1982*a* In Darkness and Light: A Study of Peasant Intellectuals in Bali. Ph.D. dissertation, University of Sydney.

1982*b* Ships of Fools and Vessels of the Divine. *Social Science and Medicine* 16(7):783–94.

1982*c* The Unbounded Self: Balinese Therapy in Theory and Practice. In A. J. Marsella and G. M. White, eds., *Cultural Conceptions of Mental Health and Therapy*, pp. 251–67. Dordrecht: Reidel.

1983 Healing as Women's Work in Bali. In L. Manderson, ed., *Women's Work and Women's Roles: Economics and Everyday Life in Indonesia, Malaysia and Singapore*, pp. 53–72. Canberra: Development Studies Centre, Australian National University.

Covarrubias, M.

1973 [1937] *Island of Bali.* New York: Knopf.

Crawfurd, J.

1820 On the Existence of Hindu Religion in the Island of Bali. *Asiatick Researches* 13:128–70.

Daroesman, R.

1973 An Economic Survey of Bali. *Bulletin of Indonesian Economic Studies* 9(3):28–61.

Forge, A.

1978 *Balinese Traditional Paintings.* Sydney: Australian Museum.

1980*a* Balinese Religion and Indonesian Identity. In J. J. Fox, R. G. Garnaut, P. T. McCawley and J. A. C. Mackie, eds., *Indonesia: Australian Perspectives*, pp. 221–34. Canberra: Research School of Pacific Studies, Australian National University.

1980*b* Tooth and Fang in Bali. *Canberra Anthropology* 3(1):1–16.

Franken, H. J.

1960 The Festival of Jayaprana at Kali Anget. In J. L. Swellengrebel et al., *Bali: Life, Thought, and Ritual*, pp. 235–65.

Geertz, C.

1959 Form and Variation in Balinese Village Structure. *American Anthropologist* 61:991–1012.

1963 *Peddlers and Princes: Social Change and Economic Modernization in Two Indonesian Towns.* Chicago: University of Chicago Press.

1967 Tihingan, a Balinese Village. In Koentjaraningrat, ed., *Villages in Indonesia*, pp. 210–43. Ithaca: Cornell University Press.

1972 The Wet and the Dry: Traditional Irrigation in Bali and Morocco. *Human Ecology* 1:34–9.

1973*a* [1964]   "Internal Conversion" in Contemporary Bali, *Interpretation of Culture*, pp. 170–89. New York: Basic Books.

1973*b* [1966]   Person, Time, and Conduct in Bali, *Interpretation of Culture*, pp. 360–411. New York: Basic Books.

1973*c* [1972]   Deep Play: Notes on the Balinese Cockfight, *Interpretation of Culture*, pp. 412–53. New York: Basic Books.

1980   *Negara: The Theater State in Nineteenth-Century Bali*. Princeton: Princeton University Press.

Geertz, H.

1959   The Balinese Village. In G. W. Skinner, ed., *Local, Ethnic, and National Loyalties in Village Indonesia: A Symposium*, pp. 24–33. New Haven: Yale University Cultural Report Series.

1963   Indonesian Cultures and Communities. In R. McVey, ed., *Indonesia*, pp. 24–96. New Haven: Human Relations Area Files Press.

1972   Bali. In F. LeBar, ed., *Ethnic Groups of Insular Southeast Asia*, pp. 60–5. New Haven: Human Relations Area Files Press.

Geertz, H., and C. Geertz

1964   Teknonymy in Bali: Parenthood, Age-Grading, and Genealogical Amnesia. *Journal of the Royal Anthropological Institute* 94(2):94–108.

1975   *Kinship in Bali*. Chicago: University of Chicago Press.

Goris, R.

1937   The Balinese Medical Literature. *Djawa* 17:281–6.

1960*a* [1935]   Religious Character of the Village Community. In J. L. Swellengrebel et al., *Bali: Life, Thought, and Ritual*, pp. 77–100.

1960*b* [1938]   The Temple System. In J. L. Swellengrebel et al., *Bali: Life, Thought, and Ritual*, pp. 103–11.

1969*a* [1937]   Pura Besakih, Bali's State Temple. In J. L. Swellengrebel et al., *Bali: Further Studies in Life, Thought, and Ritual*, pp. 75–88.

1969*b* [1948]   Pura Besakih through the Centuries. In J. L. Swellengrebel et al., *Bali: Further Studies in Life, Thought, and Ritual*, pp. 89–104.

Hanna, W.

1976   *Bali Profile: Peoples, Events, Circumstances, 1001–1976*. New York: American Universities Fieldstaff Reports.

Higginbotham, H. N.

1984   *Third World Challenge to Psychiatry*. Honolulu: University of Hawaii Press.

Hobart, M.

1975   Orators and Patrons: Two Types of Political Leader in Balinese Village Society. In M. Bloch, ed., *Political Language and Oratory in Traditional Society*, pp. 65–92. London: Academic Press.

1978*a* Padi, Puns, and the Attribution of Responsibility. In G. B. Milner, ed., *Natural Symbols in South East Asia*, pp. 55–87. School of Oriental and African Studies, University of London.

1978*b* The Path of the Soul: The Legitimacy of Nature in Balinese Conceptions of Space. In G. B. Milner, ed., *Natural Symbols in South East Asia*, pp. 5–28. School of Oriental and African Studies, University of London.

1983 Through Western Eyes: or, How My Balinese Neighbour Became a Duck. *Indonesia Circle* 30:33–47.

Hooykaas, C.
1958 *The Lay of Jaya Prana, the Balinese Uriah.* London: Luzac.
1964 *Agama Tirtha: Five Studies in Hindu Balinese Religion.* Amsterdam: Verhandelingen der Koninklijke Nederlandse Akademie van Wetenschappen, Afd. Letterkunde, n.s. 70(4).
1966 *Surya-Sevana: The Way to God of a Balinese Siva Priest.* Amsterdam: Verhandelingen der Koninklijke Nederlandse Akademie van Wetenschappen, Afd. Letterkunde, n.s. 52(3).
1973a *Kama and Kala: Materials for the Study of the Balinese Shadow-theatre.* Amsterdam: North Holland.
1973b *Religion in Bali.* Leiden: Brill.
1974 *Cosmogony and Creation in Balinese Tradition.* The Hague: Nijhoff.
1977 *A Balinese Temple Festival.* The Hague: Nijhoff.
1978 *The Balinese Poem Basur: An Introduction to Magic.* The Hague: Nijhoff.
1980 *Drawings of Balinese Sorcery.* Leiden: Brill.

Hooykaas, C., and T. Goudriaan
1971 *Stuti and Stava (Buddha, Saiva, and Vaisnava) of Balinese Brahman Priests.* Amsterdam: North Holland.

Hooykaas-van Leeuwen Boomkamp, J. H.
1956 The Balinese Realm of Death. *Bijdragen tot de Taal-, Land- en Volkenkunde* 112:74–87.
1961 *Ritual Purification of a Balinese Temple.* Verhandelingen der Koninklijke Nederlandse Akademie van Wetenschappen, Afd. Letterkunde, n.s. 68(4).

Howe, L. E. A.
1983 An Introduction to the Cultural Study of Traditional Balinese Architecture. *Archipel* 25:137–58.
1984 Gods, People, Spirits, and Witches: The Balinese System of Person Definition. *Bijdragen tot de Taal-, Land- en Volkenkunde* 140:193–222.

Korn, V. E.
1960 The Consecration of a Priest. In J. L. Swellengrebel et al., *Bali: Life, Thought, and Ritual*, pp. 131–54.

Kraan, A. van der
1983 Bali: Slavery and Slave Trade. In A. Reid, ed., *Slavery, Bondage, and Dependency in Southeast Asia*, pp. 315–40. St. Lucia: University of Queensland Press.

Lansing, J. S.
1974 *Evil in the Morning of the World.* Ann Arbor: Michigan Papers on South and Southeast Asia, no. 6.
1979 The Formation of the Court-Village Axis in the Balinese Arts. In E. M. Bruner and J. O. Becker, eds., *Art, Ritual, and Society in Indonesia*. Athens: Ohio University Center for International Studies, SEA Program.

1983*a* The Indianization of Bali. *Journal of Southeast Asian Studies* 14:409–21.

1983*b* *The Three Worlds of Bali*. New York: Praeger.

McCauley, A. P.

1984*a* Healing as a Sign of Power and Status in Bali. *Social Science and Medicine* 18(2):167–72.

1984*b* The Cultural Construction of Illness in Bali. Ph.D. dissertation, University of California at Berkeley.

McPhee, C.

1966    *Music in Bali*. New Haven: Yale University Press.

1970*a* [1936]    The Balinese Wayang Kulit and Its Music. In J. Belo, ed., *Traditional Balinese Culture*, pp. 146–97.

1970*b* [1948]    Dance in Bali. In J. Belo, ed., *Traditional Balinese Culture*, pp. 290–321.

Mead, M., and F. C. MacGregor

1951    *Growth and Culture: A Photographic Study of Balinese Childhood*. New York: Putnam.

Mershon, K. E.

1970    Five Great Elementals. *Pancha Maha Buta*. In J. Belo, ed., *Traditional Balinese Culture*, pp. 57–66.

1971    *Seven plus Seven: Mysterious Life Rituals on Bali*. New York: Vantage Press.

Miles, D.

1981    Classical Literature in an Urban Hamlet of Contemporary Bali: A Sociological Perspective. In Wang Gungwu, ed., *Society and the Writer: Essays on Literature in Modern Asia*, pp. 33–57. Canberra: Australian National University Press.

Miller, D. B.

1984    Hinduism in Perspective: Bali and India Compared. *Review of Indonesian and Malay Affairs* 18:36–63.

Noronha, R.

1979    Paradise Reviewed: Tourism in Bali. In E. de Kadt, ed., *Tourism: Passport to Development?*, pp. 177–204. New York: World Bank and UNESCO-Oxford University Press.

Pigeaud, T.

1975    *Javanese and Balinese Manuscripts, and Some Codices Written in Related Idioms Spoken in Java and Bali*. Wiesbaden: Steiner.

Poffenberger, M.

1983    Towards a New Understanding of Population Change in Bali. *Population Studies* 37:43–59.

Poffenberger, M., and M. S. Zurbuchen

1980    The Economics of Village Bali: Three Perspectives. *Economic Development and Cultural Change 29:29–133*.

Pounds, M. B.

1982    Strategies of Negotiation in Three Realms of Balinese Society. Ph.D. dissertation, University of California at Berkeley.

Ramseyer, U.

1977    *The Art and Culture of Bali*. Oxford: Oxford University Press.

Robson, S.
  1972   The Kawi Classics in Bali. *Bijdragen tot de Taal-, Land- en Volkenkunde* 128(2):308–26.
Stuart-Fox, D. J.
  1974   *The Art of Balinese Offering.* Yogyakarta: Yayasan Kanisius.
  1982   *Once a Century: Pura Besakih and the Eka Dasa Rudra Festival.* Jakarta: Sinar Harapan/Citra Indonesia.
Swellengrebel, J. L.
  1960   Bali: Some General Information. In J. L. Swellengrebel et al., *Bali: Life, Thought, and Ritual,* pp. 1–76.
  1969   Nonconformity in the Balinese Family. In J. L. Swellengrebel et al., *Bali: Further Studies in Life, Thought, and Ritual,* pp. 199–212.
Swellengrebel, J. L., et al.
  1960   *Bali: Life, Thought, and Ritual.* The Hague: Hoeve.
  1969   *Bali: Further Studies in Life, Thought, and Ritual.* The Hague: Hoeve.
Tan, R. Y. D.
  1967   The Domestic Architecture of South Bali. *Bijdragen tot de Taal-, Land- en Volkenkunde* 123:442–74.
Thong, D.
  1976   Psychiatry in Bali. *Australian and New Zealand Journal of Psychiatry* 10(1):95–7.
Tugby, D., E. Tugby, and H. G. Law
  1976   The Attribution of Mental Illness by Rural Balinese. *Australian and New Zealand Journal of Psychiatry* 10(1):99–104.
Vickers, A.
  1980   Gusti Made Deblog: Artistic Manifestations of Change in Bali. *Rima* 14(2):1–47.
  1982a   A Balinese Illustrated Manuscript of the Siwaratrikalpa. *Bijdragen tot de Taal-, Land- en Volkenkunde* 138(4):443–69.
  1982b   The Writing of Kakawin and Kidung on Bali. *Bijdragen tot de Taal-, Land- en Volkenkunde* 138(4)492–3.
Weck, W.
  1976 [1937]   *Heilkunde und Volkstum auf Bali.* Jakarta: Bap Bali and Intermasa. (Indonesian translation by W. Bhadra et al., unpublished).
Worsley, P. J.
  1972   *Babad Buleleng.* The Hague: Nijhoff.
Young, E.
  1980   Topeng in Bali: Change and Continuity in a Traditional Drama Genre. Ph.D. dissertation, University of California at San Diego.
  1982   The Tale of Erlangga: Text Translation of a Village Drama Performance in Bali. *Bijdragen tot de Taal-, Land- en Volkenkunde* 138(4):783–94.
Zoete, de B., and W. Spies
  1973 [1938]   *Dance and Drama in Bali.* London: Oxford University Press.
Zurbuchen, M.
  1981   The Shadow Theater of Bali: Explorations in Language and Text. Ph.D. dissertation, University of Michigan.

1984    Contexts and Choices: Spoken Indonesian in Bali. In S. Morgan and
        L. J. Sears, eds., *Aesthetic Tradition and Cultural Transition in Java
        and Bali*, pp. 247–66. University of Wisconsin Center for Southeast
        Asian Studies, Monograph no. 2.

FILMS

Abrams, I., and J. S. Lansing
1981    *The Three Worlds of Bali* (58 minutes, 16mm, color). Watertown,
        Mass.: Documentary Educational Resources.
Bateson, G., and M. Mead
1951    *Trance and Dance in Bali* (22 minutes, 16mm, B&W). Available from
        New York University, University of California at Berkeley, and
        Australian National University Library.
Darling, J., and L. Blair
1980    *Lempad of Bali* (56 minutes, 16mm, color). Produced by the
        Australian Broadcasting Commission and the Department of
        Prehistory and Anthropology, Australian National University.
Leimbach, B., and T. Dutton
1978    *Balinese Surfer* (52 minutes, 16mm, color). Palm Beach, New South
        Wales: Survival Films.

# Index

281